The Women Who
Made Television Funny

The Women Who Made Television Funny

Ten Stars of 1950s Sitcoms

DAVID C. TUCKER

McFarland & Company, Inc., Publishers
Jefferson, North Carolina, and London

LIBRARY OF CONGRESS CATALOGUING-IN-PUBLICATION DATA

Tucker, David C., 1962–
The women who made television funny : ten stars
of 1950s sitcoms / David C. Tucker.
p.   cm.
Includes bibliographical references and index.

ISBN-13: 978-0-7864-2900-4
(softcover : 50# alkaline paper) ∞

1. Television comedies—United States. 2. Television actors and actresses—United States—Biography. 3. Actresses—United States—Biography. I. Title.
PN1992.8.C66T83   2007
791.4502'8092273—dc22   2006101681

British Library cataloguing data are available

©2007 David C. Tucker. All rights reserved

No part of this book may be reproduced or transmitted in any form or by any means, electronic or mechanical, including photocopying or recording, or by any information storage and retrieval system, without permission in writing from the publisher.

Cover photograph: Gracie Allen from "The George Burns and Gracie Allen Show," 1950–1958 *(CBS/Photofest)*

Manufactured in the United States of America

*McFarland & Company, Inc., Publishers
Box 611, Jefferson, North Carolina 28640
www.mcfarlandpub.com*

To my mother
LOUISE CURTIS TUCKER
with love, admiration, and gratitude

Acknowledgments

I'M GRATEFUL TO A NUMBER OF PEOPLE whose help and encouragement enriched this book and kept its author on track. It was my great privilege to interview two of the leading ladies celebrated in these pages. Gale Storm was not only as charming and delightful as Margie Albright herself, but candid, funny, and extremely generous with her time. Betty White, a true class act, responded within days to my interview request, and kindly filled in some gaps in my understanding of her early television work.

Since many of their fellow 1950s sitcom stars are no longer with us, I am especially grateful for the family members and colleagues who agreed to share recollections. Douglas Brooks West, himself a busy screenwriter and producer, talked with me about his mother, Eve Arden. Actor Robert Fuller played phone tag with me for several days *not* so that he could talk about himself or his own career, but so as to sing the praises of his late friend and co-star Spring Byington. I was also fortunate to speak with the legendary comedy writer Sherwood Schwartz, who refreshed his memory on working with Joan Davis by pulling from his office bookshelves bound volumes of *I Married Joan* scripts he penned more than fifty years ago.

For most of my adult life, I've been privileged to work at the DeKalb County Public Library, and a better group of colleagues would be tough to find. My longtime boss and friend Magda Sossa, who has been supportive of me in many ways over the past ten years, spent hours proofreading and critiquing this book. Her efforts are much appreciated, as is the encouragement of people like Jane Richards and Emile Worthy, who make the workday at the Library Processing Center so much more enjoyable. DCPL's Kristi Gregory and Graham Reiney were helpful with research assistance and obtaining needed library materials, and Tamika Maddox contributed superior indexing skills. Resources available in the Woodruff Library at Emory University, and the University of Georgia Libraries, were valuable as well.

Family and friends have enriched my life in more ways than I can recount here. Among those who deserve a nod—at least—are Edward and Louise Tucker, Donna Sassone and the fabulous Sassones (Torry, Tim, and Danny), Ken McCullers, Bennie Crudup, the Gelmini clan (David, Heather, Andrew, and Tyler), Jennifer Myers,

Ron Roberts, Jacquie Roch, Joann Sexton, and Ethel Watson. A new friend, scholar and Kay Francis biographer Dr. Lynn Kear, shared her publishing expertise with me.

Finally, for reasons any media researcher or collector who reads this will surely understand, my sincere thanks to Mr. Pierre M. Omidyar, founder of eBay.

David C. Tucker
January 2007

Table of Contents

Acknowledgments vii
Introduction 1

1. GRACIE ALLEN
   The George Burns and Gracie Allen Show 5

2. EVE ARDEN
   Our Miss Brooks and *The Eve Arden Show* 21

3. LUCILLE BALL
   I Love Lucy 39

4. SPRING BYINGTON
   December Bride 59

5. JOAN DAVIS
   I Married Joan 75

6. ANNE JEFFREYS
   Topper and *Love That Jill* 93

7. DONNA REED
   The Donna Reed Show 109

8. ANN SOTHERN
   Private Secretary and *The Ann Sothern Show* 125

9. GALE STORM
   My Little Margie and *The Gale Storm Show: Oh! Susanna* 141

10. BETTY WHITE
    Life with Elizabeth and *Date with the Angels* 157

Appendix I: Casts and Credits 173
Appendix II: Chronology 179
Appendix III: Ten More Leading Ladies 183
Chapter Notes 187
Selected Bibliography 193
Index 195

Introduction

THIS BOOK PAYS TRIBUTE TO TEN PROMINENT television actresses who played lead roles in popular comedy shows of the 1950s. Pioneers in the television industry, these women created memorable characters that would have a long-standing influence on TV comedy.

Naturally any list of early female sitcom stars would have to include the magnificent Lucille Ball, and her timeless *I Love Lucy,* and indeed she and her show are prominently featured here. But Lucy was by no means the only comedic actress to headline a popular TV sitcom of that era. Among her peers who captured the attention of audiences are Gracie Allen *(The George Burns and Gracie Allen Show),* Eve Arden *(Our Miss Brooks),* Spring Byington *(December Bride),* Joan Davis *(I Married Joan),* Anne Jeffreys *(Topper),* Donna Reed *(The Donna Reed Show),* Ann Sothern *(Private Secretary* and *The Ann Sothern Show),* Gale Storm *(My Little Margie* and *The Gale Storm Show: Oh! Susanna),* and Betty White *(Life with Elizabeth).* All starred in popular shows that debuted between 1950 and 1959—in fact, most of these shows ranked among the top 25 in ratings at least once during their run—and all are profiled here.

Television comedy of the 1950s provided great opportunities for the comedic actress who could front her own show. The women featured here headlined their own sitcoms and were, with one exception, the top-billed stars of those shows. These actresses and their characters were the primary laugh-getters on some of the most highly rated sitcoms of the 1950s, shows that were noteworthy not only for their popularity, but for their innovation and creativity in the then-young medium of television. Female sitcom stars of a later generation—Marlo Thomas, Mary Tyler Moore, even Roseanne—owed a debt to these talented women who clearly demonstrated the drawing power of a funny woman.

But while Lucille Ball is still enormously popular with audiences, some of her peers from the 1950s prime time TV schedules have been neglected in recent years. *December Bride,* a Top Ten–rated CBS sitcom from the Desilu factory, is virtually unseen today, and its star, Spring Byington, is not widely known to viewing audiences.

The same is true of Joan Davis, once radio's highest-paid comedienne, whose TV sitcom *I Married Joan* has suffered a similar fate. While *I Love Lucy* is being released season by season on DVD, with episodes lovingly restored and series history and trivia carefully preserved, *Joan* scarcely exists on today's consumer DVD market, and is no longer rerun.

Like many baby boomers, I first encountered several of these actresses and their hit shows of the 1950s in syndicated TV reruns of the late 1960s and early 1970s. *I Love Lucy* and Lucy Ricardo have been part of my consciousness for so long, as they are for millions of Americans, that I can no longer remember when I first encountered that show—it's always been there. But I do remember, at the age of eleven or twelve, a local TV station's summer reruns of *Our Miss Brooks*, where I was instantly drawn to the distinctive style and dry comic delivery of Eve Arden. A year or two later, another station's rerun schedule introduced me to *Topper*, which intrigued me not only for its ghostly happenings and unique special effects, but also for its captivatingly beautiful and seductive leading lady, Anne Jeffreys.

And who could watch *Burns and Allen* without falling under the spell of the marvelous Gracie Allen, and her distinctively illogical logic? (It's infectious—one day recently, having just watched an episode, I heard someone say that their professional specialty was termite repair, and found myself thinking, "I didn't know you could repair termites.")

Back then, I was dimly aware of Joan Davis and her *Lucy*-esque sitcom *I Married Joan*, but never caught more than a few glimpses of that show, which was not so often repeated; nor was I well acquainted with *December Bride* or *My Little Margie*. One of the chief pleasures of researching this book has been the chance not only to reacquaint myself with some of the shows I loved back then, but also to discover others equally enjoyable and worthy of attention.

By the early 1970s, while the sitcoms of an earlier day were still commonly seen in syndicated reruns, the prime time sitcom landscape was increasingly the province of Norman Lear *(All in the Family, Maude, Good Times,* etc.) and other producers who, with less skill, sought to ride the coattails of his success. Also riding high was *The Mary Tyler Moore Show,* a gently realistic workplace comedy that was seen as groundbreaking for its depiction of a contentedly single career woman. That highly successful show paved the way for a host of other female characters who said and did things seldom before shown on TV—Beatrice Arthur's *Maude*, who underwent the sitcom world's first abortion, and Ann Romano (played by Bonnie Franklin) of *One Day at a Time,* considered controversial by CBS executives in 1975 because she was a divorcee raising children alone.

Unfortunately, the advent of more realistic sitcoms in the 1970s sometimes came at the expense of disparaging the work of those who had come before them. The gifted Beatrice Arthur, winding down her six-year run as Maude Findlay in 1978, said, "For the very first time, we presented somebody who wasn't just a bubblehead out to get laughs."[1]

Understandable as Ms. Arthur's viewpoint was, it does a disservice to the shows— and their leading ladies—who had preceded her. For all that they adhered to certain social norms of their time, the female characters of 1950s sitcoms, and the actresses who played them, were often trailblazers, if for no other reason than that the medium of television, and the situation comedy genre, was so new. Tracing the broadcast history of *The George Burns and Gracie Allen Show,* for instance, gives us the chance to watch the TV sitcom flourish and grow, going from a live broadcast that included integrated commercials and musical interludes, to a polished sitcom on film that still has the power to delight us with its wit and charm today.

In reading this book, you may be surprised by the variety of interesting women who were depicted in 1950s TV sitcoms. You'll meet smart and sassy career women Connie Brooks *(Our Miss Brooks)* and Katy O'Connor *(The Ann Sothern Show),* successfully negotiating the hazards of the male-dominated workplace with class and humor in a way that the 1970s heroine *Rhoda* might have appreciated. Lily Ruskin, the attractive sixty-ish widow who's the title character of *December Bride,* demonstrated that an older woman's life can still be vital, fun, and full of adventure while *The Golden Girls* were still little more than girls. And then there's Marion Kerby *(Topper),* who went a step further, still glamorous, seductive, and playful from beyond the grave.

The work these women did in the 1950s is still remarkably fresh and inventive today. Admirable as Norman Lear's campaign for realism in television was, and as skillfully as his shows were crafted, they often relied on references to current events that today make *All in the Family* seem more dated than *I Love Lucy*—and, to me, it's no contest as which is more fun to watch. Unable to fall back on strong language, racial or sexual epithets, or shock value, the shows of the 1950s entertained us because of the gifts of the actors, writers, and producers who created them, and the best of them still do so today, when we have the chance to see them.

For each sitcom star profiled in this book, a career sketch is given, concentrating primarily on her television work but also noting particular achievements in other media. Their shows, and the characters they played, are described so as to either bring back memories for longtime fans, or give a flavor of what they were like to those who haven't had the chance to see them. Information about each show's production history, ratings and notable awards won, and afterlife in syndication is given as well.

As you'll see, the actresses spotlighted were a remarkably interesting and varied bunch, whose lives often intertwined as they forged their television successes. Aside from her enormously influential *I Love Lucy,* which irrevocably changed the face of television comedy, Lucille Ball was also the vice-president of a production company that played a key role in launching other popular shows of that era, and was a lifelong friend of other sitcom stars like Ann Sothern. Actresses like Spring Byington and Joan Davis came to the world of sitcoms with impressive resumes that encompassed vaudeville, radio, theater, and movies. Troupers Gracie Allen and Eve Arden were pioneers who successfully transplanted their popular radio characters to the emerging medium of television, at a time when many of their male peers still feared to tread new territory.

Then-newcomer Betty White, one of TV's first "home-grown" stars, is still very much part of the show business scene 50 years later, as is the multi-talented actress and singer Anne Jeffreys. Oscar winner Donna Reed proved that audiences who enjoyed watching TV families headed by former male movie stars would also tune in for a show where the mother, not the father, knew best. Some of these women were longtime friends and colleagues; others found themselves inevitably situated as rivals for survival in the competitive world of prime time TV.

Their accomplishments off-screen are no less impressive than their marvelous performances. Ann Sothern was a bright, high-achieving star who headed her own production company years before Mary Tyler Moore did so, and worked steadily in a variety of roles both comedic and dramatic from the 1930s through the 1980s. Gale Storm not only juggled her TV stardom with a flourishing career as a recording artist, but bravely conquered her alcoholism, then shared her struggle with the world long before it was fashionable to do so.

So turn the page; meet the bright and talented women who made us laugh in the 1950s, and still have the power to do so today. I hope that reading this book will not only give you a new appreciation for them, but also inspire you to seek out and enjoy their work whenever possible. They were pioneers in the world of television comedy, and whenever you have an opportunity to revisit their work, you'll understand why.

❖ 1 ❖

Gracie Allen

The George Burns and Gracie Allen Show

GRACIE ALLEN BUILT A LONGSTANDING CAREER, encompassing vaudeville, radio, films, and television with a persona often described as zany, daffy, confused, or by other terms that don't generally connote intelligence. Yet Allen was in fact an innovator in the world of the television sitcom, who both alphabetically and chronologically was a leader among the actresses profiled in this book.

Part of the confusion arises from the fact that there were actually two Gracies. There was Gracie, the character, who was known to proclaim, "I'm so smart, I have brains I haven't even used yet!" Then there was the gifted actress that played her, who went by the same name, and made that character beloved by stage, film, radio, and television audiences, culminating in her eight-year run as the star of one of the most innovative and fondly remembered sitcoms of the 1950s, *The George Burns and Gracie Allen Show*.

Allen's public persona grew from a stock character type known in vaudeville as the "Dumb Dora," and was polished to a fine sheen by thirty-five years in front of adoring audiences. Although the confusion between actress and character was a commonly held assumption, those who knew Allen off-stage recognized that the public Gracie bore little resemblance to the woman who played her. Nor did her lifelong status as the second-billed member of the Burns and Allen comedy team negate the fact that she was widely viewed as the real star of the act, in whatever medium she and her husband-partner performed. Her preeminence, and the act's reliance on her talent, would be openly acknowledged in jokes on *The George Burns and Gracie Allen Show*.

Grace Ethel Cecile Rosalie Allen was born in San Francisco, to an Irish-Catholic family, near the turn of the century. Since her birth certificate was apparently destroyed in the great San Francisco earthquake a few years later, she was able to be vague about the exact date, which was usually reported during her lifetime as July 26, 1906. In fact, it may have been as early as 1895.

While still a girl, she entered vaudeville, where she originally sought work as a dancer and singer. For a time she joined sisters Bessie, Hazel, and Pearl onstage for an "Allen Sisters" quartet. But it was her comedic spark that would make her famous. Her big break came in 1922, when she joined forces with a not-very-successful comedian, George Burns. At the time, Allen was taking a hiatus from show business, and had enrolled in secretarial school in New York City. Going to the theater to see her roommate perform, she made the acquaintance of Burns, also on the bill that day, and accepted an offer to team up with him.

While Burns initially positioned himself as the deliverer of punch lines, he soon noticed that Allen could get laughs even with her straight lines, and adjusted the act accordingly. For a while, the couple got bookings mostly as a "disappointment act"— one hired at the last minute to fill in when someone more popular was ill. But with Allen in the spotlight, the couple soon found favor with audiences in the heyday of vaudeville. At first theirs was a professional relationship, but Burns proposed to his co-star in late 1925, and they became husband and wife on January 7, 1926.

Highly popular onstage, they made their film debut in the late 1920s, starring in short subjects like *Lambchops* (1929), mostly recreating their vaudeville routines. Not long afterwards, they began their radio career, beginning with Allen's solo appearance on Eddie Cantor's NBC program. Within a year, they had their own show, and would be on the air regularly until 1950. In the early 1930s, they were contract players at Paramount, first playing featured roles and eventually starring in vehicles like *Here Comes Cookie* (1935).

Gracie's carefully constructed persona was even exploited in supplementary media like a syndicated newspaper column, a mystery novel (*The Gracie Allen Murder Case*, by S.S. Van Dine) in which she was the principal character, and a comic strip featuring her likeness. A book carrying her byline, *How to Become President*, outlined her mock campaign for the 1940 presidential nomination, as a Surprise Party candidate. As Burns wryly commented, "Being dumb was a talent adaptable to every popular medium."[1]

Though her talent was the cornerstone of the success that Burns and Allen enjoyed, her own ambition played a surprisingly small role in that career. It was Burns whose show business savvy largely kept the act going, despite the frequent jokes (which he often originated) about how he merely reaped the benefits of a wife far more talented than he. Although he would come into his own after her death, he spent decades in the underrated job of straight man to his talented wife.

Like other comedians of the time period, they purportedly "played themselves," using their own names, and invited audiences to conclude that Allen really was the zany character she played so skillfully. That enabled Allen, amidst ongoing media attention, to keep a low profile for herself throughout her lengthy career. If that caused her abilities as an actress to be unfairly overlooked, it's unlikely that she worried much about it. By most accounts, performing was largely a job to Gracie Allen, one at which she excelled but did not need to be happy. Later, given the chance to walk away from her TV stardom and enjoy a quieter existence, she would do so unhesitatingly. "Fame just wasn't important to her," her husband said.[2]

In 1950, Burns and Allen were top stars on radio, and, like most radio stars, were keeping a watchful eye on a new medium, television. While recognizing its emergence as an important medium, radio performers were unsure what role it would play in their professional futures, and when would be the right time to attempt a television show. Movie stars were mostly forbidden contractually to appear in regular roles on television, which was seen as a hostile competitor by major studios. But network executives were eager to adapt their radio hits to TV.

Jack Benny, a longtime NBC stalwart, started a landslide in 1949, when he negotiated a highly lucrative deal to move his

Gracie Allen at the mike with husband George Burns for their 1940s CBS radio show.

hit radio show to CBS. That network's president, William S. Paley, didn't stop with Benny—he was after a whole slew of highly rated NBC shows, among them Burns and Allen's. Although Paley's biographer later said that his real interest was to topple NBC's dominance of the radio ratings, a notable byproduct of his campaign was to build a stable of performers who could launch a successful lineup for the fledgling CBS television schedule.

TV programming in 1950 was a smorgasbord. Program executives didn't yet know *what* people would watch on TV. Prime-time schedules stretched to fill time with documentaries, travelogues, public affairs shows, and religious broadcasts. *I Love Lucy*, which would change the face of television sitcoms, was still a year away from its debut. But Milton Berle, whose success on radio and films had been limited, was pulling high ratings on TV, proving that audiences wanted to laugh.

Benny, a longtime friend of George Burns and Gracie Allen, would dip a hesitant toe into the water of TV in the early 1950s, doing a handful of shows that supplemented his weekly radio broadcasts. Not until 1960 would he undertake a weekly TV series, and many observers felt that the video version of *The Jack Benny Show*, while quite successful, was not as natural an outlet for his gifts as radio had been. Similarly, Bob Hope, one of radio's biggest stars, would devote almost his entire television career to specials, rather than a regular series.

But Burns was confident that television was the medium of the future, and was even willing to take the radical step of giving up the team's radio show so as to concentrate on TV. Now all he had to do was convince his wife.

The new medium they would be entering, while logically turning to stars that had a following on radio, presented a set of challenges that a purely aural medium didn't, and many radio performers and producers were intimidated by the complexities of adapting their existing shows to TV. No longer could actors stand at a microphone in everyday clothes and read from a script. Now, every broadcast required decisions and preparation concerning sets and costumes, and actors would be expected to memorize their dialogue.

According to George Burns, his wife was reluctant to take the plunge into television series work. Although she had for years entrusted him with the major decisions pertaining to their career, she balked when he broached the subject of a *Burns and Allen* TV show. "This is one thing I won't be pushed into!" she declared.[3]

Like the trouper she had been since going into vaudeville as a girl, Allen eventually relented, and plans for the new show went forward. It was one of eight forthcoming shows under the supervision of CBS production chief Harry Ackerman that summer. The list also included *The Amos 'n' Andy Show* (1951–53), which because of casting problems would be delayed for almost a year.

Allen's first inkling of what the new medium would be like came in the summer of 1950, when she and her husband prepared a pilot episode of their television program. The sample show was completed in late July, recorded via kinescope so as to be shopped around to potential sponsors in New York. Trade papers made the announcement that Burns and Allen would "join other CBS radio stars in bowing into television this year."[4] In early September, Carnation signed a deal to sponsor the new show, which the company "bought on the strength of the CBS test film which won critical praise in the trade."[5]

When it premiered in October 1950, *Burns and Allen* (as it would commonly be known) bore many of the trademarks of early TV, and blurred the lines between skit comedy and sitcom. For the first two years of its run, it would be a live broadcast, seen every other week. It originally emanated from New York City, and until the completion of a nationwide coaxial cable the following year, not all parts of the country could see the show simultaneously.

The initial TV broadcast, on Thursday, October 12, was titled "The Kleebob Card Game," and must have been comfortably familiar to their longtime radio audiences. As always, the humor played on Gracie's endearingly twisted, yet strangely inarguable logic, as when she returns from visiting a friend in the hospital carrying an armful of carnations:

> GEORGE: What beautiful flowers!
> GRACIE: Aren't they? And I have you to thank for them.
> GEORGE: Me? What did I do?
> GRACIE: Well, it was your idea. You said that when I visited Clara Bagley, I should take her flowers—so when she wasn't looking, I did!

That first broadcast didn't follow the usual TV sitcom format. Allen, on making her first entrance, pauses momentarily to smilingly acknowledge the audience's applause before speaking her first lines. The first act consists of a sketch about Gracie's interaction with a door-to-door encyclopedia salesman (played by veteran character actor Henry Jones), and has little to do with the plot that will emerge in the show's second half. A musical intermission features George singing with a group called the Skylarks, before the remainder of the show introduces his strange card game, Kleebob, which is intended to help him avoid taking his wife to the movies.

Technically, the show is a bit ragged, though understandably so for such a new undertaking. Occasionally camera equipment or lights cast momentary shadows on a scene, and at one point a curtain begins to close, protruding in front of the scene then being shot. Each time that the scene shifts from George's monologue to the main living room set, the screen momentarily goes black. As for the sets, representing the homes of the Burns and their next door neighbors and friends the Mortons, they were flimsy and somewhat makeshift. Timing would continue to be a challenge during the early, live broadcasts, and sometimes George and Gracie's wrap-up at the end of the show would have to be cut short. At least once, cameras would cut away from their routine and the closing credits played over their final dialogue.

In a holdover from radio, announcer Bill Goodwin (predecessor to the better-remembered Harry Von Zell) walks into "The Kleebob Card Game" at mid-story to deliver a commercial for sponsor Carnation Milk, wrapped in a dialogue with George about his recent adventure flying a plane. Aside from this integrated commercial, there's also a running joke that painlessly plugs the sponsor, as Gracie says she likes the product, but wonders how they milk the carnations. (Later, after she comes home with the flowers from her friend's hospital room, she gives them to George to put away, saying, "We'll milk them later.") Fifty years later, ironically, sponsors would once again be seeking ways to insert their messages into the programs themselves, as viewers increasingly used technology to avoid sitting through commercials.

If the early shows seem slightly primitive today, they must have seemed quite the opposite in 1950, and not just in technical terms. By starring in her own sitcom, Allen was entering a genre occupied by few other women. In fact, there were only a handful of sitcoms of any kind on prime time schedules when *Burns and Allen* premiered, making both the show and its star pioneers.

In the late 1940s, CBS had introduced two family comedy shows that would draw large audiences, *Mama* and *The Goldbergs*, the latter based on a long-running radio hit. NBC added another domestic sitcom, *The Aldrich Family,* in the fall of 1950. One of TV's very first sitcoms, the little-remembered *Mary Kay and Johnny*, which premiered in early 1947, had already left the airwaves by the time *Burns and Allen* debuted.

Only one other sitcom spotlighting a female lead premiered alongside Allen's show—ABC's *Beulah*, starring African-American singer-actress Ethel Waters as a rather stereotypical smart-aleck maid. *The George Burns and Gracie Allen Show* would be CBS' only new sitcom entry that fall, although another well-remembered and funny show, Groucho Marx's *You Bet Your Life*, joined NBC's Thursday night schedule a week earlier, and would be *Burns and Allen*'s strongest competition that first year.

Left to right: neighbors Bea Benaderet (Blanche) and Larry Keating (Harry) pose with Gracie Allen and George Burns.

Allen quickly became one of a select number of female television stars in the early 1950s, joining the company of ubiquitous talk show hostess Faye Emerson, puppet show hostess Fran Allison, and sketch comedienne Imogene Coca, of *Your Show of Shows*, as well as the leading ladies of CBS' family comedies, Gertrude Berg of *The Goldbergs* and *Mama*'s Peggy Wood. The latter, in particular, played a character more lovable and admirable than especially funny, and Berg's show would soon fall victim to sponsor and network problems after its leading man was publicly accused of being a Communist. Until the advent of Lucille Ball a year or so later, Allen and Coca would be TV's primary female laugh-getters, and only Allen's show would be widely known to later generations through reruns.

Although Allen was the star attraction of *Burns and Allen*, the supporting cast was bolstered with several carryovers from their popular radio show, including announcer Bill Goodwin. Actors Bea Benaderet and Hal March also reprised their roles as the Mortons, George and Gracie's eternally bickering neighbors. Although Benaderet would be a cast mainstay for the show's entire run, as Gracie's best friend Blanche, there was considerably more turnover in the role of her husband Harry. March would leave the show after only a handful of episodes, and three more actors would follow in his footsteps. Each would enact the role somewhat differently, and the writers would adjust Harry's personality, until Larry Keating, who joined the show in 1953, made it his own. Benaderet, also a veteran of Lucille Ball's radio comedy *My Favorite Husband* (and countless other shows), would miss her chance to play Ethel Mertz on *I Love Lucy* because of her commitment to *Burns and Allen*, though most TV viewers would probably say that both she and Vivian Vance, who assumed the role of Ethel, ended up with the roles they should have had.

Initial response to the TV show was enthusiastic, *Variety* calling it "one of the best shows of the year," and its stars "topflight video comics."[6] The show's ratings were solid from the outset. Although never a Top Ten powerhouse like *I Love Lucy* would be, the series would nonetheless be popular enough to keep sponsors Carnation and (later) B.F. Goodrich happy throughout its eight-year run. Unlike other top radio comics like Fred Allen, who would be unable to replicate their success in the new medium, Burns and Allen were as beloved on TV as they had been on radio, and in film. Their show would become a fixture of the CBS lineup, by 1953 settling into an 8 P.M. Monday time slot that it would inhabit for the remainder of its run. That move would also help the show crack the top twenty TV ratings for the first time, placing at #20 for the 1953-54 season.

In the course of its eight-year stay on CBS, the show would edge closer to the format of a traditional sitcom, especially after its switch to film in the fall of 1952. Straddling the formative years of TV sitcoms, *Burns and Allen* would adapt accordingly, and the show would look quite different by the time it concluded in 1958. Still, as much as *Burns and Allen* might in some ways resemble the many other home and family-based sitcoms that proliferated during the mid- to late 1950s, it would always have its own unique sensibilities.

I Love Lucy would soon become the standard bearer for TV sitcoms about dizzy wives, the long-suffering men in their lives, and the muddles they created, with *I Married Joan, My Little Margie,* and others carving out their own niches with variations on this popular genre. But Allen played a character uniquely her own. Gracie wasn't Lucy Ricardo, stubbornly plotting and scheming to win her latest battle of wills with a husband who cramped her style. The element of frustration that characters such as Lucy and *Our Miss Brooks'* Connie Brooks exhibited was missing from Allen's character, who occupied her own space, in a world largely of her own making.

Unlike most comedic protagonists, she seldom had real obstacles to overcome, and if she did, she was quite capable of dealing with them in her own unique way. Cornered in her home by a vengeful bank robber (played by Sheldon Leonard) who doesn't want her testifying in his upcoming trial, she doesn't find this situation worrisome. Men who venture into her kitchen often find themselves put to work, with an apron tied around their waists (as does the real-life mayor of Los Angeles in another episode). Never does Gracie resort, as Lucy Ricardo does in a similar situation, to impulsively smashing a vase over the head of an intruder. Still less do we worry that, like Edith Bunker a generation later, that such a stranger will take liberties with our heroine.

Decades before the acclaimed *Seinfeld* declared itself "the show about nothing," *Burns and Allen* was, if not exactly that, surely the show that was about nothing much. George once remarked that the show had plots only because "it was cheaper to have them than hire a guest star"[7] (though a few of those, like their friend Ronald Reagan, did appear). Mostly the show's stories served as scaffolding, an effective frame for the flights of fancy that audiences really tuned in to see. As the seasons passed, however, and sitcoms filled the prime time schedule, *Burns and Allen* would eventually phase out some of the elements more suited to a sketch comedy or variety show, and edge closer to a standard sitcom format.

Regardless of what else might change, though, the world of *Burns and Allen* was an appealing one, and viewers were always happy to pay Gracie and George a visit. With American soldiers at war in Korea, and increasing tension at home over issues like racial segregation, school busing, and the McCarthy hearings, most viewers welcomed a show in which the most pressing problem was Gracie's effort to persuade George to finance a local ballet company (which she accomplishes by hiring dancers to pirouette through the Burns living room, serving trays and dusting furniture *en pointe*). The show drew on old husband-and-wife gags like the wife who regularly puts dents in the car, but in a playful way that let us know this plot was not intended to be taken too seriously, even by sitcom standards.

George himself never flew into the huffs that characterized Ricky Ricardo (*I Love Lucy*) or Judge Bradley Stevens (*I Married Joan*) upon learning of his wife's latest caper—he just smiled and amused himself as much as we did, even when he ended up in a jail cell somewhere along the way. (The title of Burns' 1955 memoir, *I Love Her, That's Why!*, derived from the stock explanation he gave when other characters on the show wondered why he put up with Gracie).

Nor was Gracie daunted by the prospect of dealing with policemen, bankers, or other authority figures. She kept a closet in the living room full of hats left behind when visitors beat a hasty retreat in the face of her merry madness. The audience is not surprised—just delighted—when the traffic patrolman who attempts to give her a speeding ticket ultimately goes away in search of someone less bewildering to cite.

Physical comedy, the province of several other female sitcom stars of that era, was largely absent from *Burns and Allen*. Although thought was given to how the show could be made more visually appealing when it switched from radio to TV, Allen's own comedy did not derive from the washing machine overflowing with a roomful of suds, pie-throwing, or even dressing up in wacky costumes (though George and Harry Von Zell occasionally do). Her humor was primarily verbal, and, at its best, delightfully clever. Viewers relished Gracie's sincere explanations of why she unplugged the clock (so as not to waste electricity until she *needed* to know what time it was), or her puzzled reaction to being told that someone writes for a Buffalo newspaper (she didn't realize buffaloes could read).

Allen's flawless delivery nailed even the least of the jokes, and it was a style not readily imitated, as Burns himself would discover after his wife's retirement. Seldom if ever has an actress so believably played such an unbelievable character, nor made it look as effortless as Allen did.

Like Allen's character, the show itself also had an endearing (and unusual for the time) surrealistic tone. As both our host and a character in the show that was underway, Burns was perfectly happy to let us in on the inherent unreality of the whole undertaking. In one episode, he confesses in his monologue that he could solve the basic situation quickly, but this would only make the show run short. In the early live shows, he delivers his introductory lines while standing in front of the show's living room set, then steps jauntily over the cutaway wall to join the scene in progress. This playful approach takes some of the possible detriments of live TV, such as the ramshackle sets, and turns them into a source of humor.

Later, even when the show was on film, and able to produce a more polished and realistic look, the basic tone remained unchanged. The writers gave George a magic TV on which he could observe scenes taking place in other parts of the house, and keep pace with Gracie's latest endeavor. Not until *Green Acres* (CBS, 1965–71), more than a decade later, did viewers embrace another show that so frequently reminded them of its own unreality. The factors that made *Burns and Allen* so unique among '50s sitcoms would not, despite the show's success, be widely imitated. The late 1980s cable sitcom *It's Garry Shandling's Show* would come closest to mimicking the format, in what was clearly intended by its star as an homage to Burns and Allen.

Aside from her interplay with George, Allen's most effective scenes were often opposite Bea Benaderet as Blanche Morton. Though the character of Blanche was little more than the stock sarcastic sidekick of the heroine, Benaderet enlivened the proceedings considerably with her timing, boisterous laughter, and loving acceptance of Gracie's quirks. Far from being oppressed wives, Gracie and Blanche lived well (though, in a more down-to-earth show, one might have wondered how Harry Morton's work as an accountant financed a home in the same neighborhood where television stars George and Gracie lived, or why such a skinflint would have moved there). On the verge of jumping into one of their typically outlandish schemes, Blanche and Gracie stop short, agreeing that it is their responsibility as dutiful wives not to do anything of which their husbands might disapprove—and then burst into gales of hilarity at what they've just said with straight faces.

Allen herself, though a consummate performer and the centerpiece of the show, did not take an active role in decision-making behind the scenes. It was George Burns who worked with a team of writers to devise the show's unique stories, and act as the show's executive producer. Gracie's script contributions were said to be limited to editing—weeding out an occasional joke that she thought in questionable taste, or rewriting a line that she found awkward to speak.

As a performer, however, the demands on her were considerable. Not even George received as much screen time as she did in the show's early years. Her loopy dialogue, which jumped from point to point with befuddling connections, could not have been easy to learn. Even in the live broadcasts, her performances were impeccable—there's little or nothing to betray that this is a live performance, and rarely, if ever, is she seen stumbling over a line, or ad-libbing. Her performances are relaxed, self-assured, and seemingly effortless. However, Allen told interviewers that, while she might seem the kind of performer who was immune from stage fright, it wasn't so.

"The on-stage Gracie may look poised," she said frankly, "but the real Gracie is shy, a little self-conscious, and, before every performance of my life, panicky."[8]

Her on-camera demeanor is a credit to her professionalism, but it's not surprising that she often suffered from migraine headaches that forced her to lie in bed with the shades drawn, and a damp cloth tied around her skull. Within a few years, this would not be the only health concern that she faced.

Although the show's biweekly live broadcasts were well-received, continuing even during the summer months that would later become the province of reruns, by 1952 it was evident that the trend was toward filmed TV sitcoms. The success of *I Love Lucy*'s three-camera, filmed-in-front-of-an-audience method did not go unnoticed by other sitcom producers. At first, Burns resisted making a change, feeling that the energy and spontaneity of a live performance could not be replicated in a show filmed in advance. However, it was evident not only that filmed episodes allowed for a more polished look, and eased some of the strain on performers, but also that there was a value in building a backlog of films that could be reused.

Preparing to convert the show yet again, this time into a weekly, filmed broadcast, Burns formed his own production company, McCadden Productions. Added to the payroll were several staff members with expertise in film production (including Al Simon, who as *Lucy*'s associate producer had assisted in the development of the Desilu technique).

For Allen, now inexorably committed to a career as a television star, the weekly broadcasts would remove some of the tensions of live TV, but also nearly double her workload, as she would now be expected to headline a show every week. However, not all elements of the Desilu technique were incorporated into *Burns and Allen*, which was filmed out of sequence, and without a studio audience. Although Allen had years of experience performing in front of a live audience, she disliked the pressure of it, and had suffered from "mike fright" in radio. The absence of a studio audience, once the live broadcasts were abandoned, put her more at ease when performing. Completed episodes were later shown to theater audiences so that a laugh track could be recorded.

When not performing, rehearsing, or memorizing scripts, she had other responsibilities as well. Meticulous about her appearance, she spent extra time with wardrobe people each week, insuring that she would appear in attractive and precisely fitted clothes (always being careful to avoid revealing a burn scar on her left arm, a remnant of a childhood kitchen accident). She was often called upon to participate in publicity efforts that kept her show in the public eye, as well as promotions for the show's sponsors, who billed Burns and Allen as "Carnation's own contented couple," and used them often in print ads. She regularly filmed commercials for the sponsors that would be inserted into the show in later years, once the "integrated" commercials that had been part of the live shows were dropped.

She also promoted *Burns and Allen* by making appearances on other popular CBS shows of the time, like *The Jack Benny Show*, *Toast of the Town*, and as a mystery guest on *What's My Line?* As McCadden Productions branched out into production of other shows, like the sitcom *Love That Bob* and the dramatic anthology *Climax*, Allen helped out by making guest appearances.

Though she was one of TV's best known actresses, the public knew relatively little of the real woman behind Allen's screen characterization. She did give interviews "out of character" periodically, but her image was also reinforced by gimmicks such as the syndicated newspaper column attributed to her, which was prepared by *Burns and Allen* writers, and filled with gags not unlike those heard on the show. Inexorably associated with the character who shared her name, she seldom would be seen playing other roles—her lead in the film *Mr. and Mrs. North* (MGM, 1941) being a rare exception, though not a markedly different type of character.

Away from the set, even her voice, which she raised to an unnaturally high register to play Gracie on TV, was different. Long before the era in which celebrities appeared on talk shows, wrote tell-all memoirs, or did stints in rehab, Gracie maintained a private life that seldom attracted the interest of *Confidential* magazine or other gossipmongers. She and Burns were parents to two children they had adopted in the mid–1930s, son Ronnie and daughter Sandra. Allen was careful to instill in them a strong sense of values, knowing that they were receiving an unusual upbringing in affluent Hollywood that was unlike what she and Burns had known as children. The Burns maintained a circle of show-business friends, including Jack Benny and his wife, known professionally as Mary Livingstone. (According to her husband, Allen had been known to admit, out of the earshot of others, that she wasn't really that fond of Mary, who seemed to be jealous of Gracie's accomplishments).

After his wife's death, Burns admitted in his memoir, *Gracie: A Love Story*, that he had had an extramarital affair during the early 1950s, early in the run of their TV series. His own biographer, Martin Gottfried, later reported that this was not an isolated incident, that Burns' apparently sincere devotion to his wife did not preclude him from occasional flings. Apparently Allen became aware of at least some of this, and both books contain versions of a widely repeated anecdote concerning the situation. In Burns' account, he bought his wife an expensive present out of guilt after she learned of his infidelity, causing her to tell a friend, years later, that she wished he would cheat again, because there was something else she needed for the house. Publicly, however, they remained a devoted couple, and Allen never spoke of the incident.

Gracie Allen receives a Mother's Day gift from son Ronnie and daughter Sandra in this publicity shot for *The Gracie Allen Murder Case* (Paramount, 1939).

To the actors and technicians who worked on *Burns and Allen*, she was a gracious colleague, thoughtful and professional. Fred de Cordova, who produced the show for several years, said, "Gracie was as lovely to work with as she appeared to be addle-pated on the tube."[9] However, most of her co-workers didn't seem to penetrate the façade in which she enveloped her private life. She was friendly with co-star Bea Benaderet during their long association, but they didn't often socialize away from work.

Perhaps because she "played herself," or because she had been a star for so long, Allen was often shortchanged when it came to recognizing her gifts as a performer. Although *The George Burns and Gracie Allen Show* enjoyed both good ratings and critical acclaim, its cast and crew generally went home empty-handed from the annual Emmy Awards. Gracie herself received six nominations during the show's run (including two, Best Comedienne and Best Actress—Continuing Performance, in 1956), but never received the statuette. Even those who voted on Emmy nominations seemed to be hazy as to her identity, including her one year among those nominated for Best Continuing Performance in a Series by a Woman Who Essentially Plays Herself, alongside competition such as singer and variety show hostess Dinah Shore.

"Because Gracie made playing Gracie appear to be so easy," Burns later said, "she never received the credit she deserved as an actress. One of the very few regrets I have is that Gracie never won an Emmy Award for her work on our television show, which she certainly deserved."[10]

Those in the know, however, recognized Allen's gifts. *Burns and Allen* producer-director Ralph Levy, looking back on his work with her, said, "I've often thought that Gracie was one of the finest actresses that ever lived—remember that word, *actress*, it's crucial. True, she played the silliest woman you could ever meet, but she never thought of herself as a comedienne, and George never treated her as one. In fact, there were times in radio, when Gracie was ill, and they'd use somebody like Joan Davis, a comedienne, to replace her—but it never worked properly. Only when a legitimate actress read Gracie's lines did the scenes play."[11]

During *Burns and Allen*'s eight-year run in prime time, the situation comedy genre was growing by leaps and bounds. Much had changed since the show's 1950 debut, and not just technically. As the seasons passed, the show began to more closely adhere to the prevailing standards for filmed sitcoms. Without sacrificing the show's unique feel, the writers began to compose slightly more typical sitcom plots, relying less on re-creations of Burns and Allen's vaudeville and radio routines.

By the mid–1950s, Allen, though appreciative of the show's success, and fans' adoration of her, was weary, and her health had begun to show signs of strain. At around this time, she was diagnosed with angina. Still a relatively young woman (though, if the earliest version of her birthdate is to be believed, she was in her mid-fifties when the TV show began), she had been working nonstop for more than thirty years, achieving success in at least four distinct media. Burns, insecure about his ability to survive professionally without her, admitted that, in later seasons, he often renewed the pair's contract for another year without consulting her, leery of what she might say about continuing if given the choice.

To relieve the burden on Allen, other cast members were brought in, principally George and Gracie's 20-year-old son, Ronnie Burns, who joined the show as a regular in 1955. Typical of the show's style, little explanation was given as to where Ronnie (the character) had been all those years. (In at least one earlier episode, Gracie's character had specifically stated that she and George had no children, which might have mattered in a show that had its feet on the ground more than *Burns and Allen*).

The addition of Ronnie to the cast coincided with a temporary relocation of *Burns and Allen*'s setting to New York (though it would continue to be filmed in Hollywood—somehow it seemed fitting that *Burns and Allen* would debut as a New York–based show, set in Beverly Hills, then later revert to a California-based show set in New York City). The relocation, which had the Burns and Morton families living in a hotel, allowed new opportunities for Gracie to unnerve or amuse characters like the hotel desk clerk, or the room service waiter, having leaned heavily in earlier episodes on door-to-door salesmen, policemen, and the mailman as foils for her flights of fancy. Character actor Peter Brocco had a recurring role during the 1955-56 season, playing the waiter who loved to deliver meals to her suite, where he gleefully and surreptitiously copied down her choicest remarks to share with his co-workers.

Even though the show, by 1955, was noticeably closer to the typical sitcom format than it had been during its early, live broadcasts, the surrealistic elements would continue throughout its run. In "Company for Christmas" (12/19/55), set at the hotel, George steps out on the balcony, where snow is falling, and yells to an unseen crew member, "Turn off the snow, Sidney! I wanna do my monologue." At the end of the scene, he gives the cue to resume the snow, and a pile of slush crashes down from above.

Although moments like this were still common, it was becoming more difficult for the show's writers to integrate into a sitcom format the type of routines that had made Burns and Allen famous in vaudeville, and which were used on their radio show. Later episodes drew more heavily on plot elements such as Gracie posing as a hotel maid in order to sneak into the room of another guest. Eventually a separate segment was added at the end of each show, in which the stars, in front of a curtain, performed a brief routine, often one adapted and updated from their vaudeville days, and then said goodnight to the audience.

The addition of Ronnie Burns to the cast for the last three years, and recurring story elements about his career as a dramatic student and aspiring actor, gave the show a new source of stories. The younger Burns, like Ricky Nelson on ABC's *The Adventures of Ozzie and Harriet* (1952–66), also became something of a teen idol, drawing in a new group of viewers and even enjoying a brief career as a recording artist. Towering over his mother, Ronnie played her levelheaded sidekick, as much the parent to her as she was to him. He continued with the show upon its return to a Beverly Hills setting a year later.

Working alongside his mother as a performer, Ronnie had an opportunity to see the work that her characterization entailed. "She just got very involved with the character," he said. "She would study the script for hours and hours and hours. Every time she got a new script, she had to work hard to make that script believable. She had a tough time doing it. You see, if she just read the lines naturally, people would say it didn't mean anything. She had to make it so that the audience says, 'You know? She's right.'"[12]

By this time, the show's producers and writers were making a conscious effort to lighten Allen's load. The addition of Ronnie to the cast, as well as the introduction of some recurring characters who were his friends or potential girlfriends, allowed Gracie to be deemphasized slightly. Supporting characters were spotlighted in more scenes, some of which didn't include Allen.

The leading lady of *Burns and Allen,* flanked by husband George and son Ronnie.

For example, the episode "Christmas in Jail" (12/24/56) tells how a series of holiday gift swaps and substitutions causes George to be arrested for trying to sell a phony pearl necklace back to the jewelry store where he bought the original. The story is divided among Gracie, George, the Mortons, Harry Von Zell, and Ronnie, and Allen's screen time is accordingly reduced. Viewers let the producers know that they didn't like seeing less of her, and the show's ratings began to slip a bit (dropping out of the Top 25 shows by 1957). Still, Burns hoped the changes would enable his wife to keep performing in a weekly series.

Nevertheless, by the 1957-58 season, her husband began to sense that all was not well with Allen. "I began watching her more carefully," Burns said. "Little things were different—maybe she had a little extra problem with a line, maybe she took a slightly longer break between takes. But things were different."[13]

Unlike many stars, Allen had never been given to throwing her weight around, or demanding to be the center of attention at all times. But as *Burns and Allen* neared the end of its television run, she was even more subdued than she had previously been, conserving her energy. Yvonne Lime Fedderson, later the co-founder of the ChildHelp USA charity, was among the young performers brought in for featured roles in the show's later years, and remembered Allen nearly fifty years later as "a quiet woman." Whatever difficulties she might have been experiencing, she remained gracious in her on-set demeanor. "She was pleasant and kind and I liked her very much," Fedderson says.[14]

In the spring of 1958, as the show wound up its eighth season, having done nearly 300 episodes, Burns asked his wife point-blank if she wanted to quit, and she said yes. Not only tired, she was now under the care of a cardiologist for her heart condition. Not surprisingly, the intense pressure of starring in a weekly TV show was doing little to ease her ills. McCadden and CBS announced that the show's eighth season would be its last, to the dismay of Allen's many fans.

Publicly, Allen made light of the decision, which was simply described as her retirement. "I'm going to sleep for six months," she said of her plans at the time. "I'm going to invite people in to dinner, and visit my grandchildren. And I'm going to clean out the bureau drawers."[15] Modest as ever, she was surprised by the public outcry that her decision created, with *Life* magazine, among others, covering the event of her last show.

Burns and Allen director Rod Amateau said that, even though Allen's retirement left them at loose ends professionally, the cast and crew didn't hold it against her. "Everybody was happy," he said. "Sure we all lost jobs; but we all felt so protective of Gracie, and because Gracie wanted it, everybody was happy for her."[16]

Although Allen was happy to retire, Burns wanted to continue working as a television performer. NBC, which had fewer successful sitcoms than rival CBS, quickly signed him for *The George Burns Show*, basically a continuation of the original series, minus Gracie. Unwisely, Burns surrounded himself with the same supporting cast, including his son, continued to play himself, and turned out a show that only succeeded in making viewers miss Gracie. Despite tinkering that included a mid-season change to a musical format, the show never caught on, and was canceled after one season.

Still unsure how to create a persona for himself without a dizzy dame on his arm, he drifted through the 1960s in search of substitutes—playing Vegas with Carol Channing as an ersatz Gracie, and starring in *Wendy and Me* (1964-65), an unsuccessful ABC sitcom that cast Connie Stevens as a cutely vague blonde. He also recreated some venerable Burns and Allen routines opposite Lucille Ball in a 1966 episode of *The Lucy Show*. Most of these ventures, unfortunately for him, only reinforced how unique Allen's talent was. (Even in the early 1980s, long after *The Sunshine Boys* and *Oh, God!* had revitalized Burns' career, he was still mining his past, serving as executive producer of a TV sitcom pilot, "I Love Her Anyway," that attempted to recreate the George-and-Gracie rhythm with younger performers).

While Burns faced these professional dilemmas, Allen spent the remainder of her life out of public view. Enjoying ample free time unlike she had known for most of her adult life, she played cards, shopped, had lunch with friends, and caught up on her leisure reading. She was supportive of her husband's TV ventures, but kept her distance, not tempted to make even an occasional guest appearance (although she provided a vocal track for an episode of *The Jack Benny Show*, "How Jack Met George Burns," telecast on January 7, 1964).

Unfortunately, though little was said about it at the time, her heart problems had grown increasingly serious, and she suffered a major heart attack in 1961. From that point forward, Allen stayed close to home, requiring the care of a full-time companion and venturing out only on rare occasions. On August 27, 1964, days before the premiere of George's new show *Wendy and Me*, she suffered a fatal heart attack.

Longtime friend Jack Benny, delivering her eulogy at a memorial service that drew thousands of onlookers, said, "The whole world loved Gracie ... she was recognized everywhere for her exceptional ability as a comedienne."[17]

Allen's skills as a performer would continue to be on display through filmed reruns of *Burns and Allen,* which would enjoy a long and successful run in syndication through Screen Gems (later Columbia Pictures Television), fading from the scene only in the 1970s, when black-and-white shows began to be seen as passé. Fans caught whiffs of her Gracie characterization in a host of female characters that followed in her footsteps, from *The Mary Tyler Moore Show*'s Georgette Baxter to *The Golden Girls'* Rose Nylund, though *TV Guide* readers angrily protested the insult when she was lumped alongside Chrissy Snow from *Three's Company* (ABC, 1977–84) and contemporary reality TV "performers" in an article spotlighting TV's most memorable "dumb blondes."

Unfortunately, aside from a revival on the basic cable network CBN in the 1980s, and occasional plays of a small sampling of episodes on TV Land, the classic *Burns and Allen* shows have mostly gathered dust in a vault in recent years. Only public domain DVD sets exist on today's market, mostly taken from kinescopes of a handful of early live broadcasts with variable sound and picture quality.

Although much of her TV work is difficult to see today, Gracie remains an iconic figure in American culture, 50 years after she starred in *Burns and Allen.* In 2002, impressionist Frank Gorshin starred in Rupert Holmes' *Say Goodnight, Gracie,* a one-man Broadway show in which he played George. Actress Didi Conn, best known as Frenchie in *Grease* (Paramount, 1978), represented Allen with a vocal re-creation of some radio routines. Some reviewers, while praising the show overall, commented that, as in days of yore, George was inevitably upstaged by Gracie, even in absentia. That same year, A&E's *Biography* unveiled a new documentary titled "Gracie Allen: The Better Half."

Her legacy is also denoted with the widely respected Gracie Allen Awards, given by the American Women in Radio and Television organization since 1975 to honor the professional achievements of women in broadcasting. Past winners of Gracies include Meryl Streep, Tracey Ullman, Paula Zahn, and Katie Couric, as well as numerous producers and executives who have crafted fine documentaries and public affairs shows.

At first glance, naming the prestigious awards in Allen's honor may seem a bit of an anomaly, given her stage image. But AWRT executive director Maria Efantis Brennan says the organization's membership recognized Allen's true importance as a performer and "as a pioneer in radio and television, theater and movies. She really was quite groundbreaking for her day. She created a lot of the inroads that women today have been able to follow."[18]

As for the character she played so unforgettably, Brennan believes that Allen didn't mind if people sometimes thought the star herself was that woman. "Anyone who knew her knew that nothing could be further from the truth," says Brennan of Allen's screen image. "She didn't care if people identified with her in that way, even if she was one of the smartest women you'd ever meet. She didn't mind poking fun at herself."

❖ 2 ❖

Eve Arden

Our Miss Brooks and *The Eve Arden Show*

ALONG WITH ANN SOTHERN (Q.V.), veteran film and stage actress Eve Arden provided one of TV's most prominent depictions of working women in the 1950s, with the successful adaptation of her popular radio sitcom *Our Miss Brooks*, which debuted on CBS-TV in October 1952.

Arden played Connie Brooks, English teacher at suburban Madison High School. Chief among Miss Brooks' day-to-day concerns were her prickly relationship with stuffy school principal Osgood Conklin (played by Gale Gordon), and her frustratingly unfulfilled flirtation with shy, bookish science teacher Philip Boynton (Robert Rockwell). Rounding out the regularly seen cast were Miss Brooks' elderly landlady Mrs. Davis (Jane Morgan), Conklin's pretty daughter Harriet (Gloria McMillan), and future leading man Richard Crenna, who raised his vocal chords to distressingly screechy levels as her numbskull student Walter Denton.

The show, which was a comparatively realistic, low-key situation comedy for its time, and a forerunner to the "workplace comedies" that would become popular in the 1970s, had been a favorite on CBS radio since 1948. For Arden, it offered a welcome opportunity to play a role that varied from the "type" that had begun to feel like a trap in her film career.

Born near San Francisco on April 30, 1908, Eunice Quedens was the daughter of a successful milliner, a single parent who'd divorced the girl's father over his gambling habits. With her business demanding much of her time, Eunice's mother placed the girl in a convent for a time, and later allowed her to live in rural Mill Valley, outside San Francisco, with an aunt.

From a young age, when she won a medal for a recitation to the Women's Christian Temperance Union, the future Eve Arden enjoyed performing. By the time she was in high school, starring in school plays, she was infatuated with show business. She landed her first professional gig while still a teenager, when friends of her mother took her to a local theater company and dropped her off at the front door, suggesting she get herself a job. Amazingly, she did just that.

Relocating to New York to further her stage career, she was hired for the *Ziegfeld Follies* company. It was there that, being told her real name was not suitable for a marquee, she glanced at a jar of Elizabeth Arden cosmetics and thought of a new one. Eve Arden worked on the New York stage for the next several years.

Although she made an inauspicious film debut in a long-forgotten cheapie called *Oh, Doctor!* (Universal, 1937), she first came to the attention of moviegoers with her featured role in RKO's 1937 hit *Stage Door*, a comedy-drama about the ambitious women who inhabit a theatrical boardinghouse in New York. A standout among the powerhouse cast headed by Katharine Hepburn and Ginger Rogers, and featured newcomers Lucille Ball (q.v.) and Ann Miller, Arden displayed a gift for wisecracking that would be both her claim to fame, and her *bête noire*, professionally.

During the shooting, she became acquainted with Lucille Ball, who would also receive a career boost from *Stage Door*. The aspiring actresses in the film are mostly friends, although competitive when an acting job is at stake, but Arden and Ball established a strong relationship off camera minus the rivalry. They were re-teamed in another, less successful comedy for RKO, *Having Wonderful Time,* the following year. Both still in their twenties and as yet uncertain what footholds they might find in Hollywood, they became friends, and would remain so throughout their careers. And both would ultimately find a level of career achievement and satisfaction in television that largely eluded them in movies.

For a time, Arden juggled stage work—she was featured in Cole Porter's 1941 Broadway musical *Let's Face It*—with supporting roles in films like the Marx Brothers' *At the Circus* (MGM, 1939). Although her ties to Hollywood would grow stronger in the 1940s, her passion for the stage was lifelong, and she would return to it often.

Like her friend Lucille Ball, Arden would eventually become frustrated by film studios that saw them most easily as brittle, sarcastic women who snapped off quips—Ball referred to them as "the drop-gag girls."[1] Never groomed as a leading lady, Arden nevertheless became a busy Warner Brothers contract player in the 1940s, where she specialized in supporting roles as sardonic sidekicks of leading ladies like Joan Crawford, Barbara Stanwyck, and Jane Wyman. She was Oscar-nominated as Best Supporting Actress for her role as Ida Corwin in *Mildred Pierce* (1945). Ida was the staunch ally of the heroine whose best-remembered line, referring to Crawford's wayward daughter, was "Veda's convinced me that alligators have the right idea—they eat their young."

Arden's instantly recognizable voice was also heard on popular radio programs such as *The Danny Kaye Show,* and *The Sealtest Village Store,* where she replaced Joan Davis (q.v.) when that actress was given her own show. That series kept Arden in front of audiences from 1945 to 1948.

All of these roles played on the wisecracking image of which Arden was growing tired by the late 1940s. "I just don't like that dame," she once said of her screen persona. "She is hard-boiled, unsentimental—and not me."[2] She resolved to seek out roles that would allow her to show a fuller range of emotions.

Although *The Sealtest Village Store* raised Arden's profile as a radio entertainer, she later speculated that it may have been a chance social encounter with CBS chairman William Paley that resulted in an offer to star in her own vehicle, *Our Miss Brooks*, a role for which actresses such as Lucille Ball and Shirley Booth had also been considered (and which Booth had played once in a test episode). Although the initial script didn't greatly impress her, a rewrite by writers Al Lewis and Joe Quillan, who would be associated with the show throughout its long run, made her reconsider. Chief among the show's appeals for her was the opportunity to broaden her screen image. Although the character of Connie Brooks would unquestionably trade on Arden's ability to pitch a sardonic remark, she also had a warm and likable side that the actress found greatly appealing.

In creating Miss Brooks, she drew on memories of the teachers who had an impression on her as a child. "I remember with affection those who taught me,"

Eve Arden became a CBS radio star in the 1940s with *Our Miss Brooks*.

Arden said. "I recall my third-grade teacher, umpteen years ago—Miss Ruth Waterman—she had dimples, big brown eyes, and was always smiling. I try to give Miss Brooks that same smiling quality."[3]

The radio show was a hit, and became part of Arden's professional life for the next nine years. By the early 1950s, CBS wanted to launch a video version, and looked around for a suitable television production company.

In 1951, her friend Lucille Ball's *I Love Lucy* had revolutionized TV comedy, and Ball and Desi Arnaz's company Desilu was suddenly a major force in the industry. Given Arden's extensive stage experience, it's not surprising that the notion of filming before a studio audience, as Ball and company did, appealed to her more than the one-camera, closed-set method used on other contemporary CBS sitcoms like *The Amos 'n' Andy Show*.

During early 1952, Arden was an occasional guest on the Desilu soundstage, and had an opportunity to witness how the *Lucy* shows were assembled. Two of her *Brooks* co-stars gained first-hand experience by making guest appearances on *I Love Lucy* during this apprenticeship period—Richard Crenna, who played a Walter Denton-ish lovesick teenager in an episode called "The Young Fans" (2/25/52), and Gale Gordon, who made two appearances that spring as Ricky's Tropicana boss Mr. Littlefield.

From Desilu's perspective, as company president Desi Arnaz later recalled, doing *Our Miss Brooks* offered Desilu a profitable cost-sharing opportunity. Having obtained everything necessary as an independent producer to film a weekly TV sitcom, it was easy enough to double up and shoot a second one using much of the same equipment, and many of the same crew members. For a time, the two shows would even share director William Asher, who helmed the pilot and other early episodes of the *Brooks* TV show.

The cast of the radio show, a cohesive team after four years together, would transfer to the new venture largely intact. The exception was up-and-coming leading man Jeff Chandler, not yet the movie star he would become, who had voiced the timid and square Mr. Boynton on radio. Although he was willing to continue his role, even while Universal Studios was grooming him for movie stardom, Arden and her producer knew that his look was too blatantly virile to play Boynton on TV, and recast with actor Robert Rockwell.

The pilot episode, "Trying to Pick a Fight," revolved around Walter Denton's advice to Miss Brooks that an occasional quarrel could bring a new spark to a romantic relationship. Disaster follows when Miss Brooks tests the theory, first by goading Mr. Boynton into a pointless argument, then by sharing the advice with Mr. Conklin, who uses it so thoroughly that he mistakenly thinks his wife has gone home to Mother.

The first TV episode, which took care to introduce the basic characters and situations to viewers who might not have been fans of the radio series, was vague on the exact nature of Connie's relationship with Mr. Boynton. In an early scene, it's said that they've been "dating" for four years, ever since she began teaching at Madison (and coinciding with the radio show's 1948 debut). Walter Denton alludes to their regular Friday night dinner dates. Mrs. Davis, Connie's landlady, even says that they're "going steady," though Miss Brooks disputes this, saying Mr. Boynton's greatest affection is reserved for his laboratory frog, MacDougall. For a couple who are supposedly in any kind of romantic relationship of four years' duration, though, it seems a bit odd that Miss Brooks and Mr. Boynton aren't even on a first-name basis.

If the relationship is rather unclear, Miss Brooks herself is not. From the outset, Arden plays a woman who knows her own mind, and, second perhaps only to Lucy Ricardo in 1950s sitcoms, expresses it. Her character emerges as one of the smartest and sassiest women on TV, and viewers loved her for it.

Later in the pilot episode, determined to goad Mr. Boynton into a reaction, Miss Brooks lets him have it. Finally, annoyed, he tells her—in a very mild, Boyntonish way—that she's roused him to anger. Longtime fans knew better than to expect Miss Brooks to back down:

BROOKS: You wanna make something of it, Frog-Boy?
BOYNTON: Frog-Boy?

BROOKS: Why don't you leap down to the pond, and dunk your head under a lily pad?
BOYNTON: So, you've been spying on me after school!

While she pays a surface respect to her boss, it's also apparent that Miss Brooks sees Mr. Conklin's shortcomings clearly. Her wisecracks about him, though rarely said in his earshot, nail him with telling accuracy. And, in the pilot, when he is AWOL temporarily, on the trail of his wife, Connie plops herself down in his office, trying out his desk chair for size, and identifying herself to a telephone caller as "Acting Principal Constance Brooks."

Thirty-five years before *Roseanne* (ABC, 1988–97) came on the scene, Connie Brooks was the epitome of the woman who's stronger and more able than the men in her life, both professionally and personally. Mr. Conklin is usually portrayed more as a stuffy, penny-pinching blowhard than an effective administrator, and Mr. Boynton, competent teacher though he might be, is clearly not much of a catch for a woman as bright and witty as Connie Brooks. But the lady herself is obviously a capable professional, and aggressively pursues what she wants in life, even though she doesn't always get it.

In another early episode, "Blue Goldfish" (12/5/52), when the school's lack of heat and shortage of needed equipment creates problems for Walter, Mr. Boynton, and others, it's Miss Brooks who's enlisted to broach the subject with Mr. Conklin. She's clearly the ringleader, and the one to whom others, male and female alike, look for leadership. She's also shown to be a good teacher, one who holds her students to high standards, and takes an interest in their well-being.

Arden, drawing on her experience playing brittle, caustic women in movies, as well as her own natural warmth and charm, created a character that combined the best of both. Connie Brooks doesn't suffer fools gladly, though she's often knee-deep in them. But she's also one of the more accomplished working women seen on 1950s television, and a forerunner to later TV women such as Mary Richards who had a better handle on their professional life than they did on the personal. And unlike many of TV's women, then and later, who plotted and schemed to land a man, it's always pretty clear in *Our Miss Brooks* that there's nothing wrong with Connie herself. Arden plays an attractive and smart woman, and the self-deprecating element that crept into characters like *The Dick Van Dyke Show*'s Sally Rogers, or *The Mary Tyler Moore Show*'s Rhoda Morgenstern, is largely absent here.

As the show's longtime producer Al Lewis explained to *TV Guide*, Connie Brooks "is not a man-chaser in any sense of the word. She has a deep and abiding crush on Boynton and Boynton alone.... She is strictly a one-man woman, and that's the way it's going to be."[4] Lewis' take on the situation would keep the show afloat for most of its run, until a drop in ratings led to some changes in 1955.

Away from the set, Eve Arden epitomized not only the accomplished professional—she would be a highly regarded working actress over a five-decade period—but also the woman who balances the demands of work and home. Although an early marriage to literary agent Edward Bergen ended in divorce by the late 1940s, she had become a parent with the adoption of two little girls. While touring in a summer stock production, she became friendly with her leading man, a young actor named Brooks

West, and they were married in 1951, soon adding an adopted son, Duncan, to their blended family. In 1954, Arden would give birth to a son, Douglas, completing the family that would occupy much of her energy and thought for the rest of her life.

Clearly her family life was important to her, and she devotes much space in her autobiography to accounts of bringing up her children on a ranch outside Los Angeles, their travels together, and a happy marriage. The picture that emerges is of a woman whose two greatest loves are her family, and the work she does in the theater. While television may not have been as artistically satisfying as stage work, *Miss Brooks* was important to her, not only for the professional success it represented, but also for the financial security it gave her family.

Though she says little about it in her book, Arden encountered a situation that would become much more common a generation or so later in American families— the wife who was more successful professionally, and a bigger wage-earner, than the husband. West, who was younger than she (by about eight years), was less established as a performer, and would never attain the level of fame she already had by the time they married. A few months before *Miss Brooks* made its bow on television, West was cast in a supporting role in the sitcom *My Friend Irma*, which joined the CBS schedule in early 1952. When the series underwent a format change a year or so later, West's character was written out. It was to be his only regular series role.

Meanwhile, *Our Miss Brooks*, debuting on CBS' Friday night lineup in October 1952, quickly earned a place in viewers' hearts, and received critical praise as well. "*Our Miss Brooks* had a smooth professional look, and seemed to have made the move to TV without dropping a pun or a pratfall," reported *Time*.[5]

Longtime *New York Times* TV critic Jack Gould, surveying "TV's Top Comediennes" in 1953, was not so enamored of the program itself ("hardly the best of the situation comedy shows"), but admired Arden's "brittle, caustic style and stinging delivery of a wisecrack.... If only she had a less banal vehicle to work with, Arden might be second to none."[6]

Arden's characterization also earned her praise from another constituency, as Hyman Goldberg reported rather floridly in a *Cosmopolitan* profile of the star:

"Because she has implanted in her vast following the notion that teachers bleed when they are pricked, that they occasionally find someone of the opposing sex to be not altogether revolting, and when their salaries are meager they are apt to be not very happy and even a bit threadbare, teachers everywhere regard Miss Arden, and her network alter ego, Connie Brooks, as the best thing that has happened to pedagogy since the innovation of the long summer vacation. Each week she receives several hundred letters from grateful teachers."[7]

From the show's first season, Emmy voters took notice of Arden's work, nominating her as Best Comedienne of 1952. Although Lucille Ball took home the prize that night, Arden's turn came a year later, when she was named Best Female Star of a Regular Series. She missed out on accepting her statuette in person, so sure had she been that someone else would win. She would continue to receive nominations every year that *Miss Brooks* remained on CBS.

While some reporters wondered, stereotypically, if Arden and Lucille Ball's CBS sitcoms, both for Desilu, had them engaged in a rivalry for the attention of TV audiences, the women were in fact supportive of each other's endeavors. As Ball pointed out, "Don't forget that I'm Vice-President of Desilu Productions, which means the better *Miss Brooks* does, the better off I am. That's not exactly competition, if you see what I mean."⁸ Both were also surely savvy enough to see that, for all that they had been compared in years past, they had developed personal styles, and shows, that were not particularly similar.

Mindful of her debt to Desilu, and her friendship with the Arnazes, Arden would charge them nothing for her cameo appearance in "L.A. at Last," a 1955 episode of *I Love Lucy*. One of *Lucy*'s most famous episodes, it shows Lucy, Ethel, and Fred rubbernecking at celebrities lunching at the Hollywood Brown Derby. Before Lucy has a memorable encounter with movie star William Holden and a dessert tray, she makes acquaintance with the nearby Arden, playing herself, who helpfully identifies her own caricature on the wall when Lucy mistakes it for one of Judy Holliday or Shelley Winters. Arnaz later repaid the favor with a guest stint on *Brooks*.

Eve Arden and husband Brooks West with her Emmy Award for Best Female Star of Regular Series *(Our Miss Brooks)*.

Throughout its successful four-year run on prime time television, *Our Miss Brooks* profited from the sarcastic slings and arrows that Arden handled so masterfully. This style of comedy, so associated with the actress, didn't come to her quite as naturally as people often assumed, according to her longtime colleague Richard Crenna. "There was not a lot of Brooks in her," he said years later. "She had a wonderful sense of humor, but I wouldn't say she was particularly sardonic. She never played the comedian offstage—she didn't need to be the funniest person in the room, unlike so many comics, who find it difficult to get off. She went out, got the laughs, and went back to her ranch in the Valley. She was just a wonderfully unselfish actress, and was just so up all the time; she made you feel good to be around her."⁹

Arden's son, producer/writer Douglas Brooks West, has a slightly different take on his mother's humor. Though he agrees that she rarely applied that same biting humor off-camera—"she would never say an unkind thing to anybody"[10]—he believes that it was more than a stage affectation.

"She created that persona that so many people use as an icon," West says today, adding that Arden had the character down so well that she could often contribute dialogue to scripts that needed a boost. He points to one of her best-remembered lines as Principal McGee from *Grease*—"If you can't be an athlete, be an athletic supporter!"—as an example of one of her contributions.

Although *Our Miss Brooks* unquestionably revolved around its title character, it was more of an ensemble comedy than many 1950s shows, and Arden seemed to be unafraid of letting her fellow actors shine. Gale Gordon, who practically patented the role of the irritable, blustering boss, squared off ably against Miss Brooks, a good match for Arden's strength. His character here is more varied and amusing than his later incarnations as Lucy Carmichael's (and later Lucy Carter's) constantly yelling bosses on *The Lucy Show* and *Here's Lucy*. (Had he not been under contact for *Brooks*, he might also have played Fred Mertz on *I Love Lucy*).

Robert Rockwell also deserves praise for his portrayal of Philip Boynton. The actor neatly bridges the two elements of the character that viewers need to see. He's able to play the handsome, smart, nice, if shy, man that Miss Brooks finds appealing, as well as the side of him that, consciously or not, keeps her at arms' length—and keeps the show's primary conflict alive.

In the show's early years, busy radio and TV actress Mary Jane Croft, today best-remembered for her many appearances as Lucy's pal Mary Jane on *The Lucy Show* and *Here's Lucy*, had a recurring role as Daisy Enright, fellow Madison High teacher and rival for the attentions of Mr. Boynton. Miss Enright, almost a precursor to *The Mary Tyler Moore Show*'s Sue Ann Nivens with her sweetly voiced jabs at the heroine, brought out the side of Miss Brooks most like those snappish movie roles Arden played so well.

In "Home Cooked Meal" (6/3/55), Miss Brooks and Miss Enright are both vying to impress Mr. Boynton with their domestic skills. Miss Enright ups the ante by inviting him over to watch her new TV set, leading Mr. Boynton to reminisce about the early days of TV, when there was so little of interest to watch. She quickly agrees:

ENRIGHT: Yes, in those days I remember—in my teens, there weren't very many stars on television.
BROOKS: When you were in your teens, there weren't many stars on the flag.

After three years on TV (and seven on radio), *Our Miss Brooks* underwent a major overhaul in the fall of 1955, reacting to a ratings drop that had taken the show out of the Top 25 in ratings. *I Love Lucy* had recently experienced a lift with a story arc about the Ricardos' and the Mertzes' trip to Hollywood. *Brooks* producers strove for a similar effect by introducing new storylines, and writing out some longtime cast members. In the season's second installment, aptly titled "Transition Show" (10/14/55), Connie loses her job at Madison High, which is scheduled to be bulldozed. Soon landing a new position at Mrs. Nestor's Private School, she is elated to be free of Mr. Conklin at last, until she finds that he, like she, has found a job there.

Although Gale Gordon's status on the show as Arden's chief nemesis remained intact, other featured players fell by the wayside in the new format. Almost thirty years old, Richard Crenna opted out of his role as gawky teenager Walter, who'd already been in high school for the better part of a decade on the show. The producers also elected to drop Robert Rockwell, as Mr. Boynton, from the regular cast, sending him off to a job in Arizona.

Deciding that the long, uncertain courtship of Miss Brooks and Mr. Boynton was played out, they gave Connie a succession of new love interests. Primary among them was actor Gene Barry, later TV's *Bat Masterson* (NBC, 1958–61) and the star of *Burke's Law* (ABC, 1963–65). Less retiring than Mr. Boynton, the character opened up new stories, but also removed some of the underlying tension that had been endemic to the show's humor. Other additions to the cast included Nana Bryant as school owner Mrs. Nestor, and Bob Sweeney as faculty member Oliver Munsey.

Arden did not embrace the changes. "I didn't want to leave Madison High," she told *TV Guide*, "and I didn't want to lose either Mr. Boynton or Mrs. Davis."[11] Along with the cast and character changes came a new, earlier time slot (8:30 P.M.) for *Our Miss Brooks*, replacing the just-cancelled *Topper*. But none of the changes managed to lure back the audience that was drifting away.

TV Guide, in an unusually negative review, commented on the show's ratings drop. "The reason for this isn't too hard to pinpoint. It would seem that Miss Arden and her writers don't have too much respect for their viewers' taste and intelligence. The situations, bordering on the slapstick, are too incongruous to be believable. To make certain that nobody misses the point of a gag, they run it into the ground. Sometimes they even trample on it."[12]

As the season progressed, and audiences failed to embrace the new characters and stories, some familiar elements of the original show began to resurface. In mid-season, "Mr. Boynton's Return" (2/17/56) for a visit sparked a rivalry between him and Connie's new love interest. A few weeks later, Boynton was applying for a faculty position at Mrs. Nestor's school, and Gene Barry had left the cast.

In April 1956, the sponsor renewed the show for another six months, but the deal was an unusual one, calling for only a handful of new shows. CBS began to show reruns of episodes from previous seasons, including the 1952 pilot, sometimes with a new wraparound segment featuring original cast members like Mrs. Davis. In May, the series aired its last original episodes, though reruns continued to play through the early fall. The radio show, which had survived into the twilight days of network radio sitcoms, was soon laid to rest as well.

Arden wasn't brokenhearted to see the long-running series fade to black. "I do love Miss Brooks," she said, "but enough of a good thing can be too much. Besides, the old Madison High films are going into syndication, the present show will be on all summer and RKO has just sold all those old movies to TV and I'm in most of them. People are going to have to go to Siberia to escape me."[13]

In *Our Miss Brooks'* next-to-last episode, "Principal for a Day" (5/4/56), Miss Brooks finally got her chance to sit in the administrator's office, when the new owner of Mrs. Nestor's Private School recommended her for the job. It was a long overdue promotion, albeit temporary, for the woman who'd so long demonstrated that she was just as capable, if not more so, than the men who usually held such jobs.

Today, when a long-running series comes to a close, there's usually a highly publicized final episode, which brings the show's stories to a happy conclusion. Not so

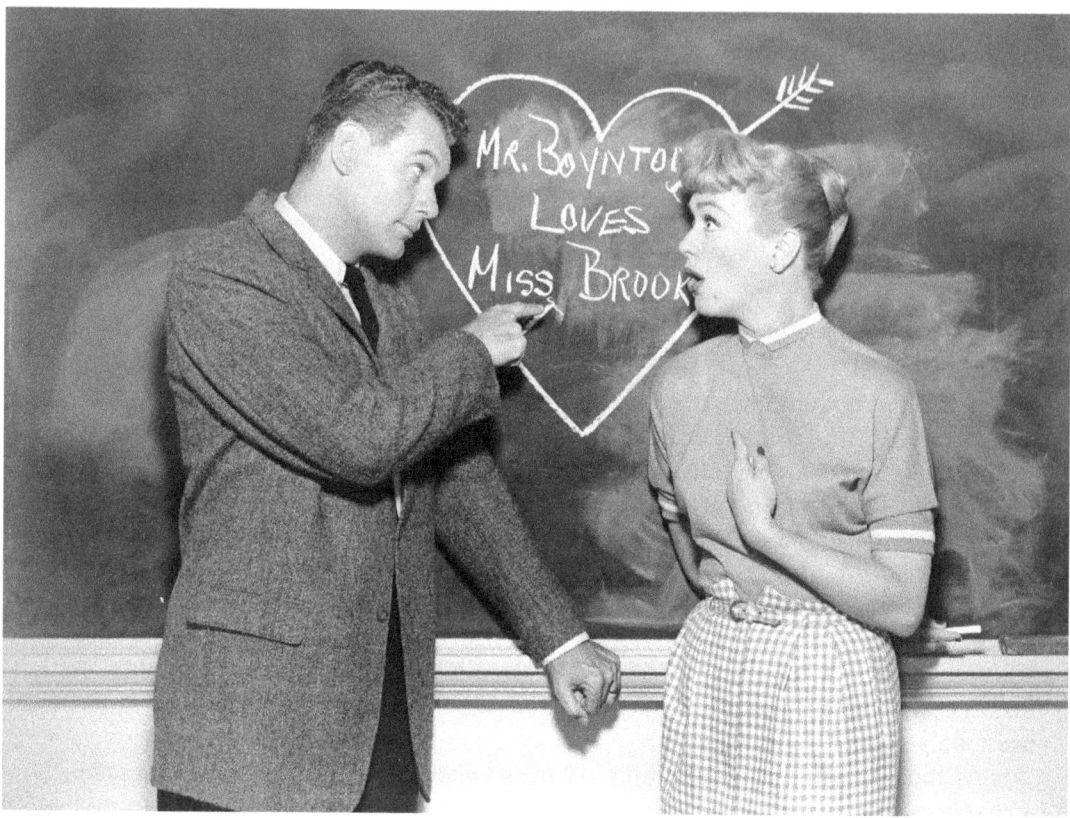

Eve Arden reunited with TV co-star Robert Rockwell (Philip Boynton) for the Warner Brothers' film version of *Our Miss Brooks* (1956).

in the 1950s, when such special episodes, and even shows with holiday themes, were often seen as detrimental to the series' afterlife in syndication.

Although the final TV episode of *Our Miss Brooks* was unremarkable, the show had an unexpected resurrection when Warner Brothers released a movie version, featuring the original cast, in 1956. Given the show's fading popularity, studio executives may well have regretted green-lighting the film by the time it hit theaters. But for *Brooks* fans, it was an unusual opportunity not only to see the stories from the series reenacted—the film opens with Connie beginning her job at Madison High School, and meeting Mr. Boynton—but also to find out the ultimate fate of Miss Brooks and her hesitant suitor, which the series had left unresolved.

Introducing a rival to Philip Boynton in wealthy newspaper publisher Larry Nolan (ironically, played by Ann Sothern's longtime co-star Don Porter), the movie escalates the basic situation that the series had so long propagated. Originally at odds with Nolan, who challenges her teaching of his teenage son, Connie gradually acknowledges an attraction to him, and sees an alternative to her stalled relationship with Mr. Boynton.

Armed with a marriage proposal from Nolan, Connie is able to stir the milquetoast Boynton into more action than she ever saw on the radio or TV episodes, sharing a fairly passionate kiss and finally getting on a first-name basis. Dreaming of the home she might someday share with "Phil" (which includes the proverbial white picket fence), Connie imagines snuggling with him in front of a roaring fire, and happily looking in on their children (eight of them!) By the movie's fadeout, after a misunderstanding with Phil threatens to break them up for good, Connie finally is on her way to marrying her man after eight years. (Although some sources report that she actually becomes Mrs. Boynton in the course of the film, this is not so, although it's clearly the expected outcome by the time the end credits appear. Only in one of the fantasy sequences is she seen in a wedding gown, being carried across the threshold).

Simultaneously with the movie's release, Miss Brooks made her debut in yet a fourth medium. Dell Comics, which published numerous movie and TV tie-ins during the 1950s, issued a one-time-only *Our Miss Brooks* comic book, which was adapted from the movie screenplay. A collector's item today, copies of the comic in mint condition sell online for $200.00 or more.

Our Miss Brooks, the movie, is an occasionally odd hybrid between the familiar characters and gags of the series, and more conventional movie plot elements. In the TV show, Connie's setbacks with Mr. Boynton typically are good for nothing more than a wisecrack. In the film, the romance is treated more conventionally, and taken more seriously. Connie's belief that she has misinterpreted Philip's intentions reduces her to tears, and the movie's final payoff threatens to turn them into a conventional romantic couple. It's just as well that the producers and writers of the TV series never allowed the marriage to happen in the show's later seasons, as it would have been as disastrous as the same happy ending was for *Rhoda* (CBS, 1974–78) twenty years later.

The movie of *Our Miss Brooks* was a box-office failure. Perhaps it came too late, after public interest in the series was on the wane. Arden herself complained that the studio publicized it insufficiently. It may also be that the failure of this film, like Liberace's *Sincerely Yours* (1955), also for Warners,' and the relatively disappointing box-office returns of Lucy and Desi's *Forever, Darling* (MGM, 1956), demonstrated that moviegoers wouldn't pay to see offshoots of current TV shows. (Although, a generation later, remakes of baby-boomer favorites like *The Beverly Hillbillies* were a much more viable option). Still, it was satisfying to see Miss Brooks land her man at last, and the movie was a better alternative than the twenty-years-later reunion shows for classic sitcoms that would be all the rage in the 1980s.

In the fall of 1956, *Our Miss Brooks* began its afterlife as a prominent feature on CBS' daytime schedule. Reruns of Arden's show, which sponsors were quick to buy, displaced a young comedian named Johnny Carson from his CBS daytime slot. Meanwhile, Arden was still under contract to CBS, and being groomed for her next project.

Even though the network considered *Our Miss Brooks* played out, executives knew that its star still had a substantial following. A year after the original series vacated the prime time schedule, Arden made a comeback to prime time TV with another CBS sitcom, *The Eve Arden Show*. The new program cast her as author and lecturer Liza Hammond (named after one of Arden's own daughters), a widow who tried to be a good mother though she was often away from home. Featured in the cast were veteran film and radio character actor Allyn Joslyn as the manager of her lecture bureau (and potential romantic interest), Frances Bavier (soon to become *The Andy Griffith Show*'s Aunt Bee), as her mother, and child actresses Karen Greene and Gail Stone as her twin daughters.

Based on a memoir by author Emily Kimbrough (whose book *Our Hearts Were Young and Gay* had already inspired another, short-lived CBS sitcom), *The Eve Arden Show* was assembled for the star by an elite pair with impeccable sitcom credentials. Sol Saks, who would later create *Bewitched* (ABC, 1964–72), created the show, and Sheldon Leonard, producer/director of another long-running hit, *The Danny Thomas Show*, (ABC/CBS, 1953–64) directed. The show was also something of a West family project—Arden and her husband Brooks West formed a company, Westhaven Productions, which co-produced the show in association with CBS. West was credited as the show's associate producer, and once again Arden chose Desilu Productions to oversee its filming.

In the pilot episode, "It Gives Me Great Pleasure" (also the title of Kimbrough's book), Arden's character, a novelist whose most recent publication is *Summer's End*, receives a visit from George Howell of the Howell Speakers' Bureau, who offers her a lecture tour. Despite the family's limited finances, Liza turns him down flat, confessing to a massive case of stage fright. After much persuasion, she makes her slightly hesitant debut as a speaker to a woman's club. Having been offered the stock advice about overcoming nervousness by imagining the audience members in their underwear, Liza gets the giggles momentarily as she gazes out into the audience of girdle-clad suburban matrons, then launches confidently into her speech.

Perhaps sensing that a bout with stage fright was by itself thin material for a series premise, Saks attempts to lay the groundwork for future stories (as well as convey a little bit of backstory) when George tells Liza, "You've been a widow for six years. You've buried yourself within these four walls [her home office], hidden in the pages of the books you write. You've been hiding from life.... When did you last have a highball? When did you last go on a date? When did you last kiss a man?" At episode's end, Liza accepts a dinner date with George, and the stage is set for a possible romantic involvement—as well as for the "adventure, glamour, romance" that he tells her will be part and parcel of her new life.

CBS executives liked *The Eve Arden Show*, and had little difficulty lining up Lever Brothers (promoting a then-new product, Dove Soap) and Shulton (hawking Old Spice products) as alternate-week sponsors for the 1957-58 season. Scheduled for an 8:30 P.M. Tuesday time slot, Arden's show would be sandwiched between two long-running CBS favorites, *The Phil Silvers Show* (1955–59) and *To Tell the Truth* (1956–68).

All signs were indicating that Arden would be launching her second hit TV series. Then came the bad news. After the deal was in place, Arden was told that neither of the two sitcom titans responsible for shepherding the pilot show would be available to assume those functions on a regular basis. Leonard was committed to *The Danny Thomas Show*, and Saks to the Ida Lupino—Howard Duff sitcom *Mr. Adams and Eve* (CBS, 1957-58).

The series went into production despite the loss of its original producer and writer. After viewing the first episode of *The Eve Arden Show*, *Variety* published a review that sounded a warning signal, saying that the show "could be in for trouble."

While acknowledging that the show had been skillfully assembled, the reviewer felt that its basic setup had "extreme limitations" that might not wear well on a week-to-week basis. As for the star, "it's regrettable that Miss Arden has become so stereotyped a TV personality, for this is a continuation of the barb-and-the-sally school of femme comedies."[14]

TV Guide's take on the show a few months later was more favorable, calling it "good clean fun" and the star "an actress of charm, restraint, style and grace."[15] Unfortunately, ratings for *The Eve Arden Show* were unimpressive, though Arden netted her fifth Emmy nomination for her work in the series. For the 1950s, the show's depiction of a working woman's conflict between home and career was downright innovative (and surely resonated with the star herself). Perhaps this worked against its acceptance with viewers, who may have preferred a more traditional maternal role model. Arden herself felt that, in the absence of director Leonard and writer Saks, there were too many voices trying to pull the show in different directions, and it never developed a clear identity. The absence of a strong romantic chemistry between Arden and co-star Joslyn didn't help matters either.

After the show's first season, CBS and the sponsors pulled the plug on *The Eve Arden Show*. Though *Our Miss Brooks* would enjoy a long afterlife in syndication through CBS Films (later Viacom) for years to come, Arden's TV career was stalled. It would be almost ten years before her next regular series role.

As she often did throughout her career, Arden went back to the theater. It may have been the variety of roles she was allowed to play that in part explained her passion for the stage. Theater engagements also offered a welcome opportunity to co-star with her husband; she and Brooks West often toured in shows together, and would continue to do so into the 1970s. She often selected shows that included a male role suitable for him as well as a juicy lead for herself.

She earned critical plaudits for her starring role in the Los Angeles company of *Auntie Mame* (with West appearing as Beauregard Burnside). Over the years, she would expand her repertoire to include *Butterflies Are Free*, *Hello, Dolly!*, *Little Me*, and other staples of community theater.

"I think that was what she loved to do the most," says Arden's son of her stage work. "I remember sitting backstage in her dressing room. That was the place she was most comfortable."

Arden also reactivated her movie career in the late 1950s with two prestigious films. Her role as lawyer James Stewart's loyal secretary in Otto Preminger's *Anatomy of a Murder* (Columbia, 1959) is relatively minor, despite her sixth billing; husband Brooks, though billed below his wife, fared better with his featured role as the prosecutor who opposed Stewart. Still, Arden's co-starring role in a hit movie that received multiple Oscar nominations, including Best Picture, represented an auspicious return to the motion picture world for the actress after an absence of several years. Arden followed that project with the film version of William Inge's play *The Dark at the Top of the Stairs* (Warners, 1960), in which her strong performance as an unhappily married woman with a weak-willed husband demonstrated that her talent extended beyond making viewers laugh.

In the early 1960s, although she was frequently visible as a guest star on television, she was unable to find another suitable series role. She teamed with husband Brooks

West for a sitcom pilot called "The Colonel's Lady," in which they played a movie star and the military man whom she marries. Unfortunately for Arden, who might have envisioned a chance to do for her actor husband what Lucille Ball had done for Desi Arnaz with *I Love Lucy,* this project never got off the ground. (In her autobiography, Arden wrote honestly, and with sympathy, about the dependence on alcohol that West developed during their marriage, and mentions career stress and frustrations as a contributing factor in his disease).

Screen Gems executive Harry Ackerman, who had been instrumental in putting together *Our Miss Brooks* as a radio show in the 1940s, signed Arden for the 1964 CBS pilot "Take Him—He's Yours," revolving around the adventures of a London-based travel agent. Nothing came of that project, nor of Universal Television's "Be Careful—It's My Art" (also known as "The Eve Arden Show"), which cast the star as a meddlesome New York widow who busied herself arranging the lives of her family.

Although not visible in her own weekly series, Arden turned up frequently as a guest star on shows like *Bewitched*, where she butted heads with Endora (Agnes Moorehead) as a vigilant baby nurse in charge of the newborn Tabitha. The 1966 appearance afforded her a professional reunion with the show's producer/director, William Asher, who had directed her on *Our Miss Brooks,* and with executive producer Ackerman. She also appeared in an episode of NBC's *Run for Your Life* (1965–68) that was designed as a pilot to star actor/singer Bobby Darin.

Desi Arnaz, who had been important to the success of *Brooks* on TV, would also be instrumental in launching Arden's last regular series role. After selling out his interest in Desilu in the early 1960s, Arnaz went into business as an independent producer, and in 1967 signed Arden as the star of a new sitcom, *The Mothers-in-Law.* Developed by longtime *Lucy* writers Bob Carroll, Jr. and Madelyn Davis, the series cast her as Eve Hubbard, middle-aged suburban mother whose daughter Susie (Deborah Walley) married the son of next-door neighbors Kaye and Roger Buell. The bulk of the show's humor revolved around Eve's prickly relationship with the other mother-in-law, played by raucous actress-comedienne Kaye Ballard.

Originally intended as a comeback vehicle for yet another Desilu star of the 1950s, Ann Sothern, the show didn't work for Arden and Sothern in tandem, who didn't create sparks together. Sothern withdrew, and Arden found herself teamed with Ballard, whose loud and boisterous style gave Arden ample opportunity for raised eyebrows, long sighs, and wry putdowns. Actor Herbert Rudley, playing Eve's rather bland lawyer husband Herb, gave Arden the first onscreen spouse of her TV career. By comparison, he made Philip Boynton seem downright exciting and personable.

Arnaz intended to sell *The Mothers-in-Law* to CBS, but executives there were not impressed, and passed on the show. With a sponsor in place, he was able to cut a deal at NBC, but found the series stuck in a difficult Sunday night time slot where it would face an uphill battle for survival opposite the second half hour of two long-running hits, ABC's *The FBI* (1965–74) and CBS' *The Ed Sullivan Show* (1948–71).

Recycling plots and gimmicks that had worked on *I Love Lucy* a decade earlier, *The Mothers-in-Law* felt passé to late 1960s viewers. Much as the writers worked to incorporate contemporary elements like rock bands, group therapy, and computer dating, the show had little to offer that was fresh or new. Executive producer Arnaz,

Eve Arden fails to appreciate the song stylings of Kaye Ballard in the pilot episode of *The Mothers-in-Law*.

struggling with alcoholism, wasn't at the top of his game, and the show didn't receive the attention it needed. NBC cancelled the series at the end of its second season of lackluster ratings.

Although *The Mothers-in-Law* was Arden's last regular series role, she would continue to be a familiar face on TV. In 1972, she starred in "A Very Missing Person," a TV-movie and series pilot. She played Hildegarde Withers, a retired schoolteacher (shades of Miss Brooks!) who teamed with a policeman to solve crimes. The character, created by mystery author Stuart Palmer, had previously been seen in a series of B-movies in the 1930s, played by elderly character actress Edna May Oliver. The series, designed to be one-third of a trio of "Great Detectives" shows, did not sell.

In 1974, Arden won the final Emmy of her career, for her title role in a 1973 *ABC Afternoon Playbreak* special called "Mother of the Bride." This short-lived series, designed as an occasional alternative to daytime TV soap operas and game shows, netted the star a perhaps-unexpected "Best Actress in Daytime Drama" award.

Arden continued to pop up in guest appearances on shows like *Maude* (CBS, 1972–78), where she played Beatrice Arthur's saucy, slightly risqué aunt. A precursor to characters like *The Golden Girls*' (NBC, 1985–92) Blanche, Aunt Lola had been around the block a time or two, and enjoyed the companionship of various men. Only in the episode's final act does Maude discover that Aunt Lola is no longer as active as her niece wishes to believe. Inclined to quote the old saw about men being like streetcars—another one comes along every few minutes—Lola ruefully admits to her niece that, like those streetcars, her escapades with the opposite sex are mostly a thing of the past.

Arden's appearance on *Maude* demonstrated that her still-sharp gifts as a performer were appreciated not just by her contemporaries like *The Mothers-in-Law*'s Carroll and Davis, who cast her in a guest role when they produced *Alice* (1976–85) at CBS, or by nostalgia fans who caught her on *The Love Boat* (ABC, 1977–86), but also by more *au courant* producers like Norman Lear. It was also interesting to see her play opposite Beatrice Arthur, who of the generation of television actresses rising to fame in the 1970s, was perhaps the most similar to Arden comedically. Both certainly shared the ability to fire off a retort.

She also remained in demand for series roles, though none of them landed a prime-time berth. Arden teamed with Don Knotts for a 1975 pilot called "Harry and Maggie," which cast them as bickering in-laws warring over the upbringing of her teenage niece. Network executives passed on the show, as they did "The Eyes of Texas" five years later, a *B.J. and the Bear* (NBC, 1979–81) spin-off in which she ran a detective agency staffed by pretty young women, and "Nuts and Bolts," a 1981 sitcom pilot about robots that found her playing opposite impressionist Rich Little.

Though Arden was always able to keep busy professionally, it's a pity that she didn't have the opportunity to cap her TV career with one last noteworthy role. *The Golden Girls*, which revitalized the careers of four older actresses and gave them a tremendous showcase for their comedic skills, came along a few years too late for Arden, but it's easy to imagine how much fun she could have been in a role of that type.

When TV producers were unable to make the best use of her comedic gifts, however, movie producers took up the slack. Her career as an educator developed a new wrinkle when Allan Carr cast her as school principal Miss McGee in *Grease* (Paramount, 1978), a role she would reprise four years later in the far less successful sequel (her final theatrical film). She also worked at Disney, where she was featured in the Kurt Russell comedy *The Strongest Man in the World* (1975), and played a key supporting role in the Chevy Chase–Carrie Fisher comedy *Under the Rainbow* (Orion, 1981), sporting a vaguely Continental accent as "The Duchess." As she had done for forty years, Arden enlivened even mediocre movies and television shows, worth watching even when the script wasn't. Even Woody Allen, at the height of his success and critical esteem, was said to be an admirer who was writing a role for her.

In 1983, Arden planned a Broadway comeback as the top-billed star of a new play, Arthur Bicknell's *Moose Murders*. Cast as Hedda Hathaway, affluent owner of a hunting lodge in the Adirondacks, in what was intended to be a spoof of murder mysteries, Arden endured a painful rehearsal and preview period in which she realized the play, which she had originally regarded as "wild and different,"[16] wasn't working. Some reports had it that Arden, then in her mid-seventies, was experiencing difficulty remembering her lines onstage.

If that was the case, the problem, according to Arden's son Douglas West, may have been the rigidity with which playwright Bicknell regarded his script. "My mother always rewrote her lines to fit her mouth," West says. But in *Moose Murders*, "he wouldn't let her contract two words." Union rules sided with the writer, leaving Arden frustrated. At odds with the creative team, she finally left the show in an unpleasant "did she quit, or was she fired?" scenario that was a sad coda to her Broadway career.

Her role recast with actress Holland Taylor, the show died on opening night amidst a critical roasting. Frank Rich of the *New York Times* wrote a stinging review, saying that attendance at its one and only performance would "separate the connoisseurs of Broadway disaster from mere dilettantes for many moons to come,"[17] and later naming it as perhaps the worst play he ever saw during his long tenure as a reviewer. *The New York Post's* Clive Barnes, calling the show "indescribably bad," reminded readers, "This was the show that parted company a few weeks back with Eve Arden. Some people have all the luck. Here it was clearly Miss Arden."[18]

The *Moose Murders* debacle must have been particularly painful for a performer who had so long valued camaraderie with her fellow cast and crew. Son Douglas West, who accompanied his parents on a number of their theatrical engagements during the late 1960s and 1970s, says that, under normal circumstances, "The cast of a play was their temporary family. People who appeared in her plays became longtime friends."

Trying to put the upsetting episode behind her, Arden turned her attention to an offer from Woody Allen, who wanted to cast her in his next film. Flattered by this opportunity to work with the critics' darling, she happily accepted. Regrettably, a family crisis caused her to withdraw from Allen's cast before she could even begin shooting. The crisis was the illness of Arden's husband Brooks West, to whom she had been married for more than 30 years. She returned home, and remained at his side until his death in February 1984. Arden's longtime manager and friend, Glenn Rose, later told the *Los Angeles Times*, "She never really quite got over the death of her husband. She was never the same after it."[19]

In 1985, her autobiography, *Three Phases of Eve,* was published. Still grieving her husband's death, she wrote fondly about their life together, and about the family they'd raised. About her work in films, surprisingly, she said, without rancor, "Outside of the money they paid me and some of the people I worked with and the time they allowed me for my child, making pictures was pretty much just a job to me."[20] Although her lifelong passion for the theater was undiminished, she also paid homage to Miss Brooks, still her best-known character, and one for whom she knew she'd be remembered.

In the late 1980s, Arden's own health took a downward turn, and she began to withdraw from the acting world. A 1987 role on *Falcon Crest* (CBS, 1981–90), reuniting her with fellow 1940s Warner Brothers contract player Jane Wyman, was one of her last television appearances. She died of heart disease on November 12, 1990, at the age of 82.

Although obituaries faithfully recorded her many professional accomplishments, and she would continue to receive posthumous tributes such as her 1995 induction into the Radio Hall of Fame, it was first and foremost *Our Miss Brooks* that would be her claim to immortality, and Arden knew that. In her autobiography she quoted an actor friend who, sensing that she didn't quite realize the impact that Connie Brooks had had on the viewing public, told her, "Don't you realize how many millions have seen you as Miss Brooks and, as long as there are reruns, will go on getting joy from them?"[21]

❖ 3 ❖

Lucille Ball

I Love Lucy

IN THE 1950S, *I LOVE LUCY,* more than any other show, demonstrated the drawing power of a funny leading lady, paving the way for most of the other sitcoms featured in this book. Because *Lucy* dominated the TV ratings for its entire prime time run, usually in the #1 spot, it popularized the domestic sitcom, filmed in front of an audience, a genre that the show's producers and writers largely invented. Decades later, the show's influence can be seen in practically every sitcom that has followed since.

Ironically, if CBS executives, and even the show's own sponsor, had had their druthers back in 1951, none of this would have come to pass. What the network asked for was a TV adaptation of Lucille Ball's radio sitcom *My Favorite Husband,* which had been playing to solid ratings since 1948. It was to co-star her radio leading man, actor Richard Denning, as her spouse, and be a live broadcast originating from New York. Lucy Ricardo had not yet been invented, and CBS certainly saw no future in starring Ball opposite her real-life husband, Latin American bandleader Desi Arnaz.

Luckily for *Lucy* aficionados, Ball was in a position to make certain demands. Although indications were that her film career had peaked, she was nonetheless one of the biggest stars to make herself available for a television series in 1951. Of the comedy shows then popular with TV audiences, which were still relatively few in number, most were adaptations of successful radio shows (i.e., *The George Burns and Gracie Allen Show, The Goldbergs),* or starred performers just becoming known to mass audiences. Milton Berle, whose sketch comedy show was still pulling large audiences, had been no more than a moderate success in radio or film, and had little to lose by toplining a TV show in the infancy of the medium. But film stars, even second-tier ones like Ball then was, were strictly hands-off where TV series work was concerned.

If Ball was being a pioneer in the early 1950s, as she undoubtedly was, it was less a career move than an effort to save her decade-old marriage. Although the unparalleled success of *I Love Lucy,* and Ball's insistence that her husband play the male lead, would ultimately only postpone the Arnazes' apparently inevitable divorce, it would provide Ball with the most unforgettable role of her long career, and provide a model from which many, many other shows would follow.

Born in Jamestown, New York, on August 6, 1911, Ball came to television after a movie career that had spanned seventeen years and dozens of films, few of them memorable. Under contract at various times to MGM, RKO, and Columbia, none of them had really known quite what to do with her, and she had circled frustratingly around top stardom without ever quite nailing it. Although her flair for comedy should have been visible from the outset, it took producers and directors a surprisingly long time to figure out what she did best.

Her film debut had been a harbinger of things of come. Cast as a beautiful slave girl in MGM's *Roman Scandals* (1933), she stood out from the crowd when she volunteered to do a bit the other pretty young actresses disdained—allow mud to be splattered on her face. The incident not only hinted at the gift for slapstick that would eventually be her stock in trade, but also showed something about Ball herself. Never one to think herself above most types of work, she would cheerfully star in mediocre B movies, pose for cheesecake photos, and generally consider herself lucky for whatever breaks she got in Hollywood.

Although it wouldn't be until *I Love Lucy* that her comedic gifts would be given free rein, Ball would have the opportunity to work with several noteworthy comedians during those early years. In the 1934 Three Stooges short "Three Little Pigskins," a young Ball found herself on the receiving end of a seltzer bottle wielded by Curly. A few years later, having worked her way up to larger roles, she played the ingénue in the Marx Brothers comedy *Room Service* (RKO, 1938), though her comedic flair wasn't readily apparent to the acerbic Groucho—"I've never found Lucille Ball to be funny on her own," he commented years later. "She's always needed a script."[1]

Off-camera, she befriended the legendary silent comedian Buster Keaton in the 1940s, when both were on the MGM payroll, he as a gag writer rather than a performer. She would later credit Keaton, and director Eddie Sedgwick, with teaching her some of the facility with props that later came in handy on her TV series. "Attention to detail, that's what it's all about," Ball later explained. "If I had to work with grapes, a loaf of bread, a cup of coffee, whatever, I had to test them first to know what I was eating or drinking, how hot or cold it was, how it got there, how it would ride on the tray."[2]

Her strong dramatic performance in RKO's *The Big Street* (1942) was critically acclaimed, but didn't lead to more roles of the same caliber. Under contract to MGM in the 1940s, she was given assignments in musical comedies like *DuBarry Was a Lady* (1942), and, for the first time, became a redhead. After freelancing for a period in the late 1940s, she signed a deal at Columbia Pictures, where she made comedies like *Miss Grant Takes Richmond* (1949). Her comedic roles of this period opened some eyes as to her comedic gifts, but films would never exploit them as well as TV did.

One of the most influential films of Ball's career, though not necessarily for career reasons, was RKO's 1940 release *Too Many Girls.* Among her co-stars in this adaptation of a successful Broadway musical was Cuban-born singer Desi Arnaz. The attraction was instantaneous, and led to marriage on November 30, 1940.

Even when her career wasn't at its peak, Ball loved show business with a fervor surpassed by few. During her tenure at RKO, according to Ball's cousin Cleo, "She was always offering to get me this role or that role, and never could understand why I wasn't interested. I could never make her understand that acting was not every girl's heart's desire. She knows, I guess, that some girls dream about other things, but I don't think she quite believes it. To Lucy everybody has that same drive, energy, concentration, and sense of purpose."[3]

By the mid–1940s, her film career still stuck in neutral, Ball was looking for other opportunities. She garnered good reviews for her supporting performance opposite Keenan Wynn in the Tracy-Hepburn comedy *Without Love* (MGM, 1945), enough so that there was interest in seeing them reunited. *Variety* reported that a Ball-Wynn radio comedy show, "The Magnificent Morgans," was being pitched to sponsors in the summer of 1945, but there were no takers.

In 1948, however, Ball debuted on CBS radio in *My Favorite Husband*, where she began to perfect her role as a zany housewife. The radio series also introduced her to producer/head writer Jess Oppenheimer, and writers Bob Carroll, Jr., and Madelyn Pugh, who would be integral to her television career.

Ironically, as plans for Ball's TV show were under discussion in the fall of 1950, Columbia released *The Fuller Brush Girl*, a raucous, high-energy comedy that came closer than most of Ball's movie assignments to demonstrating what she did best. In the movie's first ten minutes came the first of several inventive slapstick sequences—Ball's character, working as a switchboard operator, sneezes a dust cloud of face powder all over herself, sets the switchboard on fire, douses her boss with water, and shatters the glass of the office door. The sequence would have been right at home in an episode of *I Love Lucy*.

Working from a script by Frank Tashlin, whose live-action comedies were almost as animated as the cartoons

Lucy Ricardo in embryo: Lucille Ball with co-star Eddie Albert in *The Fuller Brush Girl* (Columbia, 1950), an early showcase for her slapstick gifts.

he'd previously made, Ball gave a lively performance that attracted some long overdue attention in Hollywood. "If ever there were any doubts as to Miss Ball's forte," *Variety* commented, "*Fuller Brush* dispels them. She is an excellent comedienne."[4]

The star herself made note of how well she was suited to the physical comedy the role had required. "When I decided to become a real roughhouse comedienne," she later said, "it was because I was feeling my way toward the right type of role for me. For years I had been making a big career mistake—I had faithfully followed Hollywood's idea that I was a tough, brash showgirl type.

"I was always playing uppity actresses and musical-comedy queens—which I never felt like at all. I hated being a glamour girl with never a hair out of place. Most of all, I hated those brittle lines I spoke. I guess I was a frustrated housewife, which is why I enjoy what I am finally doing on television; but for years I wasn't smart enough to do my own type-casting."[5]

Of the actresses profiled in this book, only Gracie Allen was already the star of her own network sitcom when *I Love Lucy* was in development during early 1951. The success of *The George Burns and Gracie Allen Show* may have reassured CBS executives that another half-hour comedy about a dizzy dame would be well-received by viewers. And in the early stages of developing Ball's series, the writers may have looked to *Burns and Allen* as a model for their original concept of showcasing Ball and Arnaz as a successful show business couple.

The star balked, feeling that viewers would not identify with the problems (whatever they might be) of married entertainers. But looking back on her tenure in *My Favorite Husband*, Ball recognized that she had enjoyed playing a suburban housewife, a contrast to the more glamorous, snarkier characters she had played as a movie leading lady in the 1930s and 1940s. Working with *Husband*'s producer/head writer Jess Oppenheimer and writers Bob Carroll, Jr. and Madelyn Pugh, Ball and Arnaz eventually approved a storyline that again placed her in a middle-class milieu, though everyone agreed that he could not credibly play the Midwestern banker husband that Denning had essayed in the radio show.

Eventually, Oppenheimer paid one dollar to register with the Screen Writers' Guild a brief synopsis of what would become *I Love Lucy*. Its chief characters, he wrote, "are happily married and very much in love. The only bone of contention between them is her desire to get into show business, and his equally strong desire to keep her out of it...."[6] This clever premise would allow Arnaz to be spotlighted as a singer and bandleader, at which he then had considerably more experience than he did acting, while Ball could mine comedy from the frustration of a woman continually thwarted in achieving her own ambitions.

Lest anyone doubt who was considered the star attraction here, CBS proposed calling the series *The Lucille Ball Show*, which they were willing to follow with (in smaller type) "co-starring Desi Arnaz." This no doubt struck them as a reasonable compromise, since they would have been happier with Arnaz out of the picture altogether. But Ball, aware of her husband's ego, insisted that he share the star billing, and the show was developed to showcase both family members. What CBS envisioned as a star vehicle for Ball would ultimately be announced as "the Lucille Ball—Desi Arnaz show—*I Love Lucy*." Even the "I" was intended to assuage any wounded pride on his part, as it was clearly a reference to his Ricky Ricardo character.

While trying to persuade CBS to give them a television series, Ball and Arnaz had gone on a vaudeville tour in 1950, cobbling together a well-received act that combined his singing and her clowning. Given the go-ahead on a month's notice to put together a pilot episode for *I Love Lucy,* Oppenheimer and his writers prepared a script that drew heavily on the act Ball and Arnaz had done onstage. In March 1951, the pilot episode was kinescoped from a live performance. Unlike most of today's TV pilots, the sample show was not necessarily intended to serve as the first episode of the regular series if it sold—instead, it was designed to show potential sponsors on Madison Avenue what *I Love Lucy* would be like. Believed lost for many years, a copy of the pilot episode surfaced decades later, and received its first television broadcast as a CBS special in 1990.

The pilot introduces us to what will later become some of the show's regular elements. Lucy is, of course, vying to get a place in Ricky's act, and salivates at the news that a possible TV sponsor is paying a visit to his nightclub. Ricky, setting up Oppenheimer's original premise, balks at the idea of her pursing a career: "I want a wife who's just a wife." Later, though, when the clown scheduled to perform as part of Ricky's show is injured, Lucy takes the opportunity to step in. In a dénouement that essentially contradicts much of what would take place in the regular series, Lucy's antics result in the offer of a television contract from the sponsor, which she turns down in deference to Ricky's wishes.

Although not everything about the pilot works well, Ball's chemistry with her real-life husband is immediately apparent. Always at her best when allowed ample time to rehearse, Ball shines in the show-stopping "Professor" routine, which she had perfected through hundreds of live performances. Along the way, it's obvious that she and Arnaz are struggling not to break up, especially during a moment when, as she would do in so many subsequent episodes, Ball playfully mocks her husband's accent:

RICKY: Never mind making fun of my English.
LUCY: That's English?

Watching the pilot, it's clear that Ball wanted to share the spotlight with her husband, who receives ample screen time for his singing. Although she plays most of her scenes in bulky, layered clothing (due to her real-life pregnancy), Arnaz is presented so as to showcase not only his talent but his charisma and sex appeal—it's unlikely that Richard Denning would have been directed to bare his chest in a bedroom scene, as Arnaz does in the pilot.

Some soon-to-be staples of the show surface: we hear snatches of Arnaz's signature song, "Babalu," and there's already a joke about Lucy's use of hair dye. The sets in the pilot episode bear little resemblance to the familiar Ricardo apartment seen in the series, though, and the characters of Fred and Ethel Mertz are not yet on the scene.

Shown to potential sponsors in New York that spring, the show was not particularly quick to sell, despite Ball's presence. Finally, a potential sponsor surfaced—Philip Morris. The cigarette manufacturer was willing to foot the bill for Ball's sitcom, but insisted on a weekly show instead of the every other week that she and her agent had envisioned. Ball had envisioned that her TV work could be combined with other activities if she wasn't on every week, perhaps allowing her to continue her motion picture career (as she had done during the run of *My Favorite Husband*). Nor could Arnaz continue to tour profitably as a bandleader if a weekly show was required. Rather than lose the deal, they signed on the dotted line to furnish *I Love Lucy* as a weekly entry on CBS' Monday night schedule, to debut in October 1951.

It was a busy summer—in July, Ball gave birth to her first child, daughter Lucie, after eleven years of marriage. Nonetheless, plans for the regular series went forward, and Ball began rehearsals six weeks after Lucie was born. Although network executives and the sponsor had given in to Ball's wish to co-star her husband, they made it plain that *I Love Lucy* was to be a comedy show, not a variety or musical program. Philip Morris made the point explicit by stipulating contractually that Arnaz was not to perform extraneous musical numbers in the show, singing only when it was a logical adjunct to the sitcom's storyline. Even though *Burns and Allen* was still featuring dancing and singing interludes during each live broadcast (and would continue to do so until the show converted to film in 1952), *I Love Lucy* would not follow this model.

The haphazard combinations of expediency, luck, personal motives, and creative thinking ultimately gave birth to what would become TV's premier sitcom of the 1950s. Much of this was due to Ball and her colleagues' ability to think on their feet, and develop viable alternatives when problems arose. Deciding that the Ricardos needed next-door neighbors, a setup that had worked well on Ball's radio show, Oppenheimer found that he was unable to obtain the services of well-known character actors Gale Gordon and Bea Benaderet to reprise their featured roles from *My Favorite Husband*. Gordon was committed to *Our Miss Brooks*, already a hit on radio and being eyed for a TV version, and Benaderet had already accepted a featured role on another popular CBS sitcom, *Burns and Allen*. Tackling what could have been another crisis for the burgeoning show, Oppenheimer and his stars agreed on film character actor William Frawley to play crotchety neighbor Fred Mertz, while *Lucy*'s original director Marc Daniels recommended his little-known actress friend Vivian Vance for the part of Ethel.

When Ball and Arnaz balked at relocating to New York, from which the sponsor wanted the show's live broadcasts to originate, they and their colleagues stumbled into a genre never before attempted—the sitcom filmed in front of a live audience. Film allowed them to stay home in Hollywood (one of Ball's main goals in doing the series at all), while everyone agreed that the presence of a live audience energized her performances in a way that nothing else could.

This method of making the show called for a number of technical innovations and decisions. While game shows like *Truth or Consequences* and Groucho Marx's *You Bet Your Life* (NBC, 1950–61) were being shot on film with audiences present, they generally took place on one fixed set, without the complications that *I Love Lucy* would entail. During the spring and summer of 1951, Ball and company essentially invented the method by which any number of TV sitcoms would be shot for the next several decades.

Once recorded on film, the shows were also available for rebroadcast. As ingrained into the world of the TV sitcom as reruns now are, it may be hard to imagine that this was a novelty. At that time, sitcom episodes aired once, and the shows usually took summer hiatuses during which a replacement series aired. During the run of *I Love Lucy,* especially the period in which Ball's real-life pregnancy curtailed her working hours, producer Oppenheimer would test the innovative practice of airing select episodes a second time. Surely none of those involved could have imagined how many replays *I Love Lucy* was ultimately destined to have.

By the time *I Love Lucy* premiered that fall, ironically, most of the resemblances to *My Favorite Husband,* aside from the presence of Ball herself, had fallen by the wayside. So little did it resemble the original product that CBS later launched a separate TV adaptation of *Husband,* without Ball, though it never approached the popularity of *Lucy.* Two capable leading ladies—first Joan Caulfield, later Vanessa Brown, tried in vain to make that show fly during its 1953–55 run.

Though not the first episode filmed, a segment called "The Girls Want to Go to a Nightclub" was selected as *Lucy*'s premiere episode. The episode centered on a men-vs.-women quarrel over how to observe Fred and Ethel Mertz's wedding anniversary, and culminated in a show-stopping scene in which Ball and Vance impersonate hillbilly blind dates for their husbands. The episode originally intended to be the series opener, "Lucy Thinks Ricky Is Trying to Murder Her," which was not quite as slick and skillfully shot as the one substituted, would air a few weeks later.

In changing the sequence of shows aired, the show lost the opportunity to benefit from some of the exposition and background information that had been purposely written into the first episode, such as Ricky's entrance carrying a Tropicana poster that allows him to brag about his act being held over there (an engagement that, as it turned out, would last for most of the show's run). Still, the episode that aired first effectively introduced all four principal characters, and showed that the series had grown enormously more effective since the pilot was shot.

The show's early episodes demonstrate that the producer and writers had not yet completely resolved the differences between sketch comedy and sitcom. The aptly titled "Lucy Thinks Ricky is Trying to Murder Her" asks us to believe that Lucy is genuinely afraid her husband has poisoned her, though this is blamed somewhat on her overactive imagination and professed fondness for murder mysteries. This plot would have been unlikely by the show's second or third season, when the audience knew the characters better. In another first-season episode, "The Kleptomaniac" (4/14/52), Lucy somehow transports a circus elephant into the Ricardos' bedroom, as the kicker to a joke she's playing on Ricky.

Technically, the early shows owe something to the sketch comedy format, where believability was less important. As the action switches between rooms of the Ricardos' apartment, director Marc Daniels' cameras occasionally pan past the edges of set walls, allowing us to see where they come to an end downstage. In one early episode, the effects of a gun shot through a door are represented by a patently phony-looking hole cut into the door, pulled away with a wire when the pistol is fired.

My Favorite Husband had been a moderately successful show, but hardly one that took the world by storm. Ball's most recent theatrical films had, likewise, been no more than qualified hits, and her last release under her Columbia contract, *The Magic Carpet,* which opened in the fall of 1951, had been a real stinker. Much as CBS might have hoped that *I Love Lucy* would catch on, they surely never expected the ratings phenomenon and cultural icon that it became within weeks of its premiere.

Mike Dann, a CBS program executive in the 1960s, was working at NBC when *I Love Lucy* premiered, and later remembered, "We had a show on the air [Mondays at 9 P.M.] called *Lights Out,* sponsored by Amident.... Both the show and the toothpaste were tremendously popular—everybody watched *Lights Out.*

"Then Desi and Lucy came on the air opposite that show, and *Lights Out* was canceled. We at NBC were just flabbergasted, we just couldn't believe it. Here was this girl who wasn't that famous, and this bongo player from Cuba—and it never lost its momentum. It was the first time we used the word 'runaway' to describe a show."[7]

Critics and viewers alike were flabbergasted by the raw talent that Lucille Ball displayed in early episodes of *I Love Lucy,* as showcased by the carefully structured vehicle that Oppenheimer and his staff had developed for her. The visual slapstick that would become such an important element in the TV show had played no part, obviously, in her radio work, and audiences had rarely had a chance to savor her memorable facial expressions as a comedienne. Although *The Fuller Brush Girl* traded on her visual humor in a way that had largely been unseen in the dozens of films she'd made earlier, it was the combination of visual humor, strong characterization, and emotional appeal, along with the distinctive character of Lucy Ricardo that made *I Love Lucy* irresistible to viewers. Although Ball had had no assurance that a TV series would be a wise career move, she unexpectedly hit the peak of her stardom at the age of 40.

In the show's first two years on CBS, Ball's show would deliver many of the episodes that fans would later crown as classic *Lucy.* Among the first season's highlights was "Lucy Does A TV Commercial" (5/5/52), in which Lucy had her tipsy encounter with Vitameatavegamin. The second season opener was the unforgettable "Job Switching" (9/15/52), culminating in Lucy and Ethel's losing battle with the conveyor belt at Kramer's Kandy Kitchen.

Ball embraced her sitcom work with fervor, enjoying it more than anything she had done previously. It even gave her the chance to play benefactor to friends like character actress Barbara Pepper, who turned up often on *Lucy* in minor roles. (The dedicated *I Love Lucy* watcher's version of "Where's Waldo?" is to spot either Pepper or Desi Arnaz's friend Louis A. Nicoletti in one of their frequent walk-on appearances).

Although *I Love Lucy* has been extensively analyzed, reviewed, and discussed, it is worth another look in terms of how it shaped the future of the filmed TV sitcom. TV's most popular comedy show in 1951 was still NBC's *Texaco Star Theatre,* a wild, raucous showcase for the sketch comedy of Milton Berle. Also popular was another variety show, Sid Caesar's *Your Show of Shows,* which traded in a subtler brand of sketch humor. Throughout the early 1950s, sponsors brought comedians (mostly male) to TV in hour-long formats such as *The Colgate Comedy Hour.*

I Love Lucy was the first sitcom to bring a strong element of visual humor to the format. *The Amos 'n' Andy Show,* another new sitcom on CBS' fall 1951 schedule, relied more on verbal humor than slapstick, though the latter was not completely absent from the series' scripts. *Burns and Allen* had a TV show not dissimilar from what had worked for them on radio, relying less than *Lucy* would on the visual possibilities of television.

And yet other comediennes would find that slapstick was only one element of what made *I Love Lucy* work. Joan Davis, a gifted performer who had always demonstrated a bent for physical comedy, would soon star in a show that, while it superficially resembled *I Love Lucy* in many ways (beginning with its title, *I Married Joan)*, lacked some of the other elements that made *Lucy* take flight.

In fact, while the enormous popularity of *I Love Lucy* would inevitably foster imitation, some of the elements not quite as obvious as the physical comedy would be seldom duplicated. Because the show spotlighted Ball's brilliance as a slapstick performer, some would-be imitators seemed not to notice that the audience also loved the characters on *I Love Lucy*, and rooted for them.

Lucy Ricardo, as created by Ball and her writers, was the embodiment of every audience member who longed to rebel against the mundane and ordinary in life. She has already been blessed with most of the things a woman in the 1950s was supposed to want—she had beauty, a handsome and successful husband, a happy home, good friends, and eventually a child. What Eve Arden's *Our Miss Brooks* pined for (marriage, home, and children), Lucy had. So why was she so rebellious—and so appealing to audiences?

Unlike most shows of that era, *I Love Lucy*, in its own inimitable way, acknowledged that a bright, creative woman might want an outlet for her gifts. Few TV shows at the time acknowledged as openly as *Lucy* did that housework was no big thrill for an intelligent person, or that we all sometimes long for adventure in our lives. *Lucy* also took a humorous look, through the characters of Fred and Ethel Mertz, at what middle-aged spread and twenty-five years of a humdrum existence could do to a husband and wife.

Much of the appeal of Lucy's character was to the side of us that yearns to deal with adult problems in a less-than-adult way. Can't figure out how to balance your checkbook? Throw the bills up in the air, and pay only the ones that land face-up. Wishing for some quality time alone with your husband? Lock him up in your room, and give away the key.

As producer—head writer Oppenheimer astutely observed, "To me, Lucy Ricardo represents the childish factor still a part of every adult. Most people who get into a frustrating situation may have a flash thought of some impulsive act that would be a gratifying way of coping with the situation. But they quickly put it out of their minds, the way responsible, inhibited adults are supposed to. For Lucy Ricardo, however, the impulsive thought invariably becomes the course of action. In identifying with her, the audience can vicariously enjoy exercising their own childish impulses, petty curiosities, and foolhardy but self-gratifying escapades."[8]

Along with the uniqueness of the character Oppenheimer and his colleagues created, perhaps it was the then-unusual presence of a woman writer, Madelyn Pugh (later Davis), that caused *I Love Lucy* to resonate with female viewers. Perhaps it was Desi Arnaz's status as a foreigner, in a prejudiced age, or just his status as Ball's real-life husband, that made it acceptable for Lucy to mock and defy her husband in a way that few 1950s sitcom women did. Although some of the elements of *I Love Lucy* seem dated today—the way that Lucy purports to kowtow to her husband's authority, and is prone to call him "sir" when she's in trouble—it was always pretty clear who really held the reins in that household. In "The Matchmaker" (10/25/54), after Lucy has once again dived into a situation against Ricky's wishes, they have a typical Ricardo quarrel:

LUCY: Well, for once I decided not to do what you told me!
RICKY: For *once!* You never do what I tol' you!
LUCY: Then why don't you quit tol-in' me?

My Little Margie, which came along in the flood of new sitcoms that *Lucy* inevitably spawned, transferred much of the defiance that Lucy showed her husband to Margie's father. Even Margie, though, never went as far as Lucy did—Lucy, who mimicked her husband's accent to his face, and, when competing with him for attention in front of a movie camera, reaches out and yanks his pants down.

Far from having their sensibilities affronted by this uncharacteristic husband-and-wife relationship, though, viewers ate it up. Somehow, thanks to the show's strong writing and the chemistry of its stars, Lucy and Ricky could yell at each other, make fun of each other, throw pails of water or pies in the other's face, and viewers never for a minute doubted their sincere love and affection.

Ball and Arnaz also exhibited a rapport that few other TV couples could match. For all that Ball's inimitable clowning is what most viewers most associate with the show, *I Love Lucy,* more than most sitcoms of its day, also delved into the ups and downs of married life. Though Ball's series is rarely praised as a model of reality, the scripts in fact had much to say about the day-to-day frustrations and challenges of husbands and wives, as well as the ways that women and men related to each other. In the show's first aired episode, when Lucy complains, "Ever since we said 'I do,' there are so many things we don't," the audience not only laughed but acknowledged the truthfulness behind the joke.

Although TV censorship codes were strict in the 1950s, *I Love Lucy* presented a married couple that, in the middle of the show's most absurd moments, had a natural intimacy to their interplay that could not have been achieved solely through acting, no matter how skilled. While Lucy and Ricky, like other TV couples of the day, were generally forbidden to share a bed, scenes often took place in their bedroom, and occasionally even in their bathroom, a rarity for the 1950s.

Although many TV historians credit *The Dick Van Dyke Show* (CBS, 1961–66) with breaking new ground in depicting the sexual and romantic chemistry of Rob and Laura Petrie (Dick Van Dyke and Mary Tyler Moore), *I Love Lucy* was ahead of its time in depicting a married couple whose attraction was tangible—as the results would soon be, when the star's real-life pregnancy was, despite CBS' fear of offending viewers with this frankness, written into the scripts during the show's second season.

Probably because its stars were a real-life couple, *Lucy* was occasionally permitted moments that might have been found risqué in another show. In "The Amateur Hour" (1/14/52), Ricky makes fun of Lucy's oft-repeated complaint that she doesn't own enough clothes by pretending to head out for work in his underwear, sardonically telling her, "I haven't a thing to wear!" Though Arnaz' costuming in baggy, polka-dot boxers keeps the moment seeming innocent enough, especially by today's TV standards, it's hard to envision this scene appearing in most other husband-wife sitcoms of the day.

Nor did most other shows derive so many plots from the heroine's fears that her husband might be sexually attracted to other women. From the very first episode aired,

"The Girls Want to Go to a Nightclub," the idea of Ricky's possible infidelity is a recurrent theme in the show (though he is in fact unfailingly faithful to Lucy). Although this particular issue had been a long-standing concern in Ball's own marriage, she apparently never took exception to its use as a plot point on *I Love Lucy*. Episodes such as "Don Juan and the Starlets" (2/14/55), in which Lucy wrongly believes that her husband stayed out all night with a group of beautiful models, made light of the subject while acknowledging a marital problem much less frequently discussed in other 1950s sitcoms. Did June Cleaver *(Leave it to Beaver)* or Margaret Anderson *(Father Knows Best)* ever worry that their men had wandering eyes?

The fine art of marital negotiation: the Ricardos of *I Love Lucy*.

One other unique aspect of the show received surprisingly little comment, and seemingly stirred no particular controversy with viewers—the fact that it depicted sitcom's first interracial marriage (at least by the standards of the 1950s, if not universally regarded as such today). Almost 25 years later, CBS would be extremely nervous about this aspect of two supporting roles on *The Jeffersons*—Caucasian Tom Willis and his African-American wife Helen. Series executive producer Norman Lear battled with network executives over a kiss between the two actors in the pilot episode.

Dubious as CBS was about the prospect of allowing Ball to co-star opposite her Latino husband, had Arnaz been Asian-American, or African-American, the idea would surely have been considered out of the question altogether. Because Arnaz was a relatively light-skinned Hispanic, and fit somewhat into the "Latin lover" stereotype that Hollywood had embraced in the 1940s, his casting was reluctantly approved in the face of Ball's insistence. Once that decision was made, *Lucy*'s writers played up his appeal to female viewers, presenting him as exotic and charming. The show would ultimately make him what scholar Steven Bender recently described as "arguably the most prominent media Latina/o of the last century," noting that his character was depicted as "entrepreneurial and upwardly mobile and as possessing an urban and urbane intelligence and character."[9]

Whether intentionally or not, *I Love Lucy* seemed to put much of its stars private lives on display, and viewers grew attached to Ball and her TV character to a degree that would seldom, if ever, be matched. Her real-life pregnancy was depicted in seven of the show's second-season episodes, a rarity in an era when that condition was usually represented onscreen, if at all, by the placement of a small pillow under the costume of a non-pregnant actress. Ball was visibly, unquestionably pregnant, and, far from being offended, viewers were thrilled for her. The actress and her husband, who had been childless for the first decade of their marriage, grew noticeably emotional during an *I Love Lucy* scene where Lucy tells Ricky they're "expecting" ("Lucy is Enceinte," 12/8/52), and audiences knew they were watching more than just a skilled performance. Ball would be pictured with her new baby on the cover of *TV Guide*'s first national issue, and public excitement over the event ran high in the weeks before Desi Junior's birth in January 1953.

Perfectly as Ball and Arnaz seemed to be matched onscreen, there were other elements of their real lives that peeked through as well. "Many times on the *Lucy* show," she said years later, "the script was very close to reality. In real life Desi and I had separated and reconciled many times, and the public knew this. So our writers did a script about Lucy and Ricky quarreling and separating [seemingly a reference to the "Matchmaker" episode].

"Ricky Ricardo moved out of the apartment and I was supposed to walk around the living room set, forlorn, touching each piece of furniture wistfully. To our writers' amazement, people in the studio audience took out their handkerchiefs and started weeping. Then when Lucy and Ricky were reconciled a few minutes later, in what was supposed to be a hilarious scene, nobody laughed. They were too happy and relieved to see us together again."[10]

Done as skillfully as this show did them, those elements were understandably harder for *Lucy*'s competitors to mimic. Even Ball herself, when surrounded by less inspired colleagues, would find *I Love Lucy*'s success impossible to replicate, though she would continue to be a top-rated TV star into the early 1970s with her vehicles *The Lucy Show* (CBS, 1962–68) and *Here's Lucy* (CBS, 1968–74).

Ball loved the opportunities for play that *I Love Lucy* gave her, and threw herself wholeheartedly into the show. Ironically, as joyous as the work was for her, it came during a period in her life when her own circumstances were often grimmer.

A 1953 brush with the House Un-American Activities Committee, following up on Ball's registration as a potential Communist Party voter almost twenty years earlier, threatened briefly to topple the Desilu empire. And by midway through the show's six-year run, it was becoming increasingly apparent that, for everything else *I Love Lucy* had achieved, it was not producing the desired marital harmony for Ball. An article in the January 1955 issue of the scurrilous gossip magazine *Confidential* purported to detail Desi Arnaz's frequent dalliances with other women of dubious virtue, not all of them in the distant past. The publicity embarrassed Ball, and made her realize that her husband's behavior might preclude the happy outcome she had envisioned for them as spouses and co-stars.

Ironically, the show that Ball had intended to solidify her personal life seems to have had quite the opposite effect. The longer *I Love Lucy* ran, and the more her marriage seemed to unravel, the more important her career became to her, and the greater her focus on work at the expense of her home life. Eventually the *I Love Lucy* set, or any set where she was being allowed to do the work she loved, became a safe haven that brought her more satisfaction than most other aspects of her life.

Although the three-camera method of sitcom filming was developed and perfected on *I Love Lucy*, few of the shows that followed would look as fresh and spontaneous as this one did. While later sitcoms would compile each episode from assembling the best takes from two different live performances, with the increasing sophistication of film or videotape editing allowing every blemish to be trimmed, *Lucy* maintains the feeling of a stage play. Not in the sense of playing up to the studio audience, which was perhaps most blatant in 1970s sitcoms like *The Jeffersons*, but in the choice to let slight imperfections remain in the finished product. If the *Lucy* actors occasionally stumbled slightly over a line, or reacted to something unexpected, the moment was rarely re-shot, or deleted. Though the actors never broke character, or were seen on air in the type of flubs that would be fodder for blooper shows in the 1980s, their performances gave the show a strikingly natural feel that few others replicated. Conversely, the show was never disrupted with moments such as the whoops of audience joy that eventually greeted the first entrance of almost every actor on later episodes of *Happy Days* (ABC, 1974–84). Few if any performers have ever matched Ball's ability to bring off a perfectly timed performance that looks so spontaneous—and is anything but. A fanatic about rehearsals, Ball practiced her scenes over and over each week before she was ready to face the studio audience.

By the latter half of its first season, *I Love Lucy* was setting ratings records, becoming the first TV show seen by ten million viewers with a May 1952 telecast, "The Marriage License." Not ranked as the #1 show that season, it would attain that status in 1952-53, and hold its place until it was briefly dethroned during the 1955 mania for *The $64,000 Question* and other big-money quiz shows. By the end of its run, the TV viewing audience had increased enormously, and *Lucy* was reaching more than 40 million households.

Critical attention accompanied the ratings success, and Ball would win her first Emmy for the role in 1953. Vance would take home a Best Supporting Actress trophy a year later, though Arnaz and Frawley would never be so honored.

The popularity of *I Love Lucy* even made Ball a hot ticket for movie roles again, after an absence of several years from the silver screen. In 1954, MGM released *The Long, Long Trailer*, a hit comedy that paired Ball and Arnaz as newlyweds who take a chaotic trip in their newly purchased camper. A less successful follow-up, *Forever, Darling*, was released in 1956.

One of the reasons that Ball's show stayed high in the ratings for six years was producer Oppenheimer's innovative decision to bring new story elements into the show that kept it fresh. The first of these was a happy accident, when Ball's real-life pregnancy dictated a change of course for the show's second season. That development came along just as the writers were beginning to run low on stories about Lucy trying to break into Ricky's act, and added a human element to the show that only increased its appeal to viewers.

Sometime during the 1954-55 season, with 100 episodes under their belts, he and his writers acknowledged that the show was in danger of growing stale, and brainstormed ideas for new directions. Out of that came the decision to do an ongoing story about Lucy and Ricky's trip to Hollywood, where he will star in a motion picture. The move re-energized the show, and led to some of its most memorable episodes, such as "L.A. at Last" (2/7/55), in which Lucy famously causes a tray of desserts to splatter on her idol William Holden. The gimmick worked so well that it was repeated the following season with a trip to Europe, which was slightly less effective, though giving the writers possibilities for new stories. During that season, the last of the show's true classic episodes, "Lucy's Italian Movie" (4/16/56), detailed her escapades stomping grapes in hopes of landing a film role.

Over the course of the show's run, the adventures of Lucy and Ricky in many ways mirrored the lives of the viewers who faithfully watched the show. *Lucy*'s writers found humor in Ricky's efforts at career advancement, the birth of the Ricardos' first child, the experience of sharing a vacation with friends, and ultimately, in 1957, their decision to leave New York City and relocate to the suburbs.

If *I Love Lucy*'s last season, 1956-57, was its least effective (though still top-rated), that can be attributed to several factors, one of them being the departure of producer/creator Jess Oppenheimer. Although the early episodes of *Lucy* attempted to raise Desi Arnaz's profile as an actor and singer, the show's success in fact allowed him to emerge in a completely different and unexpected role—as a studio mogul. The popularity of *I Love Lucy* inevitably led to its makers being invited to supply the networks with other shows, and by the mid–1950s Arnaz and Ball owned one of the most successful independent production companies in Hollywood. Once Ball had demonstrated that television was a viable option for a comic actress, her friends Eve Arden and Ann Sothern followed in her footsteps, turning to Desilu to further their sitcom careers.

Unfortunately, Arnaz's emerging power as Desilu president led him into conflict with Oppenheimer, who was (in today's sitcom terminology) the "show runner" of *I Love Lucy* (the executive primarily responsible for its production and creative content). The ego clash between the two men eventually resulted in Oppenheimer's decision to accept a job as a network programming executive, leaving Arnaz to produce the show's sixth season solo.

By 1957, Ball and Arnaz would make the difficult decision to end *I Love Lucy* as a weekly series, though they signed a deal to continue with occasional hour-long specials. CBS offered a record-breaking license fee for another year's worth of episodes, as the show was still firmly entrenched at the top of the ratings, but the stars were tired, and the show was exhibiting signs of age as well.

As both Ball and her husband realized, they were at a crossroads in their career. The money they had earned via *Lucy* made it entirely possible for them to walk away from the stressful business, and settle into a comfortable retirement. Arnaz later recalled that the only options available to Desilu by the mid–1950s were to wind down, or to grow into a full-fledged studio that would compete on equal footing with other major players in the television industry.

Ball, who had found her TV series more artistically satisfying and rewarding than anything else she had tried in her 25-year acting career, wasn't ready to walk away, in large part because her personal life was notably less successful.

"Desi wanted to sell everything and retire," she told her biographer Jim Brochu. "Just the word alone sent chills through my body. I loved working. I didn't want to retire ever. I told him that. I felt I didn't have a marriage anymore. Desi wasn't about to give up booze and broads, so I didn't see any reason to give up my work."[11]

During the 1957-58 season, *I Love Lucy* morphed into an occasional series of one-hour specials, aired under the title *The Ford Lucille Ball–Desi Arnaz Show*. Generously budgeted, the shows typically featured Ball and her co-stars interacting with a celebrity guest, and often a musical or dance number. Unfortunately for the sponsor, the product they were using the expensive shows to promote was the notorious Edsel, something not even Lucy and Ricky's vast audience numbers could help.

The following year, when Ford withdrew from sponsorship, Arnaz was able to incorporate the specials into a new weekly anthology series, *Desilu Playhouse*, which would last until 1960. The thirteen hour-long shows, featuring guests such as Fred MacMurray, Milton Berle, and, in the best outing, Tallulah Bankhead, were later syndicated as *The Lucy-Desi Comedy Hour*.

By the late 1950s, it was increasingly clear that Ball's marriage was on its last legs. By then far more attached professionally than they were personally, Mr. and Mrs. Arnaz were playing one of TV's most contented couples in a way they were no longer able to emulate off-camera. In the spring of 1960, faced with falling ratings for *Desilu Playhouse* and the need to separate herself professionally from Arnaz, Ball completed her contractual commitment to the show and then promptly filed for divorce. Viewers who felt they'd spent the better part of a decade peeking behind the curtain of the stars' real-life marriage were shocked by the news, though hints of marital problems for the Arnazes had begun to appear in print with some regularity by the late 1950s.

In 1960, television comedy was at a low ebb, and there were fewer series leads for funny women than there had been for years. Gale Storm's sitcom career wound down with the cancellation of *The Gale Storm Show: Oh! Susanna* after four years, and *The Ann Sothern Show* would be on the critical list by the end of the year. The failure of *The Eve Arden Show* (1957-58) had caused CBS to lose some of its faith in one of its most popular sitcom stars of the decade, and Betty White had fared no better with her first network sitcom, *Date with the Angels* (ABC, 1957-58). Only *The Donna Reed Show*, which presented its star in a more typical housewife role, was still going strong on ABC, holding fast against the array of Westerns that were filling prime time TV schedules. With the retirement of Gracie Allen in 1958, followed by the death of Joan Davis in 1961, it was as if an era in the history of television comedy was winding down with the decade.

For the moment, Ball retreated from television. She found a temporary reprieve from her troubles playing opposite Bob Hope in the United Artists film comedy, *The Facts of Life*, followed by her starring role in a mediocre stage musical, *Wildcat*, which opened on Broadway in December 1960. The show itself was forgettable, but the chance to see Lucy in person kept ticket sales brisk until illness forced Ball to close the show several months later. Although she had originally welcomed the idea of playing a fresh character, the deficiencies of *Wildcat*'s script soon became apparent to the star, and she filled the void at later performances by edging closer to her TV characterization, revamping the story of Wildy Jackson into something akin to "Lucy

Lucy the mogul: Desilu vice-president Lucille Ball pictured in 1960 with former *I Love Lucy* producer Jess Oppenheimer (at left) and actors Darryl Hickman, Marshall Thompson, and Annie Fargé, promoting the CBS sitcom *Angel*.

Ricardo Goes West." Ad-libbed in-jokes like a reference to "a fellow named Fred Mertz" drew laughs during the show's lulls.

The longest-lasting impact of her Broadway run came when the newly single Ball was introduced to comedian Gary Morton in December 1960. Their romance flourished, and culminated in Ball's second marriage the following November. She would remain married to Morton until her death in 1989, while eventually achieving a warm friendship with ex-husband Desi Arnaz.

If Ball's television career was stalled, Desilu's fortunes were also dicey by the early 1960s. The company's magic touch with sitcoms couldn't save shows like ABC's *Harrigan and Son* (1960-61) from a quick extinction. It was largely the popularity of the gangster melodrama *The Untouchables* (ABC, 1959–63) that was keeping the company afloat, and there had been signs that the show's violence and ethnic stereotyping might preclude a long TV run, despite its current high ratings. Meanwhile, *Lucy* co-creators Carroll and Martin, surely among TV's most in-demand sitcom writers, launched a CBS series called *The Tom Ewell Show,* but were unable to repeat the phenomenal success they had enjoyed with Ball. Former *Lucy* writer-producer Jess

Oppenheimer would have no better luck with his show, *Angel* (CBS, 1960-61), in which the comedy centered on a young, Lucy-ish French-born wife.

Meanwhile, though Ball had taken a hiatus from television work, she was still readily visible thanks to CBS' frequent and lucrative reruns of *I Love Lucy*. Having purchased rights to the series from Desilu in 1956, for the relatively meager price of $4.5 million, CBS opted not to put the show into syndication at the outset. Instead, repeat episodes played in prime time intermittently until 1961, and would be a staple of the network's daytime schedule well into the 1960s.

By late 1961, having tried her hand at movies and stage work, Ball was coming to the realization that no other medium suited her as well as the TV sitcom. She allowed her ex-husband, still at the helm of Desilu, to persuade her to tackle something she had initially disavowed—a second television series. Knowing Ball's hatred of change, he did everything possible to assemble a product that would be comfortingly familiar not only to viewers, but also to his jittery star, who had reason to doubt that lightning could strike twice.

I Love Lucy writers Bob Carroll, Jr., Madelyn Pugh (then Martin), Bob Schiller, and Bob Weiskopf were signed to write the new show, and many of the same crew members were recruited as well. Perhaps most importantly to Ball, since Arnaz would not appear in the show, and William Frawley was already committed to ABC's *My Three Sons*, Vivian Vance was persuaded, with a hefty salary, to sign on as Ball's co-star.

Not part of the mix, unfortunately, was Jess Oppenheimer, who had been so instrumental to the success of *I Love Lucy*. After departing Desilu in 1956, he had gone on to a lackluster career as a network executive and television producer. Not only did Oppenheimer's clashes with studio president Desi Arnaz preclude his involvement with what would become *The Lucy Show*, he would receive no credit for the Lucy Ricardo characterization that Ball would essentially reprise in her second series (and, to some degree, in all her subsequent sitcom work). Eventually, the former producer/head writer of *I Love Lucy* would sue Desilu, after the company professed that *The Lucy Show* was based on humorist Irene Kampen's book *Life without George*, and no other source.

Slotted on CBS' Monday night schedule, where *I Love Lucy* had reigned for six years, *The Lucy Show* was another hit for Ball, and would enjoy a six-year run. She took on additional responsibility a few months after its premiere, when she invoked a buy-sell agreement that ended her ex-husband's tenure at Desilu. Made unreliable by his worsening alcoholism, Arnaz disappeared from the scene for several years, and Ball was suddenly a working executive as well as the star of her own series.

During the run of *The Lucy Show*, however, many of the people both in front of and behind the camera who had been Desilu stalwarts drifted away. After the departure of Arnaz, Ball had a falling-out with her longtime writers in the spring of 1964, and replaced them with a revolving door of freelancers, supervised by Jack Benny's longtime writer Milt Josefsberg, for *The Lucy Show*'s subsequent seasons. In 1965, Vivian Vance, who had remarried a few years earlier, decided to bow out of the show, preferring to live on the East Coast full-time, and the last major holdover from *I Love Lucy* was gone.

Although Ball would continue to star in a weekly series until 1974, and would enjoy high ratings and even another Emmy victory during those years, her later work is held in significantly less esteem than *I Love Lucy*, and understandably so. By the late 1960s, Ball's TV episodes were often openly derivative of the original series, recycling plotlines, stunts, and scenarios that had been done better the first time around. Gimmicks such as the use of celebrity guests, which had been done sparingly and with skill on *I Love Lucy*, were repeated far too many times, while little or nothing that was fresh and new emerged.

The hours she spent as a studio executive cut into her rehearsal time, always a vital component in polishing her performances. Sensitive about her appearance as she headed into her late fifties, Ball would no longer allow herself to be filmed in close-up, and was more hesitant to engage in the facial gestures that had evoked so many laughs on *I Love Lucy*. Reluctant to compete with viewers' memories of Lucy and Ricky, she would play an unattached woman in all her subsequent series work, depriving the shows of the husband-wife interplay that had been so effective in the original show. Vance's absence was felt strongly as well.

Just as significantly, the departure of her original writers loosened the show's grip on what made Ball's own persona work. In the later episodes of *The Lucy Show*, and subsequently in *Here's Lucy*, the writers took a character originally limned as zany and impulsive, and gradually reinterpreted that to "stupid." While Ball herself functioned as the head of a major corporation, she spent her days playing a woman unable to grasp the complexities of routine clerical work, one who, in the absence of strong motivation in the scripts, increasingly came across as tiresomely inane and annoying.

Nonetheless, audiences' loyalty to the star, and to the ingrained Monday-night habit of watching Lucy, persisted until the early 1970s. By then, Ball, weary of the responsibility of running Desilu Productions, had sold the company to Paramount Television in a lucrative deal. *Here's Lucy* was issued under the auspices of Lucille Ball Productions, a smaller company that functioned solely to produce the star's weekly sitcom, with Ball credited as "Executive in Charge of Production."

By 1974, the changing face of television comedy (as personified by CBS' hits *All in the Family*, *Maude*, etc.) began to make Ball's shows look hopelessly passé. The show no longer

Publicity photo for *Life with Lucy*, Lucille Ball's ill-fated 1986 ABC sitcom.

in the Top Twenty-Five, Ball brought *Here's Lucy* to a stop at the age of sixty-three. Replacing it on CBS' Monday schedule that fall was Beatrice Arthur's *Maude*, the swap representing a blatant changing of the guard that some viewers cheered as laudatory and forward-thinking, and others just found sad. Ironically, *Maude* star Arthur had supported Ball in her last film role, the critically panned *Mame* (United Artists, 1974).

Aside from occasional specials, Ball would do little television work in the late 1970s and early 1980s. Unwisely, she allowed second husband Gary Morton and successful TV producer Aaron Spelling to persuade her to attempt a series comeback for ABC in 1986. *Life with Lucy*, launched when its star was 75 years old, was an embarrassing retread of her earlier shows. Initial audience tune-in was enormous, attesting to Ball's undiminished popularity, but the show seemed to sadden viewers, whose early curiosity didn't translate into ongoing success. For the first and only time in her TV career, a Ball series was cancelled due to low ratings, in late 1986.

Mostly inactive professionally after the *Life with Lucy* debacle, Ball died on April 26, 1989, at the age of 77. After decades of throwing a nearly inexhaustible supply of energy into her career, she was ill-suited for retirement, and some friends thought she was suffering from depression once she could no longer look forward to regular work. Television critic Cecil Smith, who developed a personal acquaintance with Ball during his marriage to her beloved cousin Cleo, summed her up thusly:

"To become a major star a person has to have a single purpose. Lucy's never happy unless she's working. She expends all that fantastic energy four days a week, filming her show, and comes home bruised from head to toe from pratt falls [sic] ... I say you've got to want your goal awfully bad to endure punishment like that. It's got to be your life."[12]

❖ 4 ❖

Spring Byington

December Bride

BRANDON TARTIKOFF, THE HIGHLY SUCCESSFUL programming head at NBC in the 1980s, postulated that every successful series had a Satisfying Underlying Premise, "something in the basic premise of the show that validates some reassuring notion the audience would like to believe is real." As an example, he cited his network's hit sitcom *The Golden Girls* (1985–92), which, in his words, "addressed a profound fear—the fear of finding yourself alone and unhappy in your later years," and reassured viewers "that old age and unpleasant times are not synonymous if you have good friends and a positive attitude."[1]

His theorem could have just as easily been describing a much earlier show, CBS' *December Bride* (1954–59), which starred Spring Byington as a merry, charming sixtyish widow who turned the stereotype of the nagging, annoying mother-in-law on its ear. *Bride,* in fact, offered a second SUP as well, one infrequently depicted in the sitcom world: the idea that relatives, particularly in-laws, can enjoy harmonious, mutually supportive relationships. While not an inherently funny premise, Byington and her show made it into one viewers embraced for five years, and the veteran stage and film actress became one of the most beloved sitcom stars of the decade.

December Bride was first heard as a CBS radio show, which aired from 1952 to 1953. Its premise, as described in the tagline heard at the beginning of each broadcast, was a simple one: "the story of a guy who likes his mother-in-law." The show was created by Parke Levy, who had had a long association as head writer of radio's *My Friend Irma* radio comedy, and was taken from his own family circumstances.

"*December Bride* was based upon my mother-in-law," Levy explained. "She was a widow, very attractive—not the stereotype. She was quite a gal. And being attractive and not too old, she attracted a great many men."[2]

Although *December Bride* came along in the twilight days of network radio, it

59

proved to be a popular success. By 1953, having struck gold with video adaptations of other radio shows like *Our Miss Brooks,* CBS was interested in bringing *Bride* to the tube. During preparations for its launch, however, the network and Levy reached an impasse over the casting of the show's female lead. At least one highly-placed CBS executive, for reasons not entirely clear, nixed the idea of allowing Byington to reprise her radio role.

One source said that the network nabob "wanted a bigger star."[3] Byington's friend, actress Marjorie Main of "Ma Kettle" fame, gave a different explanation: "They thought she was too old."[4] (The earlier of the two birthdates commonly cited for the actress would have made her nearly 70 when the TV pilot was being cast). Whatever the reason, series creator and head writer Parke Levy, who'd worked well with his star since launching the show on radio in 1952, was puzzled by this dictum. He opposed the idea of casting another actress. When CBS' option on the property expired during the back-and-forth over Byington, Levy took the show to TV's hottest sitcom producer, Desilu.

Studio president Desi Arnaz listened to some tapes of the radio show, liked what he heard, and signed on to co-produce with Levy a *December Bride* pilot starring Spring Byington. He and Levy agreed not to tell the star of CBS' refusal to cast her. Nevertheless, having opted for Byington, Arnaz assumed that the show would have to be sold to NBC or ABC, since he had defied CBS' preference. With some Desilu money on the line, Arnaz consulted his home oracle, wife Lucille Ball, about Byington. TV's top comedienne opined, "She'll be great in it. Film is nothing new to her."[5]

That was an understatement. Spring Byington had amassed more than 90 film credits in a career that stretched back over two decades. She had worked in everything from A films for top directors like Frank Capra and William Wyler, to horror films like Universal's *WereWolf of London* (1935), and MGM musicals like *In the Good Old Summertime* (1949). Not tied down to a contract at any particular studio, she was able to pick and choose her roles.

Born in Colorado Springs, Colorado, on October 17, 1886 (some sources say 1893), Byington moved often as a child, living with various relatives while her mother, widowed at a young age, pursued a medical degree. Rather than leaving her at loose ends, the actress later said that the transient nature of her young life made her and sister Helene resilient.

"Bad as the shifting was for our security," she said, "it was equally *good* for our mental flexibility. We had to learn to adapt to new situations. It taught us to be flexible—an important attitude in a world changing as rapidly as ours. I learned early in my life that you can't insist on everything being today as it was yesterday."[6]

Stage-struck from childhood, Byington began her acting career before graduating high school, introduced by her mother to a family friend who operated a theatrical troupe. Gaining her first professional experience with tiny roles in the Elitch Gardens Summer Stock Company, she saw firsthand the difficulties and sacrifices of a performer's life—but wasn't dissuaded. Paid a pittance of a salary, Byington didn't care—she was getting what she later described as "a three-year period of actual experience in playing which money couldn't buy."[7]

While on tour with the stock company, Byington met and married Roy Carey Chandler, who worked as a stage manager. Following their marriage in 1919, she and her new husband relocated to Argentina, and became parents to two daughters. The marriage, however, ended in divorce after only a few years, and Byington returned to New York with her children in tow, where she resumed her dormant acting career.

Cast to play a small role in a 1924 Broadway production of George S. Kaufman and Marc Connelly's *Beggar on Horseback,* Byington stepped into a bigger part after the performer originally cast fell ill. Over the next ten years, she racked up roles in some twenty productions, achieving almost constant employment throughout the 1920s and into the early 1930s. Among her noteworthy Broadway engagements was a featured part in Rachel Crothers' *When Ladies Meet,* as flighty society hostess Bridget Drake. She originated the role in the 1932-33 stage production, and would reprise it in Hollywood almost a decade later, in MGM's film adaptation.

In 1931, while still pursuing her stage career, Byington made her film debut in an obscure, Christmas-themed Vitaphone comedy short, *Papa's Slay Ride.* Two years later, she was called to Hollywood, based on a colleague's recommendation, for a key supporting role in RKO's film version of *Little Women.* As Marmee March, Byington held her own opposite a stellar cast headed by Katharine Hepburn and Joan Bennett. The high-profile role attracted the attention of other studios, and in 1935 alone Byington could be seen in eight films, among them MGM's *Ah, Wilderness!* and *Mutiny on the Bounty.*

Quickly establishing herself as a reliable character actress, she would be nominated for a Best Supporting Actress Oscar for her role in Capra's *You Can't Take It with You* (Columbia, 1938). In that memorable film, based on the Kaufman-Hart play, she was cast as Penny Sycamore, eccentric mother of the heroine. Mrs. Sycamore spends her days writing plays in the family living room, using a kitten to weight down her manuscript as she types, and all because someone mistakenly delivered a typewriter to the house eight years earlier. A year later, *The Story of Alexander Graham Bell* (Fox, 1939), paired her for the first time with actor Charles Coburn, with whom she would ultimately co-star in five more films.

Although she played a featured role in MGM's *A Family Affair* (1937), which introduced Andy Hardy and his family to movie audiences, she would not appear in the series that subsequently evolved. However, her role as the loving mother of five children in *Every Saturday Night* (Fox, 1936), with Jed Prouty cast as her husband, was popular enough to launch a similar series. What had been the Evers family in the original film was rechristened the Jones Family, and would evolve into a long-running bread-and-butter series of B films for 20th Century Fox.

The series centered on the adventures of a typical American family growing up in small-town Ohio. Byington played Louise Jones, loving and patient mother to five children—Bonnie (Shirley Deane), Jack (Kenneth Howell), Roger (George Ernest), Lucy (June Carlson), and Bobby (Billy Mahan). Prouty played John Jones, father to the brood, but it was Byington's character that held the family together.

The low-budgeted series, designed to play the second half of double bills, continued through sixteen films released between 1937 and 1940, most of them running only about sixty minutes each. The films themselves were largely unmemorable, but pleased audiences looking for light entertainment during World War II. The sixteenth and final Jones Family film, *On Their Own* (1940), was made without Prouty, whose father character was written out as being ill and confined to a sanitarium. In his absence,

Spring Byington as the loving mother of the Jones Family, with Ken Howell (left) and George Ernest in *On Their Own* (Fox, 1940).

matriarch Louise (Byington) pulls the family together despite a financial crisis, pulling up stakes to move them to a new life in California.

When she wasn't starring in B films, Byington was always in demand for supporting roles in bigger pictures. Over the course of the next fifteen years, Byington acted opposite many of the most renowned names of the era—at MGM alone, she worked with Joan Crawford (*When Ladies Meet,* 1941), Judy Garland *(Presenting Lily Mars,* 1943), and Barbara Stanwyck *(B.F.'s Daughter,* 1948). Rarely cast in unsympathetic roles (with Fox's 1946 drama *Dragonwyck* being an exception), she most often played motherly types, trading on the same charm and amiability that would later serve her well in playing Lily Ruskin. Harkening back to her appearance in *You Can't Take It With You,* she also displayed a knack for playing dithery confusion that sometimes earned her the "scatterbrain" label.

Her ego firmly in check, Byington was able to practice her craft—and attract critical attention—even when she wasn't awarded one of the starring roles. "Sometimes, young people come to Hollywood or New York after having some small success in a local company," she explained. "Their attitude is, 'I will only take a job, if such-and-such a condition is met.... My feeling is, this attitude is wrong. If you are interested in your work, your desire to do a good job comes first, your self-importance comes last."[8]

One of Byington's last films before taking the plunge into television was a Universal comedy called *Louisa* (1950), which was almost a precursor to the role she would play on *December Bride*. In *Louisa*, Byington plays a widow who has recently taken up residence with her son Hal (played by Ronald Reagan) and daughter-in-law Meg (Ruth Hussey). The elder Mrs. Norton, lonely and with time on her hands, is becoming a household nuisance, having argued with the grocer, criticized the raising of her grandchildren, and upset the family housekeeper.

Encouraged by her son to develop interests outside the home, Mrs. Norton does just that, and soon the Nortons' little boy announces, a bit taken aback, "Grandma's got a boyfriend!" When Mrs. Norton is observed holding hands with her new beau (played by Edmund Gwenn) during a movie date, and staying out until 1 A.M., the family is scandalized. Adding to the complications is Hal's boss Mr. Burnside (played by Byington's frequent co-star Charles Coburn), who also takes a shine to the attractive widow, and resolves to show up her fiancé as unworthy of her.

Although Byington unjustifiably rates only fifth billing in *Louisa*, she is actually its star, and reviewers generally singled her out for praise. The *New York Times*' Bosley Crowther, who was quite capable of skewering a performer he didn't appreciate, called Byington "darling" in the film, adding, "Her crotchetiness as a widow and then her radiance at the discovery of a new love should be more remedial than medicine in raising the spirits of people her age."[9]

The part was also a favorite of Byington's, who noted, "I liked the role because it was gay and flippant. Louisa had lots of pep, loads of charm, a wonderful sense of humor, and best of all, a universal problem to deal with in the film. She was an older woman with young ideas.... She wanted new interests in life and found them."[10] The film's popularity even led to a brief *Louisa* radio series heard on NBC in the early 1950s, with Byington and Gwenn repeating their film roles.

In 1951, Byington followed up on the success of *Louisa* with a starring role in the low-budget Monogram comedy-drama, *According to Mrs. Hoyle*. The picture cast her as a retired schoolteacher living in a fleabag hotel, who, as the film's advertising copy puts it, "turns the trick on double dealers ... and trumps the ace of every sharpie with an eye for loot or ladies!"[11] Pleased as the actress might have been by this rare instance of star billing, by then it was clear to most movie actors and executives that change was on the horizon, and that television would have a substantial impact on the careers of all but the biggest film stars.

Inevitably, Byington's film work began to slow down in the early days of TV. Rather than throwing up her hands, she gamely made tentative forays into the new medium, starting with guest appearances on early TV anthology shows like *Pulitzer Prize Playhouse*. On the filmed anthology series *Bigelow Theatre*, she starred in "Charming Billy" (6/3/51), playing "a kindly old aunt who bakes cookies for the kids in the neighborhood,"[12] and finds romance thanks to the title character, a stray dog.

In 1953, Byington made her television sitcom debut with a guest appearance on an early episode of Danny Thomas' new ABC sitcom *Make Room for Daddy*. There, she would be introduced to Desilu's methodology of filming sitcom episodes before a live studio audience. If she wasn't taking notes, she should have been. Only a few months later, she would be at work filming the pilot for the TV adaptation of *December Bride*.

Not yet a *December Bride*: Spring Byington, flanked by Edmund Gwenn and Charles Coburn, playing another eligible widow in *Louisa* (Universal, 1950).

"Lily Ruskin Arrives," shot in early 1954, opens as young architect Matt Henshaw (played by Dean Miller) accompanies his wife Ruth (Frances Rafferty) to the train station, where they will pick up Ruth's mother Lily for a visit. Having met Lily only once, briefly, at the time of his marriage five years earlier, Matt sees no reason for apprehension—until his friend and neighbor, Pete Porter (Harry Morgan) plants an idea in his head. Pete, who the year before endured a six-month visit from his own mother-in-law ("That old bat face still haunts me," he complains), warns Matt that Lily will soon settle in and rule the roost. "All beasts of prey have their natural habitat," Pete says. "The lion has its den, the leopard has its lair, and the mother-in-law has the son-in-law's home."

The comic mother-in-law figure was a sitcom staple. She was often depicted as an interloper and a fault-finder—on Desilu's *I Love Lucy*, in the episode "Lucy's Mother-in-Law" (11/22/54), Ethel Mertz warns her friend, "Honey, your mother-in-law is coming! Stand by for dust inspection!" The popular sitcom *Bewitched* (ABC, 1964–72) would offer not one but two interfering mothers-in-law—Darrin's querulous, neurotic mother Phyllis "I have a sick headache" Stephens, played by Mabel Albertson, and, even more fearsomely, *his* mother-in-law, Endora (Agnes Moorehead), who had a tendency to resolve family disputes by turning the opposition into various creatures of four or more legs. Less ominous, though undeniably of the buttinsky mold, were Eve Arden (q.v.) and Kaye Ballard in Desi Arnaz's sitcom *The Mothers-in-Law* (NBC, 1967–69).

In *December Bride,* however, Byington plays a friendly, attractive, cheerful older woman who instantly makes herself welcome in the Henshaw home. Only too happy to whip up a good meal, praise the good looks and smarts of her son-in-law, and help around the house, she's popular not only with daughter Ruth but also with Matt, who, by the series' fifth episode, "The Veterinarian" (11/1/54), will be plotting ways to extend her visit, because he so enjoys her presence. Unlike Byington's character in *Louisa,* who was initially irritable and problematic, Lily fits in beautifully from day one.

The pilot also introduces the recurring theme of Lily's status as an eligible widow, as she emerges from her trip having acquired a fiancé en route. She explains the genesis of the romance to her startled daughter and son-in-law: "He said hello to me in Buffalo, proposed in Chicago, and I said maybe in Albuquerque. Isn't it romantic?"

By episode's end, that particular romance is kaput, thanks to a misunderstanding that has Lily's family thinking her fiancé is a jewel thief. No matter—she's already snagged a date with the investigating policeman. "I'm in the arms of the law!" she says, beaming, at the episode's close, as her beau takes her out to dinner.

Aside from Byington, the TV pilot did not draw heavily on the cast of Levy's radio show. Although Levy and Arnaz had been firm that only Byington could play Lily Ruskin, they would not use the same supporting cast, populating the TV series almost from scratch. Three of radio's busiest and most highly regarded actors had been featured regulars on the original on *December Bride*—Hal March and Doris Singleton played the Henshaws, while Hans Conried had the role of Pete Porter.

While none of these actors would be a regular on TV's *December Bride,* it seemingly was not because their talents were unappreciated at Desilu. All three were seen in episodes of *I Love Lucy.* Conried memorably played Lucy Ricardo's elocution teacher ("I tippy-tippy-toe through my gaaaaaarden...") in "Lucy Hires an English Tutor" (12/29/52), while March had guest-starred as flirtatious salesman Eddie Grant, who puts the moves on Lucy in "Lucy Is a Matchmaker" (5/25/53). Singleton was perhaps even more of a familiar face to *Lucy* fans for her recurring role as the heroine's friendly rival Caroline Appleby.

For TV's *December Bride,* though, new faces filled those roles. Actor Dean Miller (born Dean Stuhlmueller), discovered by MGM talent scouts and shepherded into an acting career only a couple of years earlier, was cast as Matt, while actress Frances Rafferty, a 1940s contract player at the same studio, inherited the role of Byington's daughter Ruth. (Coincidentally, both Miller, later a local TV news anchorman, and Rafferty died in early 2004).

Character actor Harry Morgan, who'd racked up dozens of film credits since beginning his screen career in the early 1940s, was cast as Pete Porter. Morgan had already crossed paths with Byington when he played a featured role in *Dragonwyck.* (In films, he'd been billed as *Henry* Morgan, a name he changed to avoid confusion with the radio and TV comedian of that name). Morgan's role on *Bride* would be only the beginning of a long career as one of the most steadily employed actors in series television, encompassing the 1960s NBC revival of *Dragnet,* and peaking with his role as Colonel Sherman Potter in CBS' *M*A*S*H* (1972–83). On that show, he would pay tribute to his onetime co-star by displaying a photograph of Byington on Colonel Potter's desk, representing his wife Mildred whom he'd left at home.

Though not seen in the pilot, elderly character actress Verna Felton, also a veteran of *I Love Lucy* roles (most notably the crabby servant of the 4/27/53 segment "Lucy Hires a Maid"), would be another key supporting player on *Bride,* as Lily's smart-mouthed friend Hilda Crocker. Felton was familiar to Jack Benny fans for her role as Dennis Day's mother, which she had originated on Benny's radio show, and reprised on NBC's live television broadcasts of *The RCA Victor Show Starring Dennis Day* in 1952. (Explaining the origins of that character, Felton later said, "Dennis could not read lines, so the writers invented a domineering mother he only had to say yes to. That was me."[13]) Her *Bride* character, first seen by audiences in the show's second aired episode, "Lily Is Bored" (10/11/54), is described as the heroine's "oldest and dearest friend," though no explanation is offered at the time as to how Lily, shortly after relocating from Philadelphia to California, suddenly has a longtime friend living nearby.

One other character on the show, very much a presence though she was never seen, was Pete's wife Gladys. In the great tradition of unseen characters like Norm's wife Vera on *Cheers* (NBC, 1982–93), Gladys existed only in the imaginations of viewers, as summoned up by Pete's colorful descriptions. "When I married Gladys," he says, "she was a saucy bit of baggage. Do you know what she looks like today? A baggy bit of sausage." When she doesn't appear, he explains her absence with alibis like, "Gladys couldn't come over. She cooked dinner for the dog and he chased her into the closet." Not until the spin-off show *Pete and Gladys* (CBS, 1960–62) would the lady get equal time.

The three-camera system of shooting a sitcom, which Desilu had developed for *I Love Lucy* and replicated with *Our Miss Brooks,* was used for *December Bride* as well. The Henshaws' living room was the most frequently used set, with the kitchen seen almost as often. Given Byington's stage experience, which stretched back to her days as a teenager in the early part of the century, she was a natural for Desilu's method of filming before a live audience. Jerry Thorpe, who had learned the ropes as an assistant director on *I Love Lucy,* had his first assignment as a full-fledged director on the *Bride* pilot, and would continue in that capacity for numerous regular episodes of the show.

To Arnaz's surprise, the completed *Bride* pilot stirred interest at CBS, when network president William S. Paley unexpectedly expressed his enthusiasm for the show and its star. (Arnaz said that Byington, who'd been used to a certain amount of attention from CBS executives, had been mystified by their absence during filming of the pilot). Dealing from a position of strength, the savvy Arnaz agreed to give CBS back an ownership share in the show in exchange for one of the most desirable time slots on the network: Monday nights at 9:30, following *I Love Lucy.*

At that early stage in television history, programmers did not yet fully exploit the scheduling tricks that would later become commonplace, and Arnaz was ahead of his time in acknowledging what a difference the right time slot would make to the show's success. That particular time slot hardly came with a money-back guarantee: it was available only because CBS had just ousted its previous occupant, *The Red*

Buttons Show, which was not drawing a viewership level satisfactory to the sponsor. Nevertheless, that scheduling would insure that audiences would at least sample *December Bride*, which was set to debut that fall under the sponsorship of General Foods. Wanting to get Desilu's newest show off to a good start, Lucille Ball and Desi Arnaz even provided a short filmed introduction to "Lily Ruskin Arrives" when it aired on October 4, 1954.

The post–*I Love Lucy* scheduling would in fact give a substantial boost to *December Bride*, helping Byington's show land in the Nielsen Top Ten during its first season. Once viewers had seen the show, they came back for more, and it continued to climb in ratings, peaking at #5 during the 1956-57 season. Although not everyone attributed those scores to the show's own qualities—longtime CBS programmer Mike Dann dismissed it as "a terrible show [that] was a big hit because it followed *Lucy*"[14]—it did find favor with viewers.

Although Dann's judgment seems unduly harsh, the show would in fact be no critical darling, never attracting an Emmy nomination as Best Comedy Series. Contemporary reviews usually found the show pleasant if unexceptional, sometimes implying that the live studio audience's laughter had been electronically embellished. Byington, herself, though, charmed viewers and reviewers alike, much as her onscreen character did. She would be twice nominated for a Best Actress Emmy during the show's run, though she lost both times to Jane Wyatt of *Father Knows Best* (1954–60). (Supporting actors Harry Morgan and Verna Felton would also be Emmy-nominated for their work on the show, though, like Byington, they never received a statuette).

While many stars found the workload of starring in a weekly series tiring, Byington, despite her years, thrived on the schedule that TV imposed. "In New York," she told *TV Guide*, "the actors call it 'summer stock in an iron lung.' I'll buy that. It's hectic, it's rushed, it's fast; and it's just too bad if you don't like things that way. Myself, I need it. I need pace, I need tension, I need to be up and doing."[15]

The actress' status as the star of *December Bride* placed in a select group of women over the age of 50 who would star in their own television series. With the growing sophistication of television ratings surveys over time, network programmers would come to rely more heavily on demographics, and to believe that shows with older stars drew an audience less desirable to advertisers. By the mid–1960s, in fact, CBS was widely believed to have a rule against series stars being much beyond middle age. More recently, Angela Lansbury (just short of sixty when *Murder, She Wrote* premiered in 1984) and the stars of NBC's *The Golden Girls* during the same period were among the few older women to star in their own shows.

Byington's TV character was also noteworthy in that she did not follow the common TV stereotype of cranky, wisecracking older people (although Felton's character of Hilda Crocker was more in this vein). Not only did numerous episodes of *Bride* focus on Lily's dating life, a subject not commonly depicted among older characters in 1950s sitcoms, but she demonstrated a wider range of interests and activities than seen in supporting characters like *My Little Margie*'s Mrs. Odetts (played by Gertrude W. Hoffman), or *I Love Lucy*'s Mrs. Trumbull (Elizabeth Patterson).

Unusually for the sitcom world, Byington's character, though usually the center of attention, was often not the chief instigator of situations on the show. Though Lily had a slight touch of the zaniness that could be seen in Gracie Allen's TV character, she seldom concocted the type of outlandish schemes that defined the *Burns and Allen* show. Nor did she share Lucy Ricardo or Margie Albright's knack for stirring up trouble, however innocently. In fact, it was often her well-intended son-in-law and daughter who caused the trouble, which Lily resolved with her gentle, if offbeat, wisdom.

In the first-season episode "The Veterinarian," for instance, Matt worries that his mother-in-law is lonely, and plots to fix her up with a doctor he met while playing golf. Meanwhile, Lily, out shopping, meets an attractive, attentive man who seems to be a department store clerk (though he actually owns the store). When both men turn up for a dinner at the Henshaws' home, it's clear that Lily has picked the better man, unaffected by his financial prospects, while well-intended Matt's more socially worthy "doctor" friend is actually a veterinarian, who's also a boor.

In the show's early seasons, Lily's love life remained a recurrent theme of the show—as Pete Porter tells Matt in the same episode, "Your mother-in-law has become the darling of the bald head and bifocal set." Of course, none of the eligible bachelors she met turned out to be Mr. Right. One was too attached to his domineering mother, causing Lily to decide that she didn't need a mother-in-law problem at her age. Another, a wealthy oilman (played by Lyle Talbot) in the three-part "Texas Show" (originally aired from 12-22-55 through 1-14-56), turns out to be attracted to her mostly because she so resembles his late wife Kathleen. Throughout the show's early seasons, Lily continued to play the field, without ever becoming permanently attached.

However, by 1956, *TV Guide* was noting that the character's interests had broadened, lessening the emphasis on snagging a husband (though this remained a key goal for Lily's crass friend Hilda, who nursed a crush on film star James Mason, among others). Later episodes saw Byington's character directing a community theater production, taking up sports, and developing an

A woman of many interests: Spring Byington, in a 1950s pose, fueling an airplane.

interest in local politics. The 10/31/55 episode "The Shoplifter" introduced the recurring theme of Lily's job as a newspaper columnist, penning a feature for the *Westwood Gazette* called "Laughing at Life with Lily." Similarly, the actress herself was noted in magazine profiles to be pursuing a varied lot of hobbies, taking flying lessons, painting in watercolor, and indulging a fondness for reading Ray Bradbury and other science fiction writers.

Since much of the action on Byington's TV sitcom revolved around married life, and the possibility that a sixty-ish widow could find romance, it was usually noted in profiles of the actress that she herself was a divorcee. The mother of two adult daughters at the time of her starring role in *Bride*, Byington had never remarried in the years since her divorce in 1924.

Decades after *December Bride* was a Top Ten show, Byington is to modern TV viewers one of the less familiar names in this book, though several of her classic films are still in circulation. When her name does pop up in recent years, it's been in a slightly unexpected context, by authors and film historians who include her among the ranks of Hollywood's gay and lesbian performers. Byington's longtime friend Marjorie Main, her co-star in two films, including the classic comedy *Heaven Can Wait* (Fox, 1943), asked in an early 1970s interview about rumors concerning Byington's sexual orientation, responded, "It's true, she didn't have much use for men."[16]

More recently, film historian Axel Madsen, in a book about actresses and their same-sex attractions, asserted that her relationship with Main went beyond friendship. Madsen described Byington as "an active lesbian who lived with the comic Marjorie Main,"[17] stating that the women at one time shared a home in the same neighborhood as her *Little Women* director George Cukor.

In the more repressed 1950s, of course, there was no indication that Byington's private life might be in any way different from the norm, and she herself apparently had nothing to say on the subject in later years. (Pressed to expound on her late friend's orientation, Main was circumspect, saying, "Spring would roll over in her grave, bless her.")[18] Although the notorious *Confidential* magazine was "outing" celebrities as early as the mid–1950s, publishing insinuating articles about film actress Lizabeth Scott, leading man Tab Hunter, and others, Byington escaped such scrutiny, perhaps because she was not a young romantic lead like Scott and Hunter. By the time the Gay Liberation Movement began to gather momentum in the late 1960s, Byington was near the end of her life, and retreating from public view.

The publicity that Byington received during *Bride*'s prime-time run largely served to reinforce her TV image as a vital and active older woman with a myriad of interests. The actress told interviewers that she identified with her TV character. "Though I have no yearning at all to be young," she said, "I do have a great yearning to be ageless. Why look back? You can't do anything about the past, you certainly can do something about the future—for that's the direction in which we're all going. There is always something new in the future."[19]

Like Lily Ruskin, the actress dabbled in journalism, launching an advice column, "What Should I Do?," that appeared monthly in *Photoplay* magazine. Although the column surely originated as a publicity gimmick, it appears that Byington took the work seriously, and used the opportunity to share some of her own philosophy and ideas with readers. Longer than the typical newspaper advice column, her articles, which often ran to several pages in the magazine, tackled a variety of concerns.

In one 1956 issue, she responded to six reader letters, most of them from younger people, discussing such topics as shyness, physical disabilities, and parent-child relationships. To one correspondent having difficulties with her mother, Byington told a personal anecdote about a rough patch in her relationship with her own daughter. To a young man unsure how to express his interest in a slightly older woman of his acquaintance, she gives some solid advice, and concludes warmly with, "I'd like to know how this turns out."[20]

By the show's third season, the writers were in search of new ideas. Unlike many other long-running sitcoms, the cast of *December Bride* was remarkably stable, with the original five players remaining constant throughout. However, given the success that *I Love Lucy* enjoyed from the use of guest stars, it's not surprising that this trend found its way into Byington's show as well. While *Bride* would not attract the superstar names seen on *I Love Lucy* during this period—i.e., William Holden, Orson Welles—a number of familiar faces did guest stints on the show, among them Mickey Rooney, Fred MacMurray, Edgar Bergen, and Rory Calhoun, star of Desilu's Western drama, *The Texan* (CBS, 1958–60), who made two appearances.

Also seen in a guest spot was the star's friend Marjorie Main. In that 1956 episode, Lily and her friend Hilda are dazzled when it appears that an unnamed movie star, whose initials are M.M., has her eye on Matt and Ruth's house. Those anticipating a Monroe sighting, though, are taken aback to learn that it's Hollywood's Ma Kettle whom the agent represents.

Not everyone favored the guest star syndrome that became increasingly prevalent in the show's later seasons—*Variety*'s review of the fifth season opener, which featured ventriloquist Bergen, complained that he hogged the show at the expense of its star. "*December Bride* has been a TV mainstay for the past several years primarily through the efforts of scatter-brained Miss Byington. Keeping her work at a minimum may seem like a good change-of-pace idea on paper but it doesn't work out too well on camera," the reviewer commented.[21] Still, the show's third season, in which the use of guest stars was initiated, was the highest-rated of *Bride's* five-year run.

Other story elements introduced in the later seasons included a baby daughter born to neighbor Pete Porter and his unseen wife Gladys, as well as a brief engagement for Lily, depicted in a story arc that ran during the latter part of the 1956-57 season. Needless to say, the producers and writers weren't about to monkey with the hit show's premise by allowing Lily to remarry, and her fiancé soon fell by the wayside.

December Bride remained in its cozy Monday night time slot through its fourth season on CBS. After *I Love Lucy* ended its original run in the spring of 1957, it was replaced at 9:00 with *The Danny Thomas Show*, newly transferred (and re-titled) from its previous berth on ABC (as *Make Room for Daddy*). While Thomas' ratings didn't quite match Lucy's, *December Bride* continued to ride high in its 9:30 Monday slot during its fourth season, retaining the majority of viewers from its lead-in show.

In 1958, however, a scheduling change finally dislodged Byington's show from its traditional place, which was turned over to a new Desilu product, *The Ann Sothern*

Show. Bride transferred to a Thursday night slot, with reruns of the just-ended *I Love Lucy* as its new lead-in, and the ratings soon reflected the change. Whether the time change confused viewers, or they were simply growing tired of the long-running show, *December Bride* dropped from the Top Ten, and was canceled in the spring of 1959, after a five-year run. Interestingly, for all that *Bride*'s popularity was attributed to its advantageous scheduling, *The Ann Sothern Show* would perform well over the next two years in the coveted Monday-night berth, but never placed in the Top Ten as Byington's show had done.

Even though production of original episodes ceased in early 1959, *December Bride* would be kept alive in ways other than the expected reruns. Creator Parke Levy sold CBS on the idea of a spin-off show (sitcom's first), focusing on Harry Morgan's neighbor character. After five years of issuing steady putdowns about the looks, demeanor, and homemaking skills of his wife Gladys, who remained off-screen in the original show, Morgan would co-star with up-and-coming comedic actress Cara Williams in the domestic sitcom *Pete and Gladys*, which aired from 1960 to 1962 on CBS' Monday night schedule. Williams, who resembled Lucille Ball physically, and certainly seems to have been encouraged by CBS to emulate her style, played Gladys as a Lucy-esque scatterbrain, more than the battleaxe Pete had described so vividly on *Bride*. (Nowhere in sight on *Pete and Gladys* was baby Linda, born to the Porters in the original series).

Seen in the spin-off show's supporting cast were Verna Felton, reprising her role as Hilda from the original series, and eventually Frances Rafferty, who played not her Ruth Henshaw character but Gladys' buddy Nancy. As for *Bride* itself, CBS would revive the show for two prime-time rerun cycles, in the summer of 1960 and briefly in the spring of 1961 before putting the 157 episodes filmed into lucrative syndication through its CBS Films division.

Spring Byington cutting a rug with guest star Rudy Vallee in a 1956 episode of *December Bride*.

Once again at liberty after her series shut down, Byington turned up in a variety of gigs during 1959 and 1960. She, along with her *Bride* co-star Verna Felton, shot footage for the Disney classic *Sleeping Beauty*, not used in the film itself but rather as a reference for animators drawing scenes. Byington turned up as a guest star on *Alfred Hitchcock Presents,* in the episode "The Man with Two Faces" (12/13/60), again playing a mother-in-law, this time one who busts her son-in-law as a crook. She was also seen in guest appearances on *Dennis the Menace* (CBS, 1959–63) and ABC's *The Detectives Starring Robert Taylor* (1959–62).

Resuming her film career, which had been dormant during the show's five-year run, Byington landed a featured role in the Doris Day comedy *Please Don't Eat the Daisies* (MGM, 1960). Cast as the star's mother, Byington's role unfortunately allowed her few opportunities to shine. Her most noteworthy line comes when, apropos of one of Day's onscreen children, she exclaims, "You know what he did with those daisies? He *ate* them!"—thus providing a title not only for the movie itself, but also for one of star Day's musical numbers. Although *Please Don't Eat the Daisies* failed to take full advantage of Byington's gifts, it was a hit film. It was also her last theatrical release, the final entry on a filmography that boasted nearly 100 credits.

For the remainder of her career, she would concentrate her energies on television. In 1960, Byington made a bid to return to series work, co-starring opposite Charles Ruggles in a Screen Gems sitcom pilot called "Here Comes Melinda." Situation comedy was then at a relatively low ebb, especially for female stars, and the show, which aired as an episode of NBC's *Goodyear Playhouse* on May 9, 1960, under the title "The Sitter's Baby," didn't land a spot on the network schedule.

The problem, in part, may have been the glut of Westerns then occupying the prime time landscape. Having failed to beat the enemy, Byington joined them, accepting an offer the following year to join the cast of one of the better shows in the genre, NBC's *Laramie*. The hour-long Western series was entering its third season, and switching to color broadcasts (which had been highly successful for another genre show, *Bonanza*). Byington, cast as widow Daisy Cooper, would be the show's first female regular, third-billed behind series stars John Smith and Robert Fuller.

Introduced in the show's 66th episode, "Ladies' Day" (10/3/61), Daisy comes out to Wyoming via stagecoach (laden down with her substantial luggage) to inspect a store her late husband bought from "a nice man who was passing through our town" back East. She's dismayed to learn that there's no store, and no nearby town. Instead, she finds the ranch where Slim Sherman (Smith) and Jess Harper (Fuller) live, along with Mike (Dennis Holmes), an orphaned boy whom they've taken in temporarily. Hoping to be given custody of the boy, Slim and Jess have been trying in vain to hire a suitable housekeeper.

Byington's character soon bounces back from the news that she's been swindled, rolling up her sleeves and making herself useful. Before long, she's displayed her Civil War nursing skills (tidily extracting a bullet from the body of an unscrupulous bounty hunter), hustled Mike into a much-needed bath, and charmed the judge into letting the boy stay at the ranch with Slim and Jess, whom she's deemed "fine young men." Not surprisingly, Daisy is a shoo-in for the job of housekeeper and surrogate mother for the household.

Although the Western genre was one Byington had largely avoided in her film work, she settled in easily as a regular on *Laramie*, giving Daisy much of the same warmth and charm she'd given to her first floral-named TV character, Lily Ruskin. She's impressive in her ability to make the most of a small moment, as when she gently and matter-of-factly explains to Mike that she had a "very brave" son of her own, who didn't make it home from the war.

Laramie star Robert Fuller has "the fondest memories" of Byington, whose work he had known and admired before she joined the show, and whom he describes as "a marvelous actress. John Smith and I were thrilled when we found out she was going to come on," he says.[22]

Still, he remembers, "We were a little apprehensive. She was such a lady, and John and I raised a lot of hell on that show! We thought we were going to have to settle down a little bit, watch our language and all that." Instead, "it only took about a week, and she was right in the middle of it with us. She'd go along with all the gags."

On-screen, Byington played a warm and motherly woman who, nonetheless, took no guff. "She gave Slim and Jess a tough time," Fuller points out. "We had to toe the mark with her. She became the head of the family." Behind the scenes, he says, the camaraderie was equally strong, and the actress quickly grew fond of her new co-stars. "She loved both of us. She thought we were precious."

The addition of Byington brought a welcome new element to the action-oriented show. Although no longer starring in a sitcom, Byington's flair for comedy was put to good use by *Laramie* writer-producer John Champion, providing some lighthearted moments among the shoot-'em-ups. She remained a member of the show's cast for two seasons, until it was canceled in the spring of 1963.

By then at least seventy years old, the actress wasn't ready to retire, and for the next few years turned up as a guest star on some of TV's most popular shows. Her appearance on CBS' *Mister Ed,* playing a Hollywood gossip columnist in an episode called "Oh, Those Hats!" (11/17/63), was penned by two of her longtime *Bride* writers, and had the look of a series pilot, but nothing more came of it. She also popped up on a *Dr. Kildare* multi-part segment in November 1965, and played wealthy heiress and insomniac J. Pauline Spaghetti on ABC's *Batman* (12/28/66). On the *I Dream of Jeannie* episode "Meet My Master's Mother" (11/14/67), she was Tony Nelson's inquisitive mother, who doesn't want to end her visit until she is reassured that her son has met a "nice, old-fashioned girl" (i.e., Jeannie).

Byington would continue to be an active television performer until the late 1960s, one of her last appearances being a December 1968 guest role on ABC's *The Flying Nun*. Shortly afterwards, health concerns forced her into retirement, and the actress died of cancer on September 7, 1971. Obituaries, while taking note of her achievements in motion pictures and television, also pointed out that she had donated her body for purposes of medical research. She was survived by her two daughters, and several grandchildren and great-grandchildren.

Today, *December Bride* is a largely forgotten show, one of the least-often revived of any described in this book. The show has had no DVD release, and has not played even in basic cable reruns in years. Though the recipient of two stars on the Hollywood Walk of Fame (one for her motion picture career, the second for her TV work), Byington is not widely known among younger viewers today.

Nevertheless, she deserves to be remembered, and to be acknowledged for her prominence as one of the most popular sitcom stars of the 1950s, and a rare example of an actress who reaches the peak of stardom after the age of fifty. She also demonstrated that a television series about an older woman could attract a sizable audience, something that, despite the latter-day success of *Murder, She Wrote, The Golden Girls,* and others, network executives rarely acknowledge.

Busy and productive into her eighties, Byington and *December Bride* exhibited a life philosophy that she expressed thusly: "I have no patience with people, who, when their hair turns gray, think there is nothing else to learn, no new fields to explore—who ignore the future and continue to live their life of yesterday. Or, worse still, they sit around and worry about getting old!

"If there's one thing I've learned, it's this: With problems, you do what you can—those you can't change, you accept graciously. We can do nothing in the world about the passing years—but we can do something about today and keeping tomorrow alive. And that's the secret of youth."[23]

❖ 5 ❖

Joan Davis

I Married Joan

QUICK—CAN YOU NAME THE POPULAR 1950s sitcom about a zany, unpredictable wife and her patient husband? You know, the one with the three-word title that began with *I*, and included the star's first name?

For at least nine out of ten people asked that question today, the easy answer would surely be *I Love Lucy*, with a fifty-plus year track record of unparalleled popularity. But perhaps at least a handful of people, if pressed, might also remember *I Married Joan*, a not-dissimilar sitcom starring radio and film comedienne Joan Davis, which aired from 1952 to 1955 on NBC. While some observers view *Joan* as merely a second-rate knockoff of Lucille Ball's timeless sitcom, others are able to appreciate Davis as a gifted and original comic actress in her own right. Also noteworthy was the comedienne's role as the head of Joan Davis Enterprises, a production executive in an era when this was a rarity for a woman.

Unlike Ball, who struggled for almost twenty years in Hollywood to discover what she did best, being sidelined into musical comedies, *films noir*, and almost everything but the physical comedy she could do so brilliantly, Davis was making people laugh from her childhood forward. Born on June 29, 1907, in St. Paul, Minnesota, as Madonna Josephine Davis, she first hopped onstage at the tender age of seven. Assigned to give a dramatic reading, she drew instantaneous laughter from the audience. Rather than being insulted, she chose to take it as a sign, as indeed it was.

While still of school age, Davis began her professional career, after winning a succession of amateur contests, in a vaudeville act where she was billed as "The Toy Comedienne." With her mother and a tutor in tow, she toured on the Pantages circuit for a five-year period, carrying the professional responsibility for a fourteen-minute solo comedy routine. As a teenager, when she began to outgrow her original gimmick as a child comedienne, she made a brief return to full-time schooling. Although a good student, she didn't find the academic life congenial. Named class valedictorian, she had to squelch the ingrained urge to milk her acceptance speech for laughs. "I had to play it straight," she remembered years later. "Toughest assignment I've ever had."[1]

She spent much of the 1920s perfecting a style of raucous, knockabout comedy that would be her trademark for most of her career. Among her chief inspirations as she developed her skills was the comedic genius of Charlie Chaplin. For several years, Davis worked solo. Then, in the spring of 1931, she met actor Serenius (Si) Wills, and teamed with him for an act called "Wills and Davis." The two performers were married a few months later, and Davis gave birth to her only child, daughter Beverly, on August 5, 1933.

By that time, vaudeville was on its way out. Movies and radio had become the predominant entertainment media. Always astute about her career, Davis knew it was time to make a change, and relocated to California in the mid-thirties. Not immediately embraced by Hollywood, the actress took her fate into her own hands, arranging to perform at a party where Mack Sennett would be one of the guests. Sennett, best-known for his silent film comedies, liked her energetic comic style and cast her in his last two-reel comedy, *Way Up Thar,* released in 1935. The role allowed her to perform a comic juggling act with dishes (one of her favorite vaudeville routines), as well as sing.

The exposure, along with her continued popularity on the vaudeville stage, earned her an entree into movies. For a brief period in the mid–1930s, she was a contract player at RKO. Among her assignments was a minor role as a secretary in the long-forgotten comedy *Bunker Bean* (1936), appearing opposite an up-and-coming starlet named Lucille Ball. Unfortunately, the studio did not seem able to utilize its new player effectively, and before long the ambitious Davis asked for her release.

Publicity photo circa 1942, when Joan Davis was a regular on Rudy Vallee's NBC radio show.

Although her tenure at RKO was not a success, she had better luck at 20th Century Fox, where she signed a contract in 1937. Fox built up her experience with comic supporting roles in films like ice skater Sonja Henie's comedy *Thin Ice,* and the Ritz Brothers' vehicle *Life Begins in College* (both 1937). Rather than being groomed for her own starring vehicles, Davis was used as the comic relief that brightened more than two dozen Fox films during the late 1930s and early 1940s. She remained at Fox until 1941, when a couple of breakthrough roles kicked her career up a notch or two.

That year, Davis played a strong featured role opposite Lou Costello in Universal's hit haunted house comedy *Hold*

That Ghost. Cast as radio actress Camille Brewster, whose specialty is providing screams in lurid radio mystery shows, Davis' broad comedy style beautifully complements that of her co-star. Their energetic dance routine, done to the accompaniment of the "Blue Danube Waltz," showed off the amazing agility and seeming invulnerability to injury that had already become Davis trademarks.

Her other career break of 1941 was an August guest appearance on Rudy Vallee's popular radio show. Initially, there had been some doubt as to whether radio was the best medium for Davis' highly physical comedy. But playing a man-chaser with designs on star Vallee, and performing musical specialty numbers, Davis earned big laughs. After several return visits, she accepted an offer to join the cast as a regular in 1942.

In 1943, when Vallee was called up for military service, the show was revamped to put the popular comedienne front and center. Now called *The Sealtest Village Store*, the show spotlighted Davis, though the network's uncertainty about a woman carrying her own show led to the addition of comic Jack Haley to the cast as her co-star. As *Time* magazine later reported, "Everybody, including the sponsor, thought the program would collapse with just Joan Davis to hold it up. Instead, its popularity climbed. Last year [1944] Hooper for some time rated it the No. 6 attraction on the air."[2]

The character that emerged on that show was one that Davis would replicate for most of her radio career—the frantic single girl who's eager to land a husband. In a manner somewhat reminiscent of a later Joan—comedienne Joan Rivers—Davis' routines often centered on disparaging both her looks and her marital prospects. In one *Sealtest Village Store* segment, she is reluctant to attend the county fair, saying that at last year's event, "Some wise guy grabbed me by the ankles, threw me over his shoulders, and yelled, 'Hey, Joe, this certainly is a scrawny turkey we're raffling off this year!'"[3] A promotional booklet issued by sponsor Sealtest in 1944, *The Life and Loves of Joan Davis*, capitalized on her image with photos of Davis accompanied by self-deprecating jokes about her looks. Once Vallee left the show, Haley, playing the new manager she hires, would be cast as the key object of her pursuit, though she was prone to cast an eye on male guest stars like singer Dennis Day as well.

Some associated with the Sealtest show would not remember the star comedienne with much fondness. Writer Bob Weiskopf, later integral to the success of TV's *I Love Lucy*, called Davis "a difficult lady ... drove me crazy,"[4] complaining of her frequent demand for rewrites. Still, despite the network's uncertainty about starring a comedienne, it was soon clear that listeners had not abandoned *The Sealtest Village Store* in Vallee's absence, and Davis' star was on the rise again. Among those who took notice of her gifts was singer and comedian Eddie Cantor, whose own following on radio and in films was strong. Cantor offered Davis a role in his RKO comedy *Show Business* (1944).

Like many stars, Cantor didn't particularly have the reputation of sharing the spotlight, but in Davis' case he made an exception, saying later, "Joan, one of the greatest ad-lib comediennes in the business, put in many of her own lines and business and was an outstanding hit."[5] The movie did well at the box office, and reinforced Davis' position as a top comedienne. She and Cantor would later re-unite for *If You Knew Susie* (1948), in which they played husband and wife vaudeville performers.

While Cantor and Davis praised each other's work, some observers suggested that their mutual admiration society extended to the personal as well. Actress Constance Moore, who appeared in *Show Business,* later recalled, "Eddie and Joan were mad for each other. It's hard to say exactly when their relationship began, but it soon became obvious ... there was very little doubt they were having a physical relationship."[6] Whatever the truth of Davis' relationship with the married comedian, she filed for divorce from Si Wills not long afterwards, citing mental cruelty. Once their divorce became final in 1948, she would never again marry. She would, however, continue to collaborate with Wills professionally into the 1950s.

In 1945, thanks to her movie and radio work, Davis was near the peak of her fame and popularity. Her radio ratings higher than ever, she was a hot property, and in January of that year her agents at William Morris let it be known that she was open to more lucrative offers. *Variety,* in the first of a series of articles covering the star's contract negotiations, reported that two sponsors, Campbell Soup and United Drug, were competing for her services, with the program's "reputed selling price of $25,000"[7] (per week) roughly twice what her current show was costing Sealtest.

By the end of January, United Drug was reported to have the deal locked up. "Fiscal announcements were not disclosed but an announcement stated that the combination of program costs and promotion would approximate $1,000,000 per annum."[8] The lucrative deal that had been negotiated did not include Davis' Sealtest co-star Jack Haley, nor any of the other elements of that show—it was purely for the comedienne's solo services.

Within weeks, however, Davis' coup hit a snag. United had signed her without having nailed down a time slot for the new show. There were only two major networks at the time, NBC and CBS, and neither was able to clear a prime spot on its schedule. By March, *Variety* reported that "United has renewed its option of the comedienne for another 30 days, but it appears ... apparent that the whole deal, involving a four-year contract at top coin, may blow unless a suitable time is found for the show."[9] Ironically, in the midst of the crisis, Davis' Sealtest show hit #3 in the national radio ratings, surpassed in audience share only by Bob Hope and Fibber McGee and Molly.

The solution to Davis' problem, it soon became apparent, was to find a sponsor who would be willing to dump its existing show in favor of hers. Given her ratings, there were sponsors open to such a possibility, and a few weeks later, once her option with United Drug expired, Davis signed with Swan Soap. Kicked to the curb in her favor were Burns and Allen, whose Monday night show was then under Swan's sponsorship. Though that comedy team was popular enough to resurface in the fall with a new sponsor, their prime time slot would be turned over to the new *Joan Davis Show.*

Unhappy that Davis had deserted *The Sealtest Village Store,* her former sponsors forbade her to even say goodbye to her longtime listeners during her final broadcast in July 1945. Angered when it was implied that she had been disloyal to the company that had "made" her a radio star, Davis "sent back a scorching reply that jostled their memories a year when she remained with Sealtest rather than take American Tobacco's flattering deal which would have netted her a fiscal yield double of what Sealtest was paying her."[10]

Despite the gag order Sealtest placed on the comedienne, her new sponsor had no intention of letting the audience wonder what had become of her. A massive—and expensive—marketing campaign was prepared to launch not only her September premiere on CBS, but also the release of her RKO film *George White's Scandals* in theaters that fall. "Unusual angle of publication campaign inaugurated by Y[oung] & R[ubicam], agency on the Swan Soap account, aimed at a 31,000,000 readership through the nation's top mags, is that the ads are built around the comedienne and the CBS show rather than the product."[11]

The Swan Soap advertising campaign, featuring cartoons of Davis as the desperate single gal, appeared in numerous popular magazines during late 1945 and 1946. One typical ad was headlined "Attracting a man is a cinch, says Joan Davis," and showed her saying, "One good way is to lasso any man, drag him within easy reach, and put your foot on the back of his Adam's apple."

The Joan Davis Show, which would also be known as *Joanie's Tea Room*, was well-received upon its CBS premiere that September. For the next several years, Davis would not only be a leading radio performer, but also used her success and power to assume a key role behind the scenes. Her new deal had given her a large measure of creative control over her show. Forming Joan Davis Enterprises, she would rely on her own judgment and skill to present her work to the public. As she took more responsibility for her shows, there were predictions that she would move away from the focus on self-deprecating humor. Ultimately, she was reluctant to tinker with success, and the changes were minimal. Because she had built up her persona so effectively, the idea of the zany comedienne in a position of power may have seemed incongruous to some. However, Davis herself said, "In my heart I feel I am so much more than a screwball."[12]

While guiding her own fate, she also took advantage of the opportunity to help her teenage daughter, Beverly, follow her into what had become the family business. According to fan magazine accounts, Davis had originally intended to steer her daughter clear of the industry. Davis claimed that she had told her as a newborn, "For you there's going to be an established home, school and school friends, and then college. Your mother has been through the show business routine, and it's fine for those who have poster ink in their veins, but for you I want a different life."[13]

Nonetheless, when the script of *George White's Scandals* (RKO, 1945) called for a child actress to play Davis' character in a flashback scene, the comedienne gave that role to Beverly. A few years later, when the teenager, on her own initiative, won a featured role on the *Junior Miss* radio comedy show, Davis realized that her daughter shared her career goals, and was encouraging. Not only did she give Beverly parts on *The Joan Davis Show*, and share tips that would aid Beverly's own career as a comedienne, Davis would later have her daughter written into *I Married Joan* as a recurring character.

Not only was Davis' CBS radio show successful, but she was also popular enough to headline her own movies during this period. No longer under contract to Fox, she signed deals at Universal and RKO to star in her own modestly-budgeted comedy vehicles. It was also at around this time that the naturally brunette comedienne went blonde, the color she would retain for most of her subsequent roles.

Typical of the profitable B pictures she was cranking out was *She Wrote the Book*

(1946). Promoted with the tagline "Wow! Our Joan Davis goes glamorous!," the Universal comedy starred Davis as brilliant but shy college professor Jane Featherstone, who's talked into impersonating the author of a steamy bestseller, "Forever Lulu." After hearing her publisher's PR man (Jack Oakie) read a few lurid passages from the book, described as the "true confessions of an adventuress," Davis cracks, "What I want to know is, how did I find the time to write a book?" Still, she can't help being a bit intrigued, and urges him to continue reading, saying, "I want to find out who all gets the girl."

Unfortunately for Davis, her time in the top tier of radio stars was relatively short-lived. In 1947, halfway through her four-year contract, Swan Soap dropped her show, having decided that the million-dollar package was too expensive. That didn't stop her from resurfacing with a new show, *Joan Davis Time,* almost immediately, and she would continue to be a well-paid star of her own weekly radio series until 1950. But she was unable to sustain over the long haul the degree of professional success that she had reached in 1945.

While continuing her radio work, she continued with a series of film roles that displayed the slapstick gifts she had developed in vaudeville. In *The Traveling Saleswoman* (Columbia, 1950), a Wild West comedy, she played the daughter of a soap factory owner, a role that allowed her to plow through a mountain of suds after unsuccessfully attempting to operate the industrial machinery. It was a precursor of the type of comedy that she would soon bring to television. *Saleswoman* was, according to its opening titles, "a Joan Davis production," overseen by Donna Reed's neophyte producer husband Tony Owen.

Davis continued to alternate between radio and film work into the early 1950s. However, having been a radio fixture for much of the 1940s, it was only natural that Joan Davis should be a prime candidate for her own prime time television show. As far back as 1945, the authors of a book on radio comics had noted her suitability for the emerging medium, commenting, "To see her before the [radio] microphone is to watch a lot of action because she doesn't like to keep still. The mugging she does is greatly appreciated by studio audiences, and it will take television to give the full flavor of Miss Davis' work to listeners."[14]

Network enthusiasm for giving Davis a TV berth surely increased in light of the quite unexpected splash that Lucille Ball's *I Love Lucy* made during its first season (1951-52). Difficult as it may be to recognize decades later, Davis was actually better known as a comic actress than Ball was prior to *I Love Lucy.* That may explain, in part, the reaction Davis' co-workers would observe when it became clear that her TV fame was not destined to outshine that of her redheaded rival.

Davis' first stab at a television series came with a pilot she did for CBS called "Let's Join Joanie," completed in early 1951. The format cast Davis as an unmarried but man-hungry woman living in a modest rooming house, and employed as a salesgirl in a hat shop. It was an offshoot of Davis' then-current radio program, *Leave it to Joan.*

In the show's first act, Joan makes the acquaintance of studly new neighbor Jim Benson, a physical fitness nut whom she has been admiring from afar. When he drops by for a visit, and is able to lift her Murphy bed back into the wall with ease, she openly admires his strength.

Joan Davis impersonating the author of a steamy bestseller in *She Wrote the Book* (Universal, 1946).

BENSON: Oh, yes, I always keep myself in shape.
JOAN *[leering]*: You certainly picked out a nice shape to keep yourself in!
BENSON: I firmly believe in physical culture. *[Pops his biceps and poses for her]*. Look at my physique.
JOAN: Who stopped? *[Openly ogling him]*. Boy, there's acres and acres of it. You don't need a foreman, do you?

Feeling that she can land her man if she bulks up, Joan enrolls for a one-day crash course in physical fitness at Emerson's Health Farm. The majority of the show's second act consists of a lengthy routine that showcases Davis' amazing physical agility in a series of gymnasium gags involving a medicine ball, steam cabinet, and the like.

Supporting the star are character actors Joseph Kearns (later of CBS' *Dennis the Menace*) as flighty hat shop owner Antoine, and burly Hope Emerson as Davis' physical fitness trainer.

In late January, *Variety* reported that the completed show "will be flown to N.Y. this week for a looksee by the web's top brass."[15] CBS executive Harry Ackerman was high on the show once it was completed, telling *Variety* a few weeks later that it was in the process of being shopped around to potential sponsors, and that he anticipated a highly favorable response. In fact, the network was in the process of assembling several sitcoms anticipated for fall 1951 debuts, among them a TV version of

Our Miss Brooks and an as yet unnamed show that would offer "Desi Arnaz-Lucille Ball in a 'Mr. and Mrs.' format."[16]

Unfortunately, the optimism over Davis' pilot show proved unfounded, as no sponsor materialized. Another year would go by before her television series would debut, and, in that short time, much would change in the new medium. Still, it was only to be expected that Davis would eventually headline her own television comedy show, once the proper format emerged.

In 1952, *Variety* and other trade publications were full of news about the skyrocketing popularity of "vidpix"—i.e., films made specifically for television. As *Variety* reported, "it's now conceded that there's a generally fine quality in the vidpic, and the residuals matter is another strong talking point in favor of the celluloid."[17] The completion of the cross-country coaxial cable also made new options available for performers who did not wish to originate their shows as live, New York-based broadcasts.

Not only was *I Love Lucy* a TV phenomenon in 1952, but *My Little Margie*, originally set for a brief run as *Lucy*'s summer replacement that season, caught fire as well. Set to debut in the fall was Eve Arden's *Our Miss Brooks*. Clearly, funny ladies were prime time gold. Unfortunately for NBC, most of the hit sitcoms were on CBS. But if Lucille Ball could draw them in by the millions with her slapstick-oriented sitcom, who better than Joan Davis to do likewise at the rival network?

Davis cut herself a generous deal with sponsor General Electric for a sitcom to be called *I Married Joan*, which would premiere on NBC in October 1952. Aside from her profit participation in the show, Davis would collect a $7,500 per week salary (ten times what Gale Storm was then earning to star in *My Little Margie*). The new show would originate under the auspices of its star's own production company, Joan Davis Enterprises. Meanwhile, her movie career came to a close that year with the release of another budget-priced Columbia comedy, *Harem Girl*, directed and cowritten by Three Stooges veteran Edward Bernds.

Davis, as both the star and the executive in charge of producing *I Married Joan*, was under a double dose of pressure to deliver in a new medium. The show experienced some rough patches as it came together, among them the departure of original producer Dick Mack after four episodes had been filmed. Mack had been associated with Davis for twelve years, through most of her stint as a radio star.

In his place, some of the personnel eventually assembled to shoot *I Married Joan* came with valuable experience in the making of a TV sitcom. Chief among those was the show's early director Marc Daniels, previously at the helm of *I Love Lucy*. Daniels, who had departed Desilu in the spring of 1952 over a salary dispute, would similarly guide most of Davis' first-season shows (later replaced by Ezra Stone). Former *Lucy* production manager Al Simon came aboard as well.

One aspect of *I Love Lucy* that wasn't replicated on Davis' show was the presence of a live studio audience. While Ball and company felt energized by performing for a live audience, Davis, like Gracie Allen, preferred to put the shows on film without the added pressure of a stage performance.

The show that ultimately emerged was not an adaptation of the star's radio show, as were other early hits such as *The George Burns and Gracie Allen Show*. Reasoning that the new medium called for a different approach, Davis and her colleagues devel-

All eyes (and some lips) are on Joan Davis in her last theatrical release, *Harem Girl* (Columbia, 1952), with Peggie Castle and Arthur Blake.

oped a show that would draw on her capacity for slapstick in a way that radio could not. The revised format also cast aside one of her most established concepts—her radio characterization as the girl who couldn't land a man. Instead, *I Married Joan* would cast her as a zany housewife with a patient and understanding husband. To some observers, the inspiration for the new show was not Davis' own previous work, but rather a certain top-rated Desilu sitcom with a very similar title.

Each episode opened with the star, clad in a wedding gown, demurely clutching her hands, and kissing the "groom" figure from the top of the wedding cake. After a few bars of the show's theme song, performed by the Roger Wagner Chorale, the unseen announcer introduces "the Joan Davis show, *I Married Joan*," proclaiming it not only "America's favorite comedy show," but its star "America's queen of comedy" (the latter title a holdover from her radio programs). Co-star Jim Backus, the veteran radio actor who would play her husband, almost seemed an afterthought, offered the billing "and featuring...."

Like Lucy Ricardo on *I Love Lucy,* Joan Stevens was a housewife with a genius for raising a ruckus. Her husband, though often finding her antics exasperating, bore them patiently. Backus played her spouse of ten years, Judge Bradley J. Stevens, who, as the actor put it, had married airline stewardess Joan in "a moment of blinding insanity."[18] Their chaotic first meeting was depicted in a flashback scene contained in the pilot that aired as *Joan*'s premiere installment on October 15, 1952.

The format called for most episodes to open in Judge Stevens' chambers, where he was often resolving a case by telling a story about his home life, and experiences with his zany wife. This opening frame, which was usually cut from the show's later syndicated reruns, led into the main story.

Initial reaction to *I Married Joan* was generally positive, if not excessively enthusiastic. *Variety*'s review of the pilot episode said, "Miss Davis mates herself easily to the [television] medium, moves in gracefully as if nothing has changed.... She retains her sensitive ear and eye for the ridiculous and is a tongue-in-cheeker of unusual deftness."[19] The decision to use a laugh track occasionally caused reviewers to complain that the show was amusing, but not as funny as the canned laughter would seem to suggest.

Like Lucy Ricardo's husband, Brad Stevens was largely powerless to rein in his wife, who paid lip service to his manly authority (as was standard for the era), then proceeded to do whatever she pleased. A small battle of wills between husband and wife in "Joan's Haircut" (7/7/54) finds Backus' character spouting, "I happen to know a little something about the law, and as your husband, what I have to say is positive, precise, and permanent!" Unmoved, Joan retorts, "And as your wife, what I have to say is, pooh, pah, and poppycock!—and back to pooh again!"

Even the plots seen on the two shows bore some resemblance to one another, though it would be difficult to establish in some cases who got there first. *Joan*'s seventh TV episode, "Hunting" (11/26/52), about her efforts to horn in on her husband's camping trip, preceded *I Love Lucy*'s third-season episode "The Camping Trip" (6/8/53). On the other hand, Davis' episode "Bev's Boyfriend" (12/2/53), in which Joan, trying to encourage her sister's budding romance with a gawky boy, causes him to fall for her instead, seems like a cross between two earlier *Lucy* episodes—"Lucy Plays Cupid" (1/21/52) and "The Young Fans" (2/25/52). Like most 1950s sitcoms, both periodically did shows about wives who plotted and schemed to spend money in defiance of their husbands' wishes, as well the old standbys like the one about who dented the fender of the car. Both did episodes about a break in show business that required the lead character to undergo a crash diet. Although Joan doesn't quite share Lucy's obsession with getting into the act—in the first-season episode "The Acrobats" (12/31/52), she declares, "If there's anything I can't stand, it's amateur theatricals"—she's happy enough to change her tune when she learns she's wanted for the lead role.

In one of the show's funnier episodes, "Clothes Budget" (11/3/54), Brad tells Joan that the average woman "in our income bracket" spends $412 a year on her wardrobe. Claiming that she spends far less than this, Joan persuades Brad to give her the $412 in a lump sum, in exchange for which she will ask for no more money for clothes for a year. Unfortunately, Joan, who has told Brad he can give all her other clothes away to charity, goes on a shopping spree where she makes only one purchase—an evening gown that costs her entire year's wardrobe budget.

Unable to stop her old clothes being given away, Joan brings home an armload of empty boxes from the store, spends the next couple of days doing household chores like mopping the kitchen floor while clad in the evening gown, and is ultimately busted by the same catty rival who challenged her into buying the dress. This episode, more than some others, showcases not only Davis' physical comedy, but also her gift for the wry throwaway line, harkening back to her radio days:

BRAD: Joanie, you're going to serve dinner in that gown?
JOAN: I wanted to look pretty for you, dear.
BRAD: Honey, you'd look pretty to me even if you wore a flower sack.
JOAN: I wonder if they make 'em in my size.

In the final scene, as it's revealed how much Joan spent for her gown, she mutters a series of asides not unlike those that Eve Arden's Connie Brooks tossed out. Hearing the doorbell ring just as an argument breaks out, she says, "There's somebody outside—and I wish it was me." When the visitor turns out to be the operator of a newsstand, who needs to hurry back to work, Joan retorts, "If you hear of a good corner, let me know, huh?"

Subtlety was never Davis' stock in trade, and *I Married Joan* was not a low-key show. Character development and emotional content, both of which could be found to some degree on Ball's show, were largely absent from *Joan*, which existed primarily as a vehicle for its star's slapstick routines. In this respect, the show it perhaps most directly resembled was Gale Storm's *My Little Margie* (which would move into a Wednesday night slot following *Joan* in 1953). On both shows, the primary, unapologetic goal seemed to be extracting belly laughs from the viewers.

At this Davis was remarkably good. Like Ball, there was little she wouldn't do in pursuit of a chuckle. Davis considered herself the mistress of the stage fall, and she did it often. Nor was she above sharing a doghouse with two canine co-stars, snatching a bone from their owner's hand and licking that hand to show her gratitude (as she did in the 6/10/53 episode "Neighbors"). In "Acrobats" (12/31/52), she not only engages in a physical tussle with another customer over hats in a shop, but finds later herself swinging through the air as part of an acrobatic troupe.

"The Lady and the Prizefighter" (3/2/55), an episode that may have had its origin in Davis' real-life passion for boxing, has her leaping into the ring with the contestants, where she's hoisted into the air while clutching a drop-down microphone, accidentally pelts Brad with a bucket of water, and ultimately knocks the fighter out cold. Davis' comedy was arguably even rowdier than Ball's. Not surprisingly, according to Jim Backus, a nurse was present on the set at all times during filming, though Davis seems never to have sustained any serious injuries from her antics.

Whether or not the show's resemblance to *I Love Lucy*, as well as Davis' employment of some of the same personnel, made for bad feeling at Desilu is unknown. It appears, however, that Davis may have positioned herself for a rivalry, whether or not Ball chose to play along. While *I Love Lucy* topped the ratings charts, Davis' show would continue to pronounce itself "America's favorite comedy show," and bill its star as "America's Queen of Comedy." Nor did she seem eager to share the spotlight with TV husband Backus, unlike Ball or Gracie Allen, who happily shared their star billing with their straight men (also their husbands).

That choice clearly rankled with the actor, who considered himself one of the show's two leads. Writing his memoirs in the late 1980s, after Backus' recognition as "Judge Stevens" had easily been eclipsed by his later role as Thurston Howell III on

Gilligan's Island (CBS, 1964–67), as well as his fame as the voice of the cartoon character Mr. Magoo, the actor's depiction of Davis was not particularly complimentary. "Joan's behavior was enough to make a psychiatrist hit the couch," Backus wrote. "Her psyche, if indeed she had one, was as uncharted as the Sargasso Sea."[20]

One way in which Davis' peculiarities manifested themselves, in the opinion of Backus and wife Henny (who appeared occasionally on *Joan)*, was in the star's envy and resentment of Lucille Ball and the popularity of *I Love Lucy*. According to the Backuses, Davis kept a jealous eye on Ball's news-making achievements (not hard to do, since both shows were shot at General Service Studios), and reacted in kind. Seeing widespread advance publicity for Ball's MGM comedy *The Long, Long Trailer* (1954), Davis promptly had an oversized trailer of her own installed as a dressing room on the *Joan* soundstage. Likewise, the news in late 1952 that Ball was with child also gave Davis ideas, the Backuses claimed, though this proved a little more difficult to imitate.

If Davis was inclined to cast a jealous eye at Ball's success, the situation can't have been helped by the 1952 Emmy Awards, for which both performers had been nominated as Best Comedienne (Davis' only nomination). Ball, who'd already received enormous media publicity for the birth of her son Desi, Jr., a few weeks earlier, took home the first of four Emmys she would win in her long career, winning out over Davis and *Our Miss Brooks*' Eve Arden, among others.

Joan Davis dreaming up her next escapade: "Mrs. Joan Stevens" of *I Married Joan*.

If Davis expected to repeat the degree of popularity she'd experienced on radio, she was due for a disappointment. *I Married Joan,* slotted on NBC's Wednesday night schedule, drew respectable ratings, enough to keep it going, but the show never hit the Top Ten, peaking at #25 during the 1953-54 season and soon afterwards dropping out of the top thirty shows altogether. In part, this may have been due to the competition posed by CBS' *Arthur Godfrey and His Friends* (1949–59), against which Davis would face an uphill battle for viewership through *Joan*'s prime-time run.

Even more than *I Love Lucy* revolved around Ball's talents, *I Married Joan* was unmistakably a showcase for Davis. Backus' comedic talents are mostly submerged within the limitations of his straight man role, and the supporting cast largely fails to register. (One who does, in a small way, is character actress Sandra Gould, known to sitcom fans as the second Gladys Kravitz on *Bewitched*), whose immediately distinctive voice makes her a standout even in the minor scenes she's usually given).

The only featured player given a strong chance at making an impression is Davis' daughter Beverly Wills, added to the cast as a semi-regular in the show's second season. Playing Joan Stevens' gawky, college-aged sister Beverly (though introduced, oddly, in an 11/4/53 episode titled "Sister Pat"), Wills was the center of frequent stories about her dating life and school adventures. (In real life, Wills' other claim to fame was her friendship with a not-yet-known James Dean, whose oddball behavior reportedly caused Davis to throw him out of her house at least once).

Aside from Wills, the supporting cast experienced an unusual amount of turnover for a show that lasted only three seasons. The Stevens had three different pairs of friends and neighbors, none of whom had anything like the impact that Vivian Vance and William Frawley did as the Mertzes on *I Love Lucy*.

Various women had a shot at being Davis' TV sidekick, but none of them lasted long. Character actress Hope Emerson (carried over from Davis' first TV pilot, "Let's Join Joanie"), drew critical praise for her featured role as Joan's buddy Minerva Parker, but vanished from the cast after the first season. Another familiar face, actress Elvia Allman (probably best known for shouting, "Speed it up!" as the forewoman of Kramer's Kandy Kitchen on *I Love Lucy*), appeared in a few episodes as Joan's sensible Aunt Vera, alternating the role with her recurring gig playing Gracie's wardrobe mistress on *Burns and Allen*. According to *Joan* scriptwriter Sherwood Schwartz, Davis' favorite sidekick was actress Geraldine Carr, who played her friend Mabel during the show's second season, but Carr died in a traffic accident while the show was still in production.

Serious about the discipline of creating comedy, Davis "tends to tighten up on the set, is occasionally moody and at times downright depressed," said a *TV Guide* reporter who observed the making of a *Joan* episode. "But she bounces back the minute the camera starts to roll."[21]

Unlike other TV comediennes of the period, Davis made no attempt to hide, or belittle, her involvement in the creation and production of her show. Not all observers thought such involvement appropriate for a woman, in the same way that Donna Reed (q.v.) would later be criticized for being too vocal about how *The Donna Reed Show* was made. Davis' behind-the-scenes leadership sometimes had to be couched in terms thought acceptable to the public in the 1950s, as when a fan magazine profile reported her to be "crying from sheer nervous exhaustion," then stopping herself short by realizing she might hold up production. "Darn, in TV, you don't even have time to be a woman!" Davis was quoted as saying ruefully.[22]

Whatever the intent was at the time, the show that emerged as *I Married Joan*, seen today, inevitably reminds the watcher of that other *I* show. Even the same stable of character actors, who worked many of the 1950s sitcoms, can be spotted in both shows. In "Joan's Haircut," both Joan and Brad pay a visit to their respective hairstylists. Wielding the scissors at Joan's salon is actor Alvin Hurwitz, who played the manager of the employment agency in the classic "Job Switching" episode (9/15/52) of *I Love Lucy*, while Brad's barber is actor Jerry Hausner, known to *Lucy* watchers for his recurring role as Ricky's agent, Jerry, in the show's early seasons.

Just as Lucy Ricardo had an ongoing rivalry with Caroline Appleby (Doris Singleton), Joan Stevens had snooty, well-to-do "friend" Helen Cavanaugh (played by glamorous B-movie actress Adele Jergens, who had also co-starred with Davis in *The Traveling Saleswoman*).

Joan and Helen had a relationship that stopped just shy of outright hostility, as in "Home of the Week" (3/17/54), when Helen brags about photographs of her house appearing in a newspaper feature, prompting Joan to claim she'd turned down the same offer. Calling her bluff, Helen implies Joan is a liar (which she is), until Joan makes a phone call to the newspaper and talks them into the photo feature. Helen is shocked:

> HELEN: I never would have believed it! *(Pauses).* I know why they want pictures of your home—for their "Believe It or Not" column! *(As Joan fumes).* Well, I've got to be running, Joanie. I don't want to be late for my beauty appointment.
>
> JOAN *(sweetly):* Oh, no, don't be late. They'll need all the time they can get!

Knocking out scripts for Davis and company were some highly experienced radio and TV writers, among them Sherwood Schwartz, who later created both *Gilligan's Island* and *The Brady Bunch* (ABC, 1969–74). Schwartz, who'd written for Bob Hope and *The Adventures of Ozzie and Harriet,* among others, on radio, readily concedes, "She was tough."[23] Still, he remembers Davis as a star who valued his contributions.

"She insisted on the importance of writers," Schwartz says. So much so, in fact, that she wanted one within reach at all times. Each week, he or one of his fellow scripters took a turn accompanying the star to the soundstage. At any moment while the episode was being rehearsed and filmed, Davis was apt to turn to the writer on duty, declare the scene in progress unsatisfactory, and say, "Gimme something funnier!" The entire company would then sit and wait while Schwartz (or his colleague) did some fast thinking to punch up the scene.

Should that writer, as Schwartz says, be "foolish enough" to argue the need for last-minute improvements, the star would then turn to the assembled cast and crew and announce, "The writers think this is funny. I don't think this is funny!" To prove her point, Davis would deliberately do what he terms "a massacre of the script."

In her eagerness to crank up the laughs, Davis sometimes didn't know when to leave well enough alone, in Schwartz's view. "She had a tendency to overdo," he says, "and layer on things that didn't belong there." For example, in the episode "Mountain Lodge" (3/10/54), a key plot point revolves around a scheme to strand Joan and Brad at their newly purchased cabin by hiding the distributor rotor from Brad's car. The script called for Joan to nonchalantly toss the piece of hardware into the lake, unaware of its significance. On the spur of the moment, Davis decided it would be funnier if she picked up a frying pan and backhanded the rotor into the lake. Schwartz considered this "wrong from a comedy standpoint," and a distraction from the real point of the scene. Unconvinced, the star proceeded to do the scene her way.

The workload involved in making *I Married Joan* was intense, and after the first season Davis would no longer attempt to crank out 39 episodes a year, as many other shows did at that time. She cut back her schedule even further going into the show's 1954-55 season, which would consist of only 26 new segments.

Story elements introduced in the show's third season included Joan and Brad's purchase of a new home in the season opener, "New House" (9/29/54), which allowed the show's staff to revamp and enlarge the living room set where so much action took place. Along with the new house came a new set of neighbors, the Tobins (played by Sheila Bromley and Dan Tobin).

Unfortunately, despite the changes to spruce up the show, *Joan*'s third season on NBC's Wednesday light lineup soon presented Davis with a double whammy. Not only did Godfrey's competing show on CBS continue to pull strong numbers, but the mostly ratings-plagued ABC kicked in its new crown jewel, *Disneyland*, in the 7:30–8:30 time slot. *Disneyland* was a smash success, and even Godfrey felt the impact. As for Davis, the handwriting was on the wall. She wrapped up the season with "Jail Bird" (3/23/55), a funny segment about a thieving crow that hides stolen jewelry in Joan's purse, leading her to fear she's a kleptomaniac.

At the end of the show's third season on NBC, with ratings running a distant third to Godfrey and *Disneyland*, General Electric opted out of *I Married Joan*, declining to sponsor another year's worth of shows. Although it seems possible that the network could have found another sponsor to step in, especially with a less hotly contested time slot, Davis declared herself exhausted and ceased production of the show, which had 98 episodes in the can. Industry observers doubted that the star's well-being had been the principal reason for *Joan*'s windup, with one sniping, "Joan Davis got 'fatigue' right after *Disneyland* dipped her rating past the danger point."[24] Jim Backus, writing in *TV Guide* a couple of years later, was even franker: "Mr. Disney came on and our rating went down and so we were canceled."[25]

Although *I Married Joan* vacated the prime time schedule, it soon turned up in daytime reruns on NBC, one of the first TV sitcoms so reprised. The daytime repeats in 1956 and 1957 drew high ratings, allowing Davis' work to be enjoyed once again, and not incidentally setting a trend for five-days-a-week "stripping" of sitcom reruns.

On the heels of *Joan*'s demise, co-star Jim Backus landed one of his other best-remembered roles, playing father to James Dean in *Rebel Without a Cause* (Warners, 1955). Davis, however, was in fact weary from the rigors of the series, which she had found substantially more demanding than her previous radio work. For a time, she did choose to lay low, taking more time for relaxation than she had had in decades. During this period, she did turn up periodically as a guest star on the popular comedy and variety shows of the time. Although sitcoms were beginning to fall out of prime time favor, she was booked on programs hosted by Bob Hope, Dinah Shore, George Gobel, and the like.

But the veteran performer couldn't adapt to a career that was running at less than full throttle, and soon began making plans for a series comeback. In 1956, she signed a deal to develop a new show for ABC. That spring, *TV Guide* reported that the "Joan Davis Show" would include Beverly Wills as Davis' TV daughter, but few other details emerged. Ultimately, the show never found its way to the ABC schedule.

However, after leaving the NBC daytime schedule, *I Married Joan* was released for general syndication, and local station managers readily took out their checkbooks.

Joan's distributor Interstate Television was soon boasting in trade ads about the show's success in New York and other major markets.

At times during the 1950s, Davis was in the news as much for her personal life as for her professional accomplishments. The 50-year-old star's romance with a man 17 years her junior, and not a fellow actor or producer, was unusual enough to be considered newsworthy in 1957. "He's been proposing to me almost since the first day we met," Davis told reporters. "I suppose we're going to be ribbed because of the differences in age, but I don't think that will make any real difference because we're in love."[26] Unfortunately, the relationship came to a bad end a couple of years later, when Davis filed assault charges against her beau, saying he had struck her during a quarrel.

By then, although her development deal with ABC hadn't blossomed into a new sitcom, Davis was still in search of a new format for a weekly series. Her pilot film "Joan of Arkansas," a joint venture between Joan Davis Enterprises and NBC, was a candidate for the network's 1958-59 schedule. The high-concept sitcom cast its star as a dental technician chosen by computer as the ideal candidate for a flight into space. The show was conceived by writer-producer Philip Rapp, a veteran of the *Topper* series (CBS, 1953–55) who was also credited with having contributed to Fanny Brice's popular radio character Baby Snooks.

In the pilot, an enormous "electronic computer" has been programmed to identify "one perfectly normal American adult" who will undertake America's first flight into space. Thanks to a mouse who gums up the computer's works, the candidate chosen is Joan Jones of Hot Springs, Arkansas.

Project leader Dr. John Dolan (John Emery) travels to Arkansas to meet Miss Jones, who, when he arrives, is in the midst of inadvertently gluing shut a patient's mouth (allowing for the first of several Davis slapstick routines). Commandeered to travel to Washington, D.C. for this urgent mission, Joan Jones is placed under the doctor's supervision for a series of tests and exercises designed to assess her feasibility as a pioneering space traveler.

The pilot script allows Davis a frantic scene in which she's ejected from a test capsule by parachute, as well as a dream sequence that makes explicit the comparison to Joan of Arc, also, we're told, an ordinary woman who did extraordinary things. Dr. Dolan, a misogynist, is dubious about the viability of a woman for this key role, especially the impulsive, frenetic one who's been chosen.

Coming near the end of the classic 1950s age of sitcom heroines, "Joan of Arkansas" represented an admirable attempt to branch out for its star. Although the character she played was not much different from frantic housewife Joan Stevens, the setting and stories had potential to allow for new things. The supporting cast, headed by Emery as the supercilious doctor and *Topper* veteran Lee Patrick as his grumpy housekeeper Mrs. Putnam, worked well with Davis.

Although budget limitations intruded on the show occasionally—key scenes like Davis' parachute flight are largely patched together with grainy stock footage, while her anti-gravity float in the space capsule relies upon plainly visible wires from which the actress is suspended—in general "Joan of Arkansas" seemed a viable project for its star/producer. It's intriguing to consider what the storylines might have been had the show become a hit—would Davis' character have been living on an alien planet by the second or third season? Perhaps network executives, who always wanted to see that a prospective show had "legs," couldn't see how this one would sustain itself as a weekly series. Whatever the reason, NBC declined to place the show on its fall schedule, and *The George Burns Show* (minus Gracie) would be the only new comedy the network introduced in a season top-heavy with Westerns.

Davis tried once more in 1960, toplining a Paramount *Joan Davis Show* pilot in which she ran an answering service and (not surprisingly) meddled in the affairs of her clients. This, too, was rejected, and Davis' television career was finished. By then, her health also threatened to take her out of the running. Like Gracie Allen, a lifetime spent knocking herself out onstage, and then in films, radio, and television, had taken its toll on Davis, in the form of a heart ailment.

Davis abruptly disappeared from the television industry, spending her last years in seclusion at her home in Palm Springs. *I Married Joan* co-star Backus, whose follow-up venture as the star of his own sitcom, the syndicated *Hot off the Wire: The Jim Backus Show* (1960-61), was not a success, saw Davis for the last time when she attended a nightclub performance he gave in the summer of 1960. She was accompanied on the outing by a nurse-companion.

On May 23, 1961, Joan Davis was rushed to the emergency room of a Palm Springs hospital, complaining of chest pains. Early the next morning, she died, a few weeks short of her 54th birthday. Two years later, daughter Beverly Wills, who had continued to pursue an acting career on a modest scale, perished in a fire at Davis' home that also claimed the lives of the star's mother and two grandsons.

Rerun for a time on basic cable in the 1980s, *I Married Joan* is another almost "lost" 1950s sitcom. Perhaps because Davis' daughter and other family members were not around to preserve her legacy, or promote her work, she has not enjoyed the attention given to many of her contemporaries.

If *I Married Joan* is not the most memorable of the 1950s sitcoms starring funny women, it is still worth a look to observe Davis' uniquely hard-knocks comedy style. As for Davis herself, her achievements as a top-rated comedienne, augmented by her pioneering status as a producer and executive in a time when these roles were generally denied to women, makes her worthy of a place in television history.

Near the end of her life, past the peak of her popularity, Davis told an interviewer, "If show business has been good to me, it has also robbed me of many things. I'd have liked a college education, the chance to travel, and time for friends. Show business cost me my first beaux, and it eventually cost me my marriage.

"And I've been afraid all along that I just wouldn't be funny or pretty enough for the long-time bigtime. I've kept going on a mixture of gall, guts, and gumption. Faith, too—I've hung onto faith until now I realize every heartbreak has been a stepping stone."[27]

❖ 6 ❖

Anne Jeffreys

Topper and *Love That Jill*

IF ANNE JEFFREYS NEVER ACHIEVED quite the level of fame as a sitcom star that some of the other actresses in this book did, it may be because she was successful at too many different things to concentrate solely on her work in television comedy.

To some, she is best known as an RKO contract player of the 1940s, and leading lady in B Westerns and Dick Tracy films. Others remember her as a stage performer specializing in musical comedy who starred in the original Broadway production of *Kiss Me, Kate*. More recently, she has been a busy soap opera actress with recurring roles on ABC's *General Hospital* and its less successful spin-off, *Port Charles*.

But to viewers of 1950s sitcoms, she was the glamorous, playful, and charming leading lady of one of television's first fantasy comedies, CBS' *Topper* (1953–55), in which she co-starred with real-life husband Robert Sterling. Jeffreys played "Marion Kerby, the ghostess with the mostest," one of two mischievous ghosts who haunted the house and life of a conservative, middle-aged banker (played by Leo G. Carroll).

Topper, the TV sitcom, was only one of the many incarnations of Thorne Smith's classic fantasy novel (variously subtitled "A Ribald Comedy" or "An Improbable Adventure"), which was originally published in 1926. Like much of Smith's work, the novel featured a fantastic element that brought a new sense of fun and adventure to the monotony of daily life. Penned during the height of the Roaring Twenties (and Prohibition), *Topper* extolled the virtues of fast driving, glamorous nightlife, and frequent intake of alcohol, couched in the context of fantasy.

Before Jeffreys and Sterling inherited the roles of Marion and George Kerby, the characters had been adapted for a 1937 MGM film of the same name, played by Cary Grant and Constance Bennett, which resulted in two follow-ups (United Artists' *Topper Takes a Trip*, 1939, also based on a Smith novel, and *Topper Returns*, 1941). Appearing in all three films as Cosmo Topper was actor Roland Young.

The property was even adapted as an NBC radio show, *The Adventures of Topper*, which had a brief run in the summer of 1945, with Young reprising his film role opposite Frances Chaney as Marion. As noted by *Variety*'s reviewer, however, a comedy centered on the antics of appearing and disappearing ghosts "reads good on paper and was even enhanced in the film treatment," but played less well on radio, resulting in a show he found "singularly unfunny."[1] It would take television to fully exploit on a weekly basis the visual possibilities that Smith's story offered.

In 1953, producers Bernard L. Schubert and John W. Loveton secured the rights to assemble a TV sitcom version of *Topper*. Schubert's production company had already enjoyed success with another book to film to TV adaptation involving a charming couple, the amateur sleuths *Mr. and Mrs. North*. With that show already established on CBS, the producers signed George Oppenheimer as *Topper*'s head writer, and looked for a leading lady and man to star in the pilot.

Born in North Carolina on January 26, 1923, Jeffreys (originally Anne Jeffreys Carmichael) quickly proved her abilities in more than one arena, despite some health problems that sometimes kept her at home and a little lonely. Because her parents divorced when she was still a girl, and her father died a few years later, Jeffreys was extremely close to her mother, and would remain so. Discovered from an early age to possess a beautiful singing voice, she was encouraged by her mother, Kate, whose own stage ambitions had been thwarted, to perform. "I had a radio show of my own in Durham by the time I was 10," Jeffreys later recalled. "I hated it, really, but Mother kept after me and all of a sudden the fever took."[2]

Continuing her music lessons throughout her teenage years, the young Jeffreys was being directed toward a career as an opera singer, and moved to New York in pursuit of that goal. While studying music, she paid the bills as a model for the elite John Robert Powers agency. Despite her abundant musical talent, however, she soon concluded that she did not wish to pursue an operatic career, finding the work "too stiff and too confining."[3]

With her mother's encouragement, Jeffreys went to Hollywood, where she was quickly discovered and, before the age of twenty, launched on a film career. She made her film debut in 1942, playing a bit role in *Tarzan's New York Adventure* at MGM, but her agent was unable to elicit strong interest in his client at that studio. Undeterred, he took her to the more workaday Republic Studios, where she became a contract player in 1943. There, she was quickly pigeonholed into B Western films that had little use for her singing talent.

Loaned out to RKO in 1944 for a featured role in the Frank Sinatra musical comedy *Step Lively*, a remake of the Broadway hit *Room Service*, the actress made a strong impression on studio executives, who bought out her contract from Republic. Unfortunately, despite the musical talent she'd shown opposite Sinatra, her new employers continued to plop her into a series of mostly forgettable B pictures, either in-house or on loan to other studios. There were occasional highlights, such as her appearance as the "Lady in Red" who turns against her bank robber lover in the crime melodrama *Dillinger* (Monogram, 1945). Her role as Tess Trueheart in RKO's *Dick Tracy* (1945), beautiful leading lady whose boyfriend is too busy to pay her the attention she deserves, was no great acting challenge, but the film was popular enough to be reprised in a follow-up, *Dick Tracy vs. Cueball* (1946). Both films entertained

Beautiful Anne Jeffreys, reunited with *Dillinger* leading man Lawrence Tierney, in RKO's *Step by Step* (1946).

movie audiences without resulting in any noticeable career advancement for the lead actress.

Throughout the 1940s, Jeffreys' beauty and talent won her popularity with movie audiences, almost in spite of the variable scripts she was handed in mercifully forgotten epics as RKO's *Ding Dong Williams* (1946) and the Judy Canova hillbilly comedy *Joan of Ozark* (1942) at Republic. All told, Jeffreys clocked appearances in more than 30 feature films between 1942 and 1948. Despite her success in *Step Lively,* her film work rarely took advantage of her singing ability; Western films would be the genre with which she was most closely associated during this period.

Still under studio contract to RKO, Jeffreys' career received an unexpected boost in 1947, when theatrical composer Kurt Weill heard her sing, and put her musical gifts on display in the Broadway production of his show *Street Scene*. A musicalization of a previously Pulitzer Prize–winning play about tenement life, with Langston Hughes as its lyricist, *Street Scene* opened on the New York stage in January 1947. Jeffreys, cast as ingénue Rose Maurrant, earned praise from prominent critics like the *New York Times'* Brooks Atkinson, who praised the actress and her co-star Polyna Stoska for their ability to "not only sing with depth of feeling and vocal brilliance but endow the parts with loveliness of character."[4] Her performance was beautifully recorded for posterity on the original Columbia cast album, despite an attack of flu that had her "hanging onto the stool to sing it"[5] during the recording session.

Given six months' leave from RKO to appear in the Broadway production, Jeffreys completed her work on *Street Scene* in May 1947, and reported for work in Hollywood. Unfortunately, her stage triumph did little to enhance her film career, which began to wind down as the decade did. Her role in the Randolph Scott Western *Return of the Bad Men* (1948) would be her last film assignment for almost 15 years.

Once her movie commitments expired, Jeffreys focused her attentions on stage work, climaxing when she assumed the title role in the Broadway smash *Kiss Me, Kate*, which had opened in December 1948. Replacing the originally cast Patricia Morison (also a B-movie veteran), Jeffreys starred in more 800 performances of *Kate* at the New Century Theatre between 1949 and 1951, missing not a single show.

"When you get on stage, something truly magical happens," she later explained of her Broadway experience. "Adrenaline kicks in, along with something indefinable, no matter how badly you felt before. I tore ligaments in my knee during a performance of *Kiss Me Kate* and found a way to move around effortlessly on stage by putting my foot in a shoe box and sliding! I believe that it was then that I realized I could do anything under any circumstances if I put my mind to it."[6]

Cast as Lilli Vanessi, a stage star playing Katharine opposite her ex-husband's Petruchio in a musical version of Shakespeare's *Taming of the Shrew*, Jeffreys' plum role gave her the opportunity to sing Cole Porter songs like Lilli's memorable solo, "I Hate Men." The role drew on a more spirited side of Jeffreys that had not been often seen in her 1940s film work, but would surface in her portrayal of Marion Kerby on *Topper*.

Like most Broadway veterans, she would not, however, reprise her role in the film version of the highly successful musical, being replaced by longtime MGM contract player Kathryn Grayson as Kate for the 1953 release. Although Jeffreys' performance was not preserved on the original cast album, on which her predecessor Morison sings the role, Jeffreys did later record her songs for a 1959 RCA Victor album opposite Howard Keel, who starred in the movie version of *Kate*.

Jeffreys' engagement in *Kiss Me, Kate* was not only a professional success, but also resulted in a personal landmark for the actress. She'd been married briefly to Joseph Serena, a captain in the U.S. Navy, in the mid–1940s, a union that ended with an annulment. During the run of *Kate*, Jeffreys met another current Broadway performer, film actor Robert Sterling. Then appearing a few blocks away in a show called *The Gramercy Ghost*, Sterling had been divorced from actress Ann Sothern (q.v.) in 1949. Jeffreys and Sterling fell in love, and their relationship culminated in marriage on November 21, 1951, *Kate* having closed in July. Their union would not only be a source of great personal happiness for Jeffreys, but also set the stage for her transition to television work.

Following a brief stint in another musical comedy, *Three Wishes for Jamie*, during the spring of 1952, Jeffreys teamed with her new husband, developing a nightclub act that would allow them to work together. Like Lucille Ball and Desi Arnaz had done a couple of years earlier, they used the act as an opportunity to display their chemistry as a team. The popularity of their nightclub act led to an out-of-the-blue television offer to star in the Schubert-Loveton *Topper* pilot.

Anne Jeffreys with real-life husband and frequent co-star Robert Sterling about a year after their marriage, enjoying cocktail chat with actress Nancy Carroll.

"So we came back and played the Coconut Grove at night and shot the pilot during the day," Jeffreys later explained. "Then we went up to the Fairmont in San Francisco. They called and said it was the quickest selling pilot of that time—only two weeks after they got it all together, it sold! So we canceled the rest of our club acts to come back and do *Topper*."[7] The show had been sold to sponsor R.J. Reynolds Tobacco (promoting Camel Cigarettes), and would debut on CBS' Friday night schedule in October 1953.

As in Smith's novel, and the original MGM film, the series would revolve around the adventures of a rather straitlaced suburban husband whose life was complicated by the presence of two sexy and playful ghosts. However, the TV pilot, "Topper Meets the Ghosts," provided a backstory slightly different than the previous versions.

In the film, Cosmo Topper (played by Roland Young) knows George Kerby as a young, rather irresponsible playboy whose wealth has earned him a position as one of the trustees at the bank where Topper is an executive. Playful George (Cary Grant) and his glamorous wife Marion (Constance Bennett) meet an untimely end when his reckless driving results in a car wreck. Purchasing the sleek car from the Kerbys' estate, Topper is shocked to find that George and Marion's restless spirits still inhabit it.

TV's *Topper* brought the characters together in a completely different fashion. In the pilot, George and Marion perish in a skiing accident, as does their guide dog, a Saint Bernard named Neil. When Cosmo Topper and his wife Henrietta (played by Lee Patrick) purchase the Kerbys' house, the stodgy banker learns that his house is haunted by its previous occupants, who take it upon themselves to brighten his dreary existence.

Topper, as played by Young in the 1937 film, is on the verge of what would later be described as a "mid-life crisis." Entrenched in a rut of monotonous daily life, and kept firmly under the thumb of his fussy wife (played by Billie Burke), Topper buys the Kerbys' sleek roadster as an act of rebellion. Though basically devoted to his wife, he is charmed by the young and flirtatious Marion, who unleashes an unexpectedly adventurous and playful side of the dignified businessman.

For TV, the character relationships were slightly different. While TV's Cosmo Topper, being unable to oust the Kerbys from his home, ultimately learns to enjoy their company, the comedy in *Topper* usually takes the form of his embarrassment and discomfort at their antics. Jeffreys, although glamorous and stunningly beautiful as TV's Marion Kerby, plays a character toned down a bit to be acceptable to 1950s viewing audiences.

In TV's *Topper*, George and Marion are fun-loving, slightly bored ghosts who cheer up their daily existence with mischief and playfulness. Almost akin to poltergeists, though not of the deliberately malicious ilk, the couple (seen, as the show's announcer says, "by only three people on Earth—you, me, and Cosmo Topper") make various objects fly unexpectedly through the air, play invisible games of badminton, and otherwise wreak havoc in the previously sedate Topper household.

Not surprisingly, the "dead" characters on *Topper* were distinctly more lively and animated than the live ones. The Kerbys' untimely demise didn't seem to interfere with their abilities to eat, drink, and not surprisingly, considering the sponsor, smoke—the latter an especially neat trick for characters presumably no longer breathing. The real-life romantic chemistry and charm of Jeffreys and her husband Robert Sterling make TV's George and Marion appealing and glamorous, to the degree that prevailing standards allowed.

Completing *Topper*'s main cast were two veteran film actors, Leo G. Carroll and Lee Patrick, playing Mr. and Mrs. Topper. Carroll, whose credits stretched back to MGM's *Sadie McKee* (1934), played Topper as a genial, patient, and rather unassuming man. His portrayal was not unlike that of Roland Young, who'd played the role in all three of the *Topper* films, though Carroll's version was less inclined to break out of his middle-class rut than Young's had been. (Young, after a long film career, had died in the summer of 1953, causing some critics to criticize Carroll's portrayal of Topper as being imitative of his recently deceased predecessor).

Cast as Mrs. Topper, Lee Patrick would also contribute strongly to the show's humor and appeal. In the TV series, much of the Kerbys' antics took place in the Toppers' living room or kitchen, and required frequent impromptu explanations from Mr. Topper whenever something bizarre took place in front of his wife's eyes. TV's Henrietta was a rather dizzy, vague woman who readily accepted her husband's rather suspect cover-up stories for whatever she'd just seen.

Patrick, a Warner Brothers contract player in the 1940s, was versatile enough to play Mrs. Biederhof, the chilly, snooty mistress of Joan Crawford's onscreen husband in *Mildred Pierce* (1945), as well as Sam Spade's assistant in *The Maltese Falcon* (1941). In her early fifties when *Topper* began, the actress had already made a successful transition to character roles, and was the veteran of a previous comedy series, NBC's *Boss Lady*, which had had a brief run in the summer of 1952. Rather unjustifiably relegated to featured billing in *Topper*'s closing credits, Patrick was a major factor in the show's success, with her comedic reactions to the strange goings-on that constantly surrounded her.

Also regularly plagued by the Kerbys' shenanigans were the Toppers' cook Katie (an early role for the veteran comedic supporting player Kathleen Freeman), and Topper's even stuffier boss at the bank, Mr. Schuyler (played by Thurston Hall). Henrietta's friend Thelma (Mary Field) turned up now and then as well.

To everyone around him, Topper would eventually become adept at the impromptu explanation for what they'd walked in just in time to see him do. As on the later *I Dream of Jeannie*, the magical characters on *Topper* had a habit of vanishing just as the hero's friends and co-workers arrived on the scene, leaving him holding the bag—and making scarcely plausible explanations for what they'd witnessed. (Seeing Mr. Schuyler's eyes bug out at the file floating off his desk toward the file cabinet, Topper helpfully explains that there's "a bank draft.")

Like Wilbur Post of *Mister Ed* (CBS, 1961–66), Major Anthony Nelson of *I Dream of Jeannie* (NBC, 1965–70), and Tim O'Hara of *My Favorite Martian* (CBS, 1963–66), Cosmo Topper was a man who spent much of his time trying to keep a whopper of a secret. Even when he does decide to tell the truth, as in "The Diamond Ring" (3/19/54), it doesn't help. Readily confessing to his doctor that he's bedeviled by the three ghosts who inhabit his house, Topper is merely advised to consider a relaxing stay in a sanitarium. In the same episode, a police psychiatrist and his colleagues similarly refuse to believe Topper's story, even as one of them has his hair rumpled by the invisible Marion, another's cigarette is snatched out of his hand by George, and a third feels Neil's warm, wet tongue slurping against his cheek.

Contributing to several of the first-season *Topper* scripts was a then-unknown Stephen Sondheim, hired after meeting head writer George Oppenheimer at a dinner party. In those days, it was still expected that a small, in-house writing staff could churn out weekly TV episodes with no difficulty, even on top-rated shows like *I Love Lucy*. Busy at the typewriter during the summer of 1953, the young Sondheim found the pace of TV work daunting, telling friends, "The schedule calls for an entire program to be shot every two and a half days. I don't know how the hell they're going to do it."[8]

Somehow, the cast and crew managed. Not only did the *Topper* pilot quickly attract a sponsor, but its critical reception was largely enthusiastic as well, reviewers recognizing a show quite unlike most other comedies on the tube in 1953. *Variety*'s reviewer deemed the series opener "a socko start" that promised to be "one of the most diverting skeins of the year," praising Jeffreys and Sterling as "a charming couple, whether on the cafe circuit or this debut in a regular teleseries."[9]

Viewers agreed, and *Topper* became a popular success for CBS and Camel Cigarettes, despite competition that first season from another new sitcom, NBC's *The Life of Riley* (1953–58), which starred film actor William Bendix. Although *Riley* emerged the initial ratings victor in the 8:30 time slot, *Topper* had its own following that kept it afloat, part of a solidly developing block of CBS Friday-night comedy that also encompassed *Mama* and Eve Arden's *Our Miss Brooks*.

While not every couple might have relished the amount of togetherness that came as co-stars in a television series, Jeffreys said she and Sterling thrived on it. "It's true Robert and I are together far more than most married couples, but this has helped our marriage," she said. "I enjoy his company, I'm never bored around him, and I think he feels the same way. And even though we're at the studio together all the time that doesn't mean we are never apart. Some days Robert does not have the time to do more than speak casually to me. He has his duties—and I have mine. But this does not break the togetherness we always feel."[10]

For the early 1950s, *Topper* was an extremely ambitious and innovative TV sitcom. While many prime time shows still aired live, making do with primitive sets and simple staging, Jeffreys' show was a sophisticated special effects comedy ten years prior to the flurry of such shows (*Bewitched*, *My Favorite Martian*, *I Dream of Jeannie*) that would fill network schedules in the 1960s. Utilizing stop motion photography, double exposures, tricks with piano wires, and the like, *Topper*'s special effects crew dazzled audiences of the era with visual wizardry untried on any other show of the period. The show's achievements would be recognized with an Emmy nomination for Best Situation Comedy that first season.

"Although the technical work at that time was really extraordinary," remembered Jeffreys' co-star Kathleen Freeman, "there was still none of the technological expertise that's available today, so everything had to be done manually. For instance, floating glasses in front of a mirror usually required a couple of people high above with strings—or this special wire they used—and, of course, they had to make sure the wire didn't show. Making the ghosts invisible or semi-invisible all took a great deal of time, too. It was very exhausting, as a matter of fact."[11]

With the format of the show ruling out the possibility of it being filmed before a live studio audience, the producers utilized a laugh track that may have been generated by screening completed films for an audience. This method of gathering audience response was a popular practice at the time, before it became routine for TV sitcoms to simply use a laugh track compiled by a sound engineer from a library of responses to older shows. Adding to the implication, if not the reality, of a live audience, on *Topper* was the sound of listener applause at every commercial break, as if the curtain had just fallen in a theater.

As for Jeffreys herself, there were few, if any, sitcom leading ladies of the era more glamorous or captivating. Because she was playing a fantasy figure, rather than a (supposedly) real woman, she was permitted to sip martinis, wear slinky and seductive outfits, and drape herself across the lap of an older, married man, as she does in the first-season episode "George's Old Flame" (7/2/54), breathing, "Oh, Topper darling, aren't you attracted to me?" In Jeffreys' capable hands, though, this was always playful, rather than offensive.

Unusual though their roles may have been, she and Sterling in fact played one of the most charismatic couples seen in 1950s sitcoms. Although the scripts sometimes called for the characters to be at odds, as in "The Proposal" (2/19/54), when, in *Topper*'s twist on a typical sitcom plot, Marion has a fight with George over his inattentiveness to his wife, Jeffreys and Sterling parlayed their real-life relationship into an onscreen chemistry that enriched the show. She would later remember "The Proposal" as her favorite *Topper* episode.

In a very different way from Lucille Ball's Lucy character, Marion and her husband often settled the hash of overly pretentious, nosy, or unpleasant characters. Taking time out from their self-appointed roles as Topper's new best friends, the Kerbys could be counted on in a pinch to triumph over a burglar, a swindler, or even a badly behaved child. Although they regularly bewildered and unnerved Henrietta and maid Katie, the Kerbys also geared up for action anytime a stranger made himself unwelcome in "their" home, as in the episode "Henrietta Sells the House" (4/9/54), when they declare war on a retired military man who buys the Toppers' home and threatens to separate Cosmo from his ghostly friends.

Depending on the needs of any individual *Topper* scene, Jeffreys' Marion Kerby might be partially visible, pop in or out, be see-through, or be represented only by her voice. Given the complexities of shooting such scenes, even a trouper like Jeffreys found some difficulty in meeting the demands of *Topper*'s schedule. Filming 39 episodes per year, laden with special effects, meant long hours on the set. For the actress, accustomed to quite a different routine—and working hours—as a Broadway performer, filming *Topper* was a challenge.

"I'm a workhorse," she told *TV Guide*. "Always have been. But it's taken a long, long time to get used to this 6:45 A.M. business. In New York we never got to bed until around 4:00 in the morning. We'd sleep all day, have lunch at 5:00 or 6:00 in the afternoon, get to the theater at 8:00, have a snack after the show and then party a bit until 4:00. Nice normal Broadway routine."[12]

Despite her busy schedule, Jeffreys concluded her first season as a sitcom star with happy news on the personal front. As the show's 1953-54 season wound down, the actress announced that she was pregnant with her first child. Acknowledging the collaborative effort involved in this as well as their television work, she and her husband named their son, born on August 2, 1954, Jeffreys Sterling. He was the first of three sons Jeffreys would have over the next several years.

With the show's second season came one cast change. Actress Kathleen Freeman departed her recurring role as maid Katie, turning up in a prominent assignment opposite Thomas Mitchell on the syndicated sitcom *Mayor of the Town* (1954-55). Replacing her on *Topper*, as a gawky but similarly spooked cook named Maggie, was actress Edna Skinner. Skinner, previously a stage actress, is better known to baby boomers for her later role as wry, shopaholic Kay Addison in the early years of CBS' *Mister Ed* (1961–66). Stepping in for Freeman could have been an awkward situation, but Skinner didn't find it particularly worrisome: "There's always going to be the comparison [to the original performer] and you have to realize that that's going to happen. And so, rather than do an aping of anything, you must bring your own interpretation to the role."[13]

Otherwise, there were few changes to *Topper*'s proven formula in its second season on CBS. Behind the scenes, original writers Oppenheimer and Sondheim gave way to a team headed by veteran comedy writer Philip Rapp. Rapp, who'd begun to contribute scripts to *Topper* during the latter half of the first season, soon became the show's supervising story editor (i.e., head writer). He brought with him a substantial

Cast of *Topper:* Anne Jeffreys and Robert Sterling (standing) with Leo G. Carroll and Lee Patrick (Cosmo and Henrietta).

resume that included the development of the hit radio comedy *The Bickersons*, as well as screenplays for several inventive Danny Kaye film comedies of the 1940s.

In search of new stories, *Topper*'s rejuvenated writing staff would eventually take Cosmo and his companions further and further from home, the scripts incorporating trips to Las Vegas, a desert island, and even Lisbon—though, in this case, Lisbon was a town in South Carolina. Although the first-season episode "Henrietta Sells the House" tells us that, should the Toppers move to a new house, George and Marion won't be able to come along (it's "against the rules," she explains), those rules apparently don't preclude them from taking an occasional trip with their friend.

One such outing, "Topper Goes West," was a flashback to Anne Jeffreys' days as a Western actress, the episode mocking genre stereotypes as "Calamity Marion," George "Tall in the Saddle" Kerby, and Cosmo "The Dude" Topper showed off their prowess with trick riding, quick-draw gunplay, and a showdown with a bad guy in the saloon. The episode also, intentionally or not, reflected the ongoing popularity of a genre that would soon threaten to take over prime time TV altogether, leaving sitcoms and comedic actresses in short supply.

Retaining the same Friday time slot, and the same competition from *The Life of Riley,* Jeffreys' show in its second year began to challenge its highly rated NBC competition. Though *Riley* still emerged the victor in the 1954-55 ratings race, it lost several points in the Nielsen ratings, and the gap between it and *Topper* narrowed considerably, with both shows ranking among the season's Top Twenty-Five.

Although Camel continued its sponsorship of *Topper* into a second year, the company took advantage of a then-new wrinkle among TV sponsors when it relinquished a half-interest in the popular show to an alternate-week sponsor, General Foods, in early 1955. Although the TV medium was still young, changes such as this one were becoming increasingly common, as the typical single-sponsor pattern of early TV gave way to the reality that not every company could, or wanted to, assume sole sponsorship of an expensive weekly series.

Solidly popular with viewers, *Topper* by all indications should have been settling in for a multi-season run. Instead, in the late spring of 1955, trade papers printed the surprising news that the show's second season on CBS would be its last. Having cut its sponsorship of the show in half only a few months earlier, Camel was the instigator of this move, declining to sign on for a third year as sponsor. Although General Foods was happy with the show, and willing to foot half the bill for a third year of episodes, Camel's pullout cost *Topper* its spot on the CBS schedule, where it aired for the last time in September 1955.

The cigarette company's surprising decision to relinquish sponsorship of a hit series was probably for reasons similar to its rival Philip Morris' abandonment of an even more popular CBS show, *I Love Lucy,* the same year. In the early days of TV, sponsors paid for a network time slot in the hopes of reaching the largest possible audience, with the assumption that, given exposure to enough potential customers, their products would sell accordingly. Despite *Topper*'s sophistication, however, it shared with *Lucy* a considerable appeal to kids, who loved the ghost-com's special effects and made up much of the audience available in the show's early-evening time period.

Topper may simply have failed to draw the type of viewers inclined to smoke, though in those days before the Surgeon General's warnings and the eventual banning of cigarette advertising on television, Jeffreys and Sterling made sophisticated and elegant spokespeople for the brand in *Topper* commercials and related magazine advertisements. Though it would remain legal for quite some time to advertise tobacco products on TV, there was also much in the news in 1955 about the possible health risks of smoking, and this resulted in some rethinking by R.J. Reynolds and other manufacturers about the substantial budgets they were sinking into the sponsorship of television shows.

Reynolds would eventually decide that a show targeted primarily at male viewers would be a better investment of its advertising dollars, allowing *Topper* to fall by the wayside despite its more-than-acceptable ratings. That fall, Reynolds would assume sponsorship of a new CBS sitcom, *The Phil Silvers Show*—a.k.a. *You'll Never Get Rich*— as a promotional vehicle for Camel cigarettes.

For Jeffreys, the surprise cancellation of *Topper* despite its healthy ratings interrupted plans to combine her career and raising a family. She and Sterling had already planned to enlarge their family, hoping to time things so that she could be pregnant again during the hiatus between the show's second and third season. As it turned out, she would have more time than she'd realized to devote to her family, though unfortunately at the expense of some career momentum.

If *Topper* was unable to land a deal to continue production of new episodes, it did not, nonetheless, vacate the prime time schedule. In two seasons, the cast had completed 78 episodes, and Loveton and Schubert quickly leased rerun rights to ABC. The third-place network made no new episodes of *Topper*, but scheduled an entire season of repeats of the CBS episodes in a 7:30 P.M. Monday time slot, where it aired through the spring of 1956 under the sponsorship of Standard Brands. That summer, NBC took its turn with *Topper*, scheduling yet another round of reruns in an early Sunday evening slot and giving the show a rare distinction of having played in prime time on all of the "Big Three" networks of the time.

Although it seems odd today that such a popular show would be relegated to reruns, rather than finding a sponsor willing to keep it going, 1955 was also the year when TV decision-makers seem to have fully embraced the viability of the filmed sitcom rerun. In 1952 and 1953, trade papers were full of items about the growing popularity of filmed shows over lived ones, and the realization, not then taken for granted, that they could profitably be shown more than once. Original syndicated sitcoms like Guild Films' *Life with Elizabeth*, starring Betty White (q.v.), were snapped up by stations around the country, where they were seen as an easy alternative to locally produced live broadcasts.

By 1955, if anyone had ever doubted viewers' willingness to watch filmed sitcom episodes more than once, they no longer did. Early network sitcom hits like Joan Davis' *I Married Joan* were among the first to demonstrate the popularity of the sitcom rerun that year, and such shows were hugely popular with both networks (for daytime schedules) and local stations starved for programming to fill the hours that networks didn't. The decision to cease producing new *Topper* episodes, and lease rerun rights to the episodes already available, may have been made by the packagers with an eye to quick profit.

Although those 78 episodes comprised a smaller number than would later be deemed necessary for the syndication market (where at least 100 episodes to re-play were preferred), that would not keep *Topper* off the air. After finally leaving the primetime schedule in 1956, having played all three networks, syndicated *Topper* reruns would be a staple of local programming for another decade.

Added to the show for its rerun cycles was the opening sequence familiar to baby boomer rerun watchers, in which Jeffreys' and Sterling's names first appear onscreen while they remain invisible, their presence represented only by free-floating accoutrements like opera gloves and a cigarette. Only in the intro's closing seconds, as the letters spelling out *Topper* slide across screen, do the actors "materialize" alongside co-star Leo G. Carroll, Jeffreys sporting a beguiling Cheshire Cat grin. The sequence replaced the opening titles used during the show's CBS run, which included a prominent plug for the original sponsor's cigarettes.

Not only would the original show remain popular with viewers, but networks would make two attempts to revive the *Topper* franchise in the 1970s. A 20th-Century Fox TV-movie and series pilot, *Topper Returns,* starring Stefanie Powers as Marion and Roddy McDowall as Cosmo, aired on NBC in 1973. A few years later, ABC gave Kate Jackson a stab at Jeffreys' old role, starring the *Charlie's Angels* veteran opposite her then real-life husband, Andrew Stevens. Neither pilot landed a series slot on the prime time schedule, nor did the leading ladies' performances erase the image of Jeffreys as Marion Kerby.

Topper's influence would also be seen in the plethora of fantasy comedies that populated network TV in the mid–1960s. The resounding success of *Bewitched* (ABC, 1964–72), whose star Elizabeth Montgomery even resembled Jeffreys somewhat, paved the way for Barbara Eden's *I Dream of Jeannie* (NBC, 1965–70) and others less successful. A few years later, *The Ghost and Mrs. Muir* (1968–70), which played a season each on NBC and ABC, also mined the vein that had begun with *Topper.* For much of the decade, comedies laden with special effects would be a viable commodity on TV.

Meanwhile, although *Topper* had met an early demise, Anne Jeffreys was still popular with viewers, and it didn't take long for her to resurface on prime time TV. Even before *Topper* wound down, she displayed her musical comedy gifts in a 90-minute "Max Liebman Presents" special that aired on NBC, "The Merry Widow" (4/9/55). When that show was well-received, she returned for "Dearest Enemy" (11/26/55), in which she co-starred with Robert Sterling. ("The Jeffreys-Sterling team delivered the pop song material in tuneful style," *Variety* commented).[14] For viewers who knew her only as Marion Kerby, the musical "spectaculars" were a revelation.

Having enjoyed their first collaboration as sitcom co-stars, Mr. and Mrs. Sterling soon signed to re-team for a new series assembled by producer Alex Gottlieb *(The Gale Storm Show),* under the auspices of the Hal Roach studios. Originally announced as "Jacques and Jill," a test film of the romantic comedy show had been completed by the spring of 1957, and was being shopped to sponsors.

Jeffreys' new vehicle didn't surface that fall, however. By the time it ultimately made its bow on ABC, in early 1958, it had been re-titled *Love That Jill,* and would be sponsored by Max Factor Cosmetics. Network publicity for the new sitcom proclaimed of the show's stars, "She's lovely! He's in love! You'll love them!"

Premiering on January 20, 1958, with an episode titled "Tonight's the Night," Jeffreys' new show cast her as Jill Johnson, owner of a Manhattan modeling agency, Model Girls, with Sterling heading a rival firm. The supporting cast, aside from the beautiful models who would be seen regularly, included Jimmy Lydon as Jill's male secretary, Richard, and Betty Lynn (later Thelma Lou of *The Andy Griffith Show*) as Jack's assistant. *Jill* would be competing with the final episodes of *The George Burns and Gracie Allen Show* on CBS, and a Western drama called *The Restless Gun* on NBC, for viewers' attention.

Unfortunately, the show Jeffreys and Sterling had envisioned didn't really materialize. *Variety*'s review of the series opener complained that the script unwisely "inject[ed] sillyisms into a sophisticated farce about dog-eat-dog New York business society," and carped that Jeffreys' contributions to the proceedings were "a sly grin and a silly wiggle."[15]

Before long, nobody was happy, especially the stars. "We got into big altercations about how the scripts were going," Jeffreys later remembered. "They started out very good ... slick and well written. Then they became slapstick, incomprehensible and stupid, really. Finally, after we did the twelfth show, we went to Hal Roach, the head of the studio at the time, and expressed our unhappiness. He expressed his unhappiness, and we said, 'Why don't we just call it quits.'"[16]

With ratings unimpressive, neither the network nor the sponsor was inclined to disagree. The new show was off the ABC airwaves by April, not even kept around for a summer rerun cycle.

For a time in the early 1960s, in the wake of *Love That Jill*'s quick demise, Jeffreys concentrated on raising her family, which grew to include sons Jeffreys, Dana, and Tyler. While Robert Sterling tried another sitcom without his wife, *Ichabod and Me*, which aired on CBS in the 1961-62 season, before making a mid-life career change out of show business, Jeffreys was seen on TV only in occasional guest spots for the next several years. She made a brief return to the film world in 1962, after an almost fifteen-year absence, playing the wife of suburban husband and wannabe playboy Howard Duff in MGM's *Boys' Night Out*.

By the mid–1960s, she had resumed work in the theater, touring in productions of musicals like *Camelot* and *The King and I*. In 1965, she was onstage at the Music Theater of Lincoln Center, co-starring opposite Alfred Drake in a revival of *Kismet*. She supplemented her stage work with occasional guest appearances on popular series like *Wagon Train* (NBC and ABC, 1957–65).

Not until the early 1970s did the actress resume regular TV work, when she took on a recurring role in the NBC daytime soap opera *Bright Promise*. Cast as well-to-do Sylvia Bancroft, Jeffreys was part of a then-current trend for name actors finding a second career in daytime television. Following in the footsteps of film stars Joan Bennett *(Dark Shadows)* and *Promise*'s original top-billed star, Dana Andrews, Jeffreys took on the grind of a daily show like the trouper she had always been. Her work on that show was short-lived, as was the show itself, cancelled in 1972, but the industry was on notice that Jeffreys, still beautiful at fifty, was ready to work in television again.

A year later, she was seen as co-star to Laurence Luckinbill in ABC's spy thriller *The Delphi Bureau* (1972–73), part of a rotating trio of one-hour shows seen under the umbrella title *The Men*. Her role as a mover and shaker on the Washington, D.C., social scene traded on Jeffreys' trademark style and charm, and netted her a Golden Globe nomination as Best TV Actress (Drama), but the series was not a hit.

In the late 1970s and 1980s, Jeffreys was a favorite of mega-producer Aaron Spelling, who used her often as a guest star in his crowd-pleasing ABC shows, with her appearance in a first-season episode of *Fantasy Island* (1978–84) followed by a return visit, as well as stints on *Vega$* (3/7/79) and *Hotel* (1/11/84). Other producers followed suit, with Jeffreys seen in multiple episodes of CBS' prime time serial *Falcon Crest* during the 1983-84 season, playing Amanda Croft, romantic rival to series lead Angela Channing (Jane Wyman). On NBC's *Buck Rogers in the 25th Century*, she played the regal Prime Minister of an alien world in "Planet of the Amazon Women" (11/8/79).

Having populated the ABC schedule with the aforementioned hits, Aaron Spelling tried yet another three-vignettes-per-hour anthology show in the fall of 1984, with Jeffreys among the regular players in his *Finder of Lost Loves*. The show starred Tony Franciosa as the self-appointed title character, who took on the task of reuniting lovers separated by circumstance. Jeffreys played his office manager in the series, which vanished after one season of so-so ratings in the Saturday night time slot long held by *Fantasy Island*.

The cancellation of her prime time show left Jeffreys free to resume another role she had begun a year or so earlier. Cast as wealthy widow Amanda Barrington of ABC's *General Hospital*, Jeffreys launched what would be an almost twenty-year association with ABC's daytime lineup. Originally cast by producer Gloria Monty (who'd worked with Jeffreys on *Bright Promise*) as part of a short-term storyline about a handsome and unscrupulous spa masseur who seduced and then blackmailed his older female clients, Jeffreys remained part of the soap's landscape for the next several years. Not under full-time contract to the show, she worked on it sporadically over the next fifteen years, simultaneously juggling other recurring assignments like her role as David Hasselhoff's mother on the syndicated *Baywatch*. For a time, she also served as a hostess introducing nostalgic films on the American Movie Classics network.

Anne Jeffreys as the regal Amanda Barrington of the daytime soap *Port Charles*.

Unlike many actresses whose careers are unfairly curtailed after they reach the age of forty (sometimes sooner than that), Jeffreys maintained a busy professional schedule throughout her sixties and seventies. Her glamour, cultured speaking voice, and air of sophistication made her a natural for roles as worldly, often affluent mature women, her characters tending mostly toward the upper end of the economic scale.

In 1999, Jeffreys' daytime character, Amanda Barrington, was transferred to the *General Hospital* spin-off, *Port Charles*, where she would appear more frequently than she had in recent years on the original series. Her most prominent storyline, in the early 2000s, positioned her as the source of conflict in her young granddaughter's star-crossed romance with a working-class African-American boyfriend. In her mid-seventies, Jeffreys was still not only the picture of elegance but astonishingly beautiful, causing the decades-younger actor who played her granddaughter's love interest to comment publicly on what a stunner she was.

Not every actress whose credits stretched back to the classic films of the 1940s would relish the grueling work schedule of daytime television. As *Port Charles'* former casting director Mark Teschner points out, "You have to come in and be ready to act. It's all about the work." But Jeffreys, he says, was up for the challenge. "She's an actress that loves to work. She is tireless, in the best sense."[17]

As it happened, *Topper,* popular and innovative as it was, would be only one of the many roles Anne Jeffreys would inhabit in a career that lasted more than fifty years. Still highly visible in her early eighties, she regularly attends Broadway openings and has received awards for her extensive work with charities like ChildHelp USA, and serves on the board of nonprofit organizations such as the Young Musicians' Foundation. Her happy marriage to Sterling lasted nearly 55 years, until she was widowed on May 30, 2006.

The cancellation of *Port Charles* in 2003, shortly after Jeffreys' 80th birthday, might have been expected to bring the veteran star's career to a close. While she stayed closer to home during Sterling's last years, Anne Jeffreys remained game for new adventures nonetheless. Not ready to call her career finished, she told a *Playbill* reporter who asked about her future acting plans, "Make me an offer."[18] A year or so later, writer-director Scott M. Anderson did exactly that, casting Jeffreys in a key role as the Duchess of York in his film adaptation of Shakespeare's *Richard III,* scheduled for 2007 release.

The timeless appeal of fantasy has kept *Topper* and its beautiful leading lady popular with audiences for more than fifty years. Jeffreys may have best explained the show's lasting appeal when she said, "We live in a real world. Why do we have to take that as our entertainment?"[19]

As for Jeffreys herself, her star quality remains undiminished. Says her soap opera colleague Teschner, "Without even trying, she is innately stylish and glamorous. She still retains that special aura about her that she's always had. She is one of a kind."

7

Donna Reed

The Donna Reed Show

CHRONOLOGICALLY THE LAST MAJOR 1950s female sitcom star to appear on the scene, Donna Reed was also, paradoxically, the one whose show most closely conformed to stereotyped views of the era. Yet Reed herself, whose name would eventually become synonymous with the warm and loving TV mother, was in fact a more complicated person than that image suggests, and quite capable of standing up for herself in order to achieve her goals. Nor was Donna Stone, the lead character of *The Donna Reed Show*, as one-dimensional as her critics would later imply.

Born Donnabelle Mullenger on January 27, 1921, Reed's old-fashioned upbringing on a farm in Iowa, where she was the eldest of five siblings, would stand her in good stead to play the matriarch of a loving TV family. Looking back on it, however, she was careful to emphasize that her early life and adolescence during the Depression had been anything but idyllic. "It may have been good training for life," she later said of her upbringing, "but we had few good times and very little money."[1] As a teenager, Reed moved into town and lived with her grandmother while attending high school. It was in school that she acted for the first time, on the recommendation of a teacher who thought it would help Donna overcome her shyness.

Given her family's financial status, college might not have been an option for her. However, offered the opportunity to live on the West Coast with an aunt, Reed was able to enroll in Los Angeles City College, entering as a freshman in the fall of 1938. While there, she appeared in a couple of plays, but was not terribly serious about an acting career. Her coursework was designed to prepare her for a secretarial career, which she considered a more realistic goal.

However, in late 1940, while still a college student, Reed entered a beauty pageant, and was named Campus Queen of Los Angeles City College. The victory landed her picture on the front page of the *Los Angeles Times*. Although she had dabbled in acting at school, she otherwise had little preparation for the expressions of interest from movie studios that resulted from the publication of her photo. But her innocence and beauty were captivating.

MGM casting director Billy Grady later commented, "I remember this beautiful, wide-eyed, frightened child walking into my office. I was struck by her look of—quality. Please underline that 89 times: quality."[2] She was soon given a screen test, in which her co-star was another young hopeful, actor Van Heflin. The test was a success for both Reed and Heflin, and in 1941, she became an MGM contract player for a modest $75 per week. If not a fortune, it was nonetheless quite respectable money for a woman who'd lived in near-poverty as a child.

At MGM, which routinely renamed its actors with monikers more suitable for a marquee, she didn't remain Miss Mullenger for long. First christened Donna Adams, she soon underwent another change, adopting the stage name she would use for the remainder of her career, though she professed no fondness for it. "I hear 'Donna Reed' and I get a picture of a tall, chic, austere blonde, which isn't me," she later said. "I've *never* liked that name. It has a cold sound. Donna Reed."[3]

Despite her lack of experience, Reed's work at MGM got off to a quick start. Rather than breaking her in slowly with minor roles, she was quickly cast as one of the key players, along with Robert Sterling and Dan Dailey, in a gangster flick called *The Get-Away* (1941). From there, she soon went on to appearances in some of the studio's most popular series, racking up credits in *Shadow of the Thin Man* (1941), *The Courtship of Andy Hardy* (1942), and two entries in the "Dr. Gillespie" films that were made after Lew Ayres left the Kildare series.

While working at MGM, she met and befriended a studio makeup artist, William Tuttle, whom she married in 1943. Having kept her burgeoning relationship under wraps, the marriage came as a surprise to many of the actress' colleagues, as did the divorce that followed in 1945. According to Reed's biographer Jay Fultz, she became pregnant during her first marriage, but underwent an abortion out of fear that a pregnancy would cost her the career that was then on the upswing.

Reed would remain an MGM contract player through the late 1940s. In 1945, she landed two of her best-remembered roles. She played Gladys Hallward, innocent niece of the artist who painted *The Picture of Dorian Gray,* and co-starred as a dedicated nurse in John Ford's war drama *They Were Expendable*. It was also the year that, having recently divorced Tuttle, she married her agent, Tony Owen, with whom she would later produce *The Donna Reed Show*. In 1947, they began a family, adopting a son they named Tony, Junior.

Her most iconic movie role, as Jimmy Stewart's leading lady in the ubiquitous *It's a Wonderful Life* (1946), was not then the career triumph that its latter-day following might suggest. In fact, the film received lukewarm critical notices, and was something of a box-office disappointment, failing to live up to the expectations created by the teaming of Stewart and director Frank Capra. Stewart, though liking Reed personally, associated her with the movie's poor showing. He would later veto re-teaming with her in films like *The Stratton Story* (1949), preferring June Allyson. (In later years, with the critical reputation of *It's a Wonderful Life* quite different, Reed was often invited to testimonial dinners and tributes to Stewart, to which she was known to reply waspishly, "Have you asked Miss Allyson?"[4]).

Barely out of her teens, Donna Reed makes her film debut in MGM's *The Get-Away* (1941), with Dan Dailey.

Reed's seven-year contract with MGM expired in 1948. She left the studio with few regrets, bored with the roles she was getting. For the next couple of years, she free-lanced, and concentrated on family life, giving birth to son Timothy in the summer of 1949. Thanks in part to husband Tony Owen's association with Columbia Pictures, where he served as an assistant to studio head Harry Cohn, she signed a contract there in 1950.

Initially, her assignments at Columbia were unmemorable. But it was there that, in 1953, she would land the last of her memorable movie roles, cast against type as Alma Burke, a woman of easy virtue, in the World War II drama *From Here to Eternity*. In James Jones' novel, the character was bluntly called a whore, albeit one with "a face like a Madonna,"[5] but movie censorship codes of the 1950s did not allow for quite this level of candor.

The movie Alma, formerly a poor but respectable girl from a small town, works at the New Congress Club, "two steps up from the pavement," which advertises drinks, dancing, and recreation, but whose owner "pays us to be nice to all the boys." Having been rejected by the man she loved, Alma (known on the job as Lorene) is working at the club only until she can go back home with enough money to support herself and her mother in style, and rejects the idea of marrying Prew (Montgomery Clift), the decent soldier who's fallen in love with her.

It was a role unlike anything Reed had ever played. She was intrigued by its possibilities, but knew it would be a long shot to beat out more blatantly sexy actresses also in the running. Director Fred Zinnemann, who'd directed Reed a decade earlier in a minor thriller, *Eyes in the Night* (1942), liked her work but wasn't enthusiastic about casting her as Alma. Had Reed not already been on the payroll at Columbia, she probably would have been bypassed for the meaty role. Having won some of his casting preferences, however, Zinnemann acquiesced where Reed was concerned.

Her performance was a revelation, playing the outwardly tough character "so touchingly and so well,"[6] as her director later admitted. On March 25, 1954, she was named Best Supporting Actress at the annual Academy Awards. This should have raised her stock considerably at Columbia, but it didn't. Reed was mystified by the lack of follow-up, and angered by the mediocre Western scripts sent to her in the wake of her Oscar win. She asked for, and obtained, her release from the Columbia contract, but was no happier in her subsequent stint at Universal Pictures, where she undertook legal proceedings when they offered her supporting roles rather than the starring vehicles she'd signed to do.

By the mid–1950s, Reed could see her movie career winding down, and was giving serious attention to television, tempted largely by the financial prospects associated with a hit series. With her husband, Tony Owen, Reed formed a production company, Todon of California, Inc., to assemble a series vehicle for her. Owen was by then a producer in his own right, though none of his projects had really struck fire. Their first project together for Todon was an African adventure film, *Beyond Mombasa* (1956), which did little to enhance the career of either its leading lady or producer. But what would ultimately emerge from their professional partnership would be *The Donna Reed Show*, which would be done in collaboration with Screen Gems (ironically, the TV arm of Columbia Pictures, where Reed had been dissatisfied as a contract player).

She was still somewhat leery about a full-time venture into television. By that time, with her movie career slowing down, she had already tried a couple of TV guest-starring roles, and wasn't terribly impressed. In late 1954, she made her television acting debut on *Ford Television Theatre*, playing the title role in "Portrait of Lydia" (12/16/54). Of her 2/24/57 appearance on *General Electric Theater*, cast as an Amerasian woman in an episode called "Flight from Tormendero," Reed later said, "It's the worst thing I've ever done, but I'm told it got one of the series' highest ratings. Personally, I think people were fascinated by how bad it was, too hypnotized to turn it off."[7]

Surprisingly, given the popularity she would achieve with the relatively simple format of *The Donna Reed Show*, casting the star as a wife and mother wasn't the slam-dunk one might assume. In fact, she wasn't sure the sitcom format was for her, telling one of the series' early directors, "I'm nervous—I can't do comedy."[8] But on network television in the late 1950s, there seemed few viable options except sitcoms and Westerns, the latter a genre that rarely placed women in lead roles. After Owen and Reed had considered various roles she might play in a weekly sitcom, it was an executive at Screen Gems, seeing a photo of the star with her real-life family, who suggested the proper setting for *The Donna Reed Show*.

Family sitcoms were a firmly established subgenre in the 1950s, and Reed would be entering a crowded field with hers. Prior to *The Donna Reed Show*, most would center on fathers, who were either of the bumbling-but-lovable variety (NBC's *The Life of Riley*), or the all-knowing patriarch typified by the enduring *Father Knows Best* (1954–60). Lead actresses like *Best*'s Jane Wyatt or Harriet Nelson *(The Adventures of Ozzie and Harriet)* were usually the adjunct to the father figure. Reed's series would be different, in that it established the primacy of the mother on the domestic front.

Ironically, in taking that stance, *The Donna Reed Show* would establish a linkage with a later ABC sitcom with which it otherwise had virtually nothing in common— the phenomenally popular *Roseanne* (1988–97). On the surface, Roseanne, wryly promoted by ABC upon her debut as "June Cleaver, Donna Reed, and Harriet Nelson all rolled into one," played a mother who would have sent Donna Stone reeling in shock. Still, both shows revolved around a dedicated mother, and shared to some degree a worldview that, according to Roseanne, the men who worked in television had difficulty understanding—"that the female character could drive scenes, that the family functioned *because* of her, not in spite of her."[9]

The pilot of *The Donna Reed Show* sold to ABC, to debut in the fall of 1958, under the sponsorship of Campbell's Soup. The stakes were high, and Reed would have no assurance that her TV series would be a hit. The beleaguered ABC, in fact, was firmly in third place with TV viewers, and had never before been home to a hit TV sitcom starring a woman. (*The Real McCoys*, starring Walter Brennan, and Danny Thomas' *Make Room for Daddy*, which jumped to CBS in its fifth season, were among ABC's few sitcom successes). So many ABC shows, comedic or otherwise, tanked that a comedian's much-repeated joke in the 1960s was, "Want to end the Vietnam War? Put it on ABC, it'll be over in thirteen weeks!"

The Donna Reed Show cast its star as Donna Stone, an upper-middle-class housewife and mother living in suburban Hilldale, in an unspecified Midwestern state, where her husband Alex was a successful practicing pediatrician. His busy career would be the explanation for the wife's primacy in the Stone household. Unlike Ozzie Nelson of ABC's other family sitcom hit, *The Adventures of Ozzie and Harriet* (1952–66), who was so little identified with work that viewers never knew what, if anything, he did for a living, Dr. Alex Stone was a professional whose work life often prevented him from being front and center at home.

Reflecting Reed's primary status, the actor cast as Dr. Stone, Carl Betz, was a relative newcomer, whose biggest TV credit was a running role in the daytime soap opera *Love of Life*. While Reed would be billed above the title ("Donna Reed in..."), her TV husband would be credited initially with "featuring Carl Betz." Rounding out the cast were juvenile actors Shelley Fabares as daughter Mary, and *Mickey Mouse Club* veteran Paul Petersen as her brother Jeff.

The show's original opening titles showed Reed, as Donna Stone, seeing her family out of the house in the morning, lunches prepared for the kids, and receiving a goodbye kiss from Dr. Alex. (A later version would show that, having seen her husband and kids safely off, Donna herself had somewhere to be, and hurried out the door behind them).

Although later critics would deride *The Donna Reed Show* for presenting an extremely stereotypical and outdated picture of American womanhood, its creators thought of it quite differently. Series creator William Roberts, a longtime screenwriter whose credits included *The Magnificent Seven* (United Artists, 1960), intended the role of Donna Stone to show the many demands placed on stay-at-home moms, who were expected to be "wife, mother, companion, booster, nurse, housekeeper, cook, laundress, gardener, bookkeeper, clubwoman, choir singer, PTA officer, Scout leader, and at the same time effervescent, immaculate, and pretty."[10] Years before it became trendy once again to respect the workload and demands involved in being an at-home mom, Reed played a TV character that depicted the job with respect.

Reed herself saw the series as progressive. "We started breaking rules right and left," she said of assembling *The Donna Reed Show*. "We had a female lead, for one thing, a strong, healthy woman. We had a story line told from a woman's point of view that wasn't soap opera."[11]

Nor did Reed suffer from the typical actress wish to appear younger than she was. Still in her mid-thirties when *The Donna Reed Show* was being developed, she had no qualms about playing the mother of a teenager, though her own children were younger. Roughly a decade younger than TV moms like Harriet Nelson and Jane Wyatt, she gave motherhood a tinge of glamour it usually lacked on TV.

In the show's opener, "Weekend Trip," the Stones are trying to get away for a mini-vacation, but are impeded by circumstances. Chief among them is Alex's inability to correctly diagnose the illness of one of his young patients. His medical training notwithstanding, it's Donna who figures out that the boy isn't ill at all, just faking because he's afraid to confront a bully at school.

The Donna Reed Show premiered on September 24, 1958, at 9 P.M., with little fanfare. ABC's scheduling indicated great faith in the

Donna Reed with her original TV family (left to right): Shelley Fabares (Mary), Carl Betz (Alex), Paul Petersen (Jeff).

show—or perhaps simply desperation. It would play opposite the long-running anthology series *The Millionaire* (1955–60) on CBS, and, on NBC, the return to a weekly series of television's first superstar, Milton Berle, in *The Kraft Music Hall*. A lead-in from the similarly themed *Ozzie and Harriet* was hoped to deliver a suitable audience to *The Donna Reed Show*'s doorstep, but clearly Reed was in for a challenge.

ABC's promotional ads tied its new show to the long-running *Ozzie*, billing the hour of family-oriented comedy with the tagline "TWO big happy families." Of *The Donna Reed Show*, the network's copywriters said, "Donna's married to a handsome baby doctor—and the whole show is one howl after another."

Initial critical reaction found little to shout about in Reed's show, though *Variety* deemed it "a pleasant family situation comedy," and said it had "a good plus in pert, likeable Miss Reed."[12] Nor, judging from early ratings scores, were viewers immediately drawn in. In October, Berle's ratings were three times what Reed was pulling in. By all indications, ABC programmers were standing alongside the Wednesday night scheduling board with a wet rag, ready to erase *The Donna Reed Show* and try again. Resisting network pressure to tinker with the show's format, Reed and Owen were nervous nonetheless.

Fortunately for Reed, executives at Campbell's Soup liked the show, if not its ratings, and were willing to give it a little breathing room to see if the audience would find it. If Reed was worried, she didn't show it. "I'm hopeful," she told *TV Guide* that fall. "I think the novelty will wear off for Milton Berle after a month or so and we'll come out on top."[13]

By the latter half of the 1958-59 season, in fact, the tide was turning. Word of mouth may have come into play; whatever the reason, ratings for *The Donna Reed Show* were climbing. In the spring of 1959, ABC and the sponsor renewed the show for a second season. Berle's highly touted show would not be so fortunate.

After a shaky start, in fact, *The Donna Reed Show* would become one of the mainstays of ABC's schedule, lasting for eight years. In its second season, it would be partially responsible for the sitcom failure of another movie veteran, the competition from Reed's ratings spelling doom for CBS' *The Betty Hutton Show* (1959-60). By then, Reed and Owen had successfully lobbied ABC for an earlier time slot (8 P.M.) that allowed family members of all ages to tune in.

Although Reed's work in the series would disprove her assertion that she wasn't funny, she would be presented quite differently from the major female sitcom stars that had preceded her. Largely eschewing slapstick or broad comedy, Reed played a somewhat idealized middle-class mother whose stock in trade was warmth, charm, and a facility for making viewers smile.

In a typical episode, "Tony Martin Visits" (3/2/61), Donna insists she has been wrongly issued a ticket for letting her parking meter expire while she shopped. Insisting on having her day in court, she meets singer Tony Martin, who was cited for speeding on his way through town. Both believe they are innocent, and ask to be given trials—but the date selected for Donna's hearing will cause the family to postpone a much-anticipated skiing trip. Donna, who insists that the meter malfunctioned—"we have too many machines telling us what to do!" she complains—believes it's a matter of principle not to pay her $2 fine without having her story heard. She must then decide which is more important—her principles, or the plans with her family.

Though, as the above synopsis suggests, the stories on *The Donna Reed Show* hardly delved into the more controversial or painful aspects of family life, the depiction of Donna Stone was not really as bland and lifeless as later commentary on the show implied. The show derived gentle humor from her pragmatic approach to child-rearing. In "The Broken Spirit" (1/7/60), when Alex is calling to Jeff upstairs, and annoyed by the lack of response, Donna steps in neatly, saying, "There's an easier way, dear." Raising her voice slightly, she calls, "Dinnertime, Jeff!," which promptly brings him running.

Reed's light touch even allowed humor a bit stronger, without ever being offensive. In another episode, she cheerfully tells a visitor that she's not much given to shouting at her children—"a rubber hose is just as effective, and it doesn't leave marks," she says, smiling gently as she delivers a line that could almost have come from a *Roseanne* script.

From the show's early days, Reed would rack up Emmy nominations for her skillful portrayal of Donna Stone. All in all, she received four Lead Actress nominations, but never emerged victorious. Reed, competing opposite the likes of the much-admired Barbara Stanwyck (for her 1960-61 NBC anthology series), felt critics underestimated the difficulties of playing light comedy, and wasn't surprised to go home empty-handed.

By the time *The Donna Reed Show* went into its second season, however, it was firmly established as a hit, and critics were developing an appreciation of its low-key style. A trade paper review of the season opener noted, "Show may actually be classed as bonafide domestic comedy, distinguished from the garden variety situationer in that its characters, although idealized, are not daffy or given to doing silly things for silly reasons. Motivation is generally accounted for here, and the comedy, slight as it is, comes from recognizing h[o]me situations that conceivably may, and often do, occur."[14]

Ironically, the woman who would become an icon of American motherhood would feel conflicted about the time that she spent away from her own children while filming *The Donna Reed Show*. Reed and Owen had four children, two of them adopted. When her ABC series began, the oldest was twelve; the youngest, her daughter Mary Anne, was only a year old.

Spending long hours on the set was sometimes difficult for the star. "Donna misses her children," said TV spouse Betz. "Some days it's obvious that she's depressed, although she'll deny it."[15] Husband Tony Owen would boost his wife's spirits with unannounced set visits from their children, as well as flowers delivered with notes counting down how many more episodes she had to go before completing the season's work.

Though Reed, like Lucille Ball at the time, disavowed strong involvement behind the scenes in the show that bore her name, being careful to credit husband Owen as the producer, she admitted that the fast pace of television work had put new responsibilities on her that she hadn't had as a movie actress.

"I've learned how to make decisions," she said, "and I mean decisions right now—not tomorrow morning or next week. I don't mean that I'm running the show—anything but—but Tony consults me, the director will ask me for an opinion, casting wants to know what I think about this or that actor. At MGM all I ever had to worry about was who sent the flowers to the dressing room and did I know my lines for the next scene."[16]

Without fanfare, Reed used her ownership of the show to give opportunities to some longtime friends and colleagues. Actor Jimmy Hawkins, who'd played her son in *It's a Wonderful Life*, would have a recurring role as Mary Stone's off-and-on boyfriend. "The Career Woman" (4/28/60) featured a guest appearance by Reed's fellow MGM alumna Esther Williams. Buster Keaton, another friend from MGM, turned up as well.

Pleased as Reed was that her series was a success, she didn't anticipate that she would be doing it as long as she ultimately did. "I think three years is ideal for a TV series," she told a reporter in the late 1950s. "If you can manage to keep going for three years, you're doing very well. After that, you're under great pressure to keep up whatever standards you've set."[17]

The Donna Reed Show was hard work, and at times it appeared that the star's enthusiasm for her series was waning. In 1962, it took a reduction in the number of episodes filmed per season, and a revamping of the shooting schedule that shortened her work hours, to get Reed to agree to a fifth year of the show.

"Every year since the fourth season Donna has wanted to quit," said Screen Gems executive William Dozier rather patronizingly in 1964. "But all of us knew it was a game. She wanted to be coaxed. She wanted more money. She's a woman. We'd settle it, then await the end of the next season when the music would start, and we'd all waltz around again."[18] Reed herself never denied that the financial motive in doing a series was strong, though she cared about the quality of her work nonetheless.

As time went on, however, she mastered the complications of balancing work and home. TV's most nurturing stay-at-home on-screen, Reed herself was in fact re-thinking some of her own assumptions about the role of women in society. Pioneering feminist Betty Friedan, who'd created a controversy with her book *The Feminine Mystique* in 1963, surveyed television's images of women in an article for *TV Guide*, and, without specifically citing *The Donna Reed Show*, asked, "Why is there no image at all on television of the millions and millions of self-respecting American women who are not only capable of cleaning the

"Well stocked to throw in the towel," according to the original caption for this *Donna Reed Show* publicity photo.

sink, without help, but of *acting* to solve more complex problems in their own lives and in society? That moronic housewife image denies the 24,000,000 women who work today outside the home, in every industry and skilled profession, most of them wives who take care of homes and children too."[19]

Friedan might have been taken aback to learn that the actress who played TV's premier housewife shared some of her misgivings about forcing women into traditional roles. "Maybe the 'experts' are crazy wrong when they say an unmarried woman is 'unfulfilled,'" she told an interviewer in 1964. "Maybe every woman *shouldn't* necessarily be married and have children—and a lot of women would be happier and more fulfilled if they didn't."[20] As for herself, she came to realize after working on *The Donna Reed Show* for several years that she could be a good mother even though she wasn't at home all day every day.

If the woman Reed played onscreen was a diplomat, charmingly soft-spoken, and seemingly no challenger of societal norms of the day, interviewers and colleagues were sometimes surprised to find that the actress herself was a bit more complicated. Nor did she hesitate to speak her mind. Explaining why she had largely abandoned film work, aside from a cameo in the Columbia Pictures comedy *Pepe* (1960), Reed said disdainfully of contemporary movies, "They're terrible. Directors seem to hate women—make them look as if they'd never seen a comb, and give them roles of unwed mothers and tramps. There's nothing left for families but Walt Disney and Doris Day."[21]

Even by the standards of the early 1960s, however, *The Donna Reed Show* was often criticized as unrealistic, an idealized portrait of family life that had no real-life counterpart. It was commonly mocked with titles such as *The Madonna Reed Show*, or *Mother Knows Best* (in fact, *Mother Knows Better*, though meant facetiously, was briefly considered as a title for the series). Producer Tony Owen, while not denying that the show accentuated the positive, said he and Reed made this choice consciously. "There's a good side and a bad side to everyone," he said. "Sure, they'll go for the nasty stuff at first, but you *have* to give them an ideal to look up to."[22]

By the 1970s, with the Women's Liberation Movement in full swing, "Donna Reed" became shorthand for the cliché of the impossibly perfect TV mother, an icon to which no human could possibly compare. Unlike her contemporary Barbara Billingsley, who played another idealized TV mother, June Cleaver of *Leave it to Beaver* (CBS and ABC, 1957–63), Reed's own name was usually invoked, rather than that of her character, Donna Stone.

Today, the show is often derided as high camp. In the 2/22/01 episode of *Gilmore Girls*, the WB series about a thirty-something divorcee and her teenage daughter, Lorelai and Rory (Lauren Graham and Alexis Bledel) are watching *Donna Reed Show* reruns. Visitor Dean isn't familiar with the show:

> LORELAI: You don't know who Donna Reed is? The quintessential 50s mom with the perfect 50s family?
> RORY: Never without a smile and high heels?
> LORELAI: Hair that, if you hit it with a hammer, it would crack?
> DEAN: So ... it's a show?
> RORY: It's a lifestyle.
> LORELAI: It's a religion.

The title of this particular episode, incidentally, is "That Damn Donna Reed."

Like other shows of its kind, *The Donna Reed Show* profited from viewers' comfort level in watching a familiar TV family growing up year by year. Taking a leaf from the book of shows like *Ozzie and Harriet,* Reed and Owen also appealed to younger viewers by spotlighting its teenage cast as singers. Shelley Fabares' "Johnny Angel," which briefly hit #1 on the *Billboard* charts in 1962, was soon followed by "My Dad," which Paul Petersen sang in a *Reed* episode of the same name (10/15/62). Both actors recorded for the Colpix label, a division of Columbia.

In 1963, with Reed's original TV children headed toward adulthood, producer Owen introduced a new member to the Stone household—adopted daughter Trisha, played by Paul Petersen's young sister Patty. First seen in "A Way of Her Own" (1/31/63), Trisha helped fill the gap when, later that year, Shelley Fabares, ready to pursue other career options, left the show's regular cast. Mary was sent away to college, though Fabares would return to the show occasionally.

Other cast changes in 1963 included the introduction of Bob Crane (pre–*Hogan's Heroes*) and Ann McCrea as the Stones' neighbors, the Kelseys. Crane, then a Los Angeles disk jockey, made his *Donna Reed Show* debut, as Dr. Dave Blevins, in the 3/14/63 segment "The Two Doctors Stone." His guest appearance went over well enough that he was asked back for another episode, "Friends and Neighbors" (4/4/63), in which his character, re-christened Dr. Kelsey, had just married Midge (McCrea) and bought the house next door to the Stones.

Crane and McCrea were signed as full-time regulars that fall, and Midge quickly became Donna Stone's best friend. The cast additions eventually led to yet another update of the show's opening titles. In this version, while Donna is, as always, ushering her husband and children out of the house in the morning, neighbors Dave and Midge poke their heads in long enough for the new cast members to be billed as well.

According to series co-star Paul Petersen (Jeff), it was an ABC edict that led to the cast changes—"The network thought we needed neighbors to add a new twist to the show after Shelley left." Petersen grew fond of Ann McCrea, whose professionalism he admired, but not of Crane, whom he later described as "a really detestable person"[23] who brought tension to the working atmosphere at *The Donna Reed Show.*

The presence of these new characters, however, as well as the advancing age of Donna Stone's "kids," did allow for some for more adult-centered stories that were less focused on child rearing. One such episode was "The Tycoons" (10/22/64), which revolves around Alex and Dave's ups and downs playing the stock market, and the awkwardness that both couples feel when Alex is more successful. (With his winnings, Alex and Donna buy their first color TV set, though *The Donna Reed Show* itself would remain a black-and-white broadcast for its entire run).

Another, "Peacocks on the Roof" (3/4/65), centers on the family's concern that Alex, who's been working long hours, is hallucinating. After falling asleep during a showing of Dave and Midge Kelsey's vacation slides, Alex sees a peacock in the backyard that eludes everyone else's view. Dave insists on giving his overworked colleague a physical, but it isn't until Alex meets a neighbor with a large menagerie of pets that he's able to prove to Donna that he wasn't seeing things.

Reed was invigorated by the addition of new characters, telling a journalist, "I think we picked up more viewers because we brought in Bob Crane and Ann McCrea as neighbors. I had been brainwashed to think our audience is mostly kids. Now I'd like to run an even wider gamut with our stories."[24] She became friendly with McCrea off-camera as well. In 1965, when Bob Crane left *The Donna Reed Show* to star in CBS' *Hogan's Heroes* (1965–71), the most logical explanation for his absence would have been for the Kelseys to move away. But Reed, who enjoyed working with Ann McCrea, insisted that she be retained through the show's 1965-66 season.

Though she welcomed the opportunity for new stories, Reed had no desire to hog the spotlight. At one time, when she was thinking of quitting her long-running show, she rejected a proposal by husband Owen that would have allowed her to sit out some episodes altogether. While she thought that unfair to the audience, Reed encouraged the writers to develop scripts that gave her co-stars a chance to be front and center. In "Who's Rockin' the Partnership?" (1/16/64), for example, Paul Petersen as son Jeff is the pivotal character, the story depicting his summer job running a gas station with friend Smitty. Reed has a secondary role, mostly as observer and commentator on the problems at hand.

Otherwise, the show changed little. Idealized as her character was, Reed gave Donna Stone humanity, as in "When I Was Your Age" (1/22/66), when son Jeff impulsively announces his intention to marry girlfriend Bebe (Candy Moore). Husband Alex tries to be reassuring, but Donna is unnerved nonetheless:

> ALEX: Now, darling, all teenagers go through this marriage thing.
> DONNA: Yeah, and a lot of them get married!
> ALEX: But remember Mary? She made the same announcement when she graduated from high school.
> DONNA: Well, I was panic-stricken then, and I'm panic-stricken now!

The Donna Reed Show continued to grow in popularity as the seasons passed. During the 1963-64 season, six years into its run, the show was in the Top Twenty in national ratings, clocking in at #16. It became a staple of ABC's Thursday night schedule, retaining its 8 P.M. time slot, where it was often hammocked by shows of similar appeal like *Ozzie and Harriet* and *My Three Sons* (ABC and CBS, 1960–72). In January 1965, ABC added reruns of *The Donna Reed Show* to its daytime schedule.

Enjoying a long run on ABC, *The Donna Reed Show* would amass more than 250 episodes before it wore out its welcome. By the fall of 1965, however, ratings were falling, with unexpected competition from CBS' critically assailed *Gilligan's Island* (1964–67). In December, trade papers reported that *Reed* was on ABC's chopping block.

Ozzie and Harriet was also fading in popularity, and the network opted to retire both long-running shows in the spring of 1966. In fact, a number of marginally popular black-and-white sitcoms were departing the network schedules—*The Patty Duke Show, My Favorite Martian, The Munsters*, etc.—often because studios and network executives couldn't come to terms over the now-mandatory conversion to color broadcasting, and the additional costs associated with it.

Celebrating the end of filming *The Donna Reed Show* with a wrap party in late 1965, Reed shed a few tears, but had no real regrets about putting her series to rest.

"I am happy to have finished that eight-year episode of my life," she wrote to a friend at the time. "I was eight years at MGM, four years at Columbia, four years at Universal; wonder what the next four or eight years will bring?"[25]

Professionally, Reed entered a quiet period. She did no guest star appearances on television, had no particular desire to launch a second series, and steered clear of movies as well. "I just wouldn't do the junk I was offered," she later explained. "I didn't like the way films were treating women. Most of the roles were extremely passive—women in jeopardy, poor stupid souls who couldn't help themselves."[26]

For the rest of the 1960s and into the early 1970s, she would add virtually nothing of note to her acting resume, although she would be highly visible in reruns of *The Donna Reed Show*. The show's daytime network reruns continued until 1968, after which Screen Gems successfully placed it into syndication. With so many episodes available and legal complications surrounding some of the 1960s segments, the syndication package mostly excluded the sixth and seventh season episodes, though the final season was used.

Like *Leave it to Beaver* (1957–63) and *Gilligan's Island*, *The Donna Reed Show* would be seen daily on the afternoon rerun schedules of countless local stations. Among those stations, by the 1970s, was Ted Turner's independent Channel 17 in Atlanta, which he would convert to the enormously successful TBS superstation, with reruns like *Reed* among the key building blocks.

Her co-stars continued to pursue acting careers post–*Donna Reed Show*. Carl Betz, after playing second fiddle for so many years, became the star of his own well-received dramatic series, *Judd, for the Defense*. Betz played a Texas-based criminal attorney in the show, which enjoyed a two-year run on ABC from 1967 to 1969, and netted its star an Emmy Award. Shelley Fabares would continue to be in demand, particularly for sitcom roles, seen as a regular cast member in *The Little People/The Brian Keith Show* (NBC, 1972–74), *The Practice* (NBC, 1976-77), and, most notably, *Coach* (ABC, 1989–97), as leading lady to star Craig T. Nelson.

Petersen, outgrowing his teen idol stage, found acting work less plentiful, and eventually changed careers. Today, he is the founder and director of A Minor Consideration, an advocacy group focused on protecting the interests of child actors. Though he is passionate about the wrongs perpetrated on young performers, he has been quick to clarify that his own experience with Reed and TV father Carl Betz was an exception to the norm.

"They meant the world to me and always will," Petersen said. "Without their love and rock-solid support, you would not be talking to me. I would be a memory. I'd be one of those Hollywood tragedies."[27]

As for Reed herself, when she re-emerged into public view, it was in perhaps the last way her fans might have expected, short of taking a role in the original off–Broadway production of *Hair*. In 1967, at the urging of former *Donna Reed Show* scriptwriter Barbara Avedon (later the creator of *Cagney & Lacey*), Reed became co-chairman of the newly formed Another Mother for Peace, an organization of women opposing U.S. involvement in the Vietnam War. Attending the 1968 Democratic National Convention and other political rallies, she campaigned for politicians who proposed cutting off funding for the war, and did interviews endorsing AMP's slogan, "War Is Not Healthy for Children and Other Living Things."

Explaining the genesis of her unexpected activism, Reed said, "I'd been overwhelmed by hopeless despair over the war, having two sons who might have to go to Vietnam to fight in a war I don't believe in. Then one night at a rally for Eugene McCarthy, a mike was put in front of me unexpectedly, and I heard myself speaking what I thought."[28]

In 1971, in a controversy not unlike the ones that would confront a different Republican regime thirty-odd years later, AMP's discovery of maps showing offshore oil deposits surrounding Vietnam led Reed to co-author a widely disseminated article in the organization's newsletter titled, "Are Our Sons Dying for Offshore Oil?" The organization, still active today, would later turn its attention to other issues, including nuclear proliferation, but still maintains its original focus as well, and has protested the U.S.' involvement in Iraq.

If her antiwar activism wasn't enough to show that Reed wasn't the woman she played on TV, her decision in 1970 to file for divorce from Tony Owen clinched the deal. Over the years, many had thought that she was ill-suited to her brash, flashy husband. After 25 years of marriage, with their children mostly grown and out of the house, America's beloved TV housewife concluded that their differences were too much for them. A year later, she would meet Colonel Grover Asmus, whom, despite their original differences of opinion concerning the Vietnam War, she married on August 30, 1974. He had been proposing to Reed on an almost-daily basis for the past three years.

In the mid–1970s, amidst a nostalgia boom, plans for a *Donna Reed Show* reunion reached the discussion stage. A similar *Father Knows Best* special on NBC had pulled high ratings, and there was network interest in a *Reed* revival. Before it could be done, however, Carl Betz was diagnosed with lung cancer. After his death in 1979, Reed and her co-stars decided not to proceed with the project.

However, after more than a decade of professional inactivity, Donna Reed the actress returned to television in the late 1970s, starring in Ross Hunter's miniseries adaptation of Helen Van Slyke's 1976 popular novel *The Best Place to Be*. Hunter, whose specialty as a producer was glamour (among his biggest successes was the 1959 remake of *Imitation of Life*, toplining Lana Turner), was more to Reed's taste than the filmmakers who coaxed older actresses into campy, axe-wielding star turns in horror movies. Reviews were mixed, but Reed was happy with the program, which drew ample ratings for NBC, and represented a rare showcasing of a woman over fifty in a starring role. Given her background with AMP, she was intrigued with the possibility of playing antiwar activist Peg Mullen in ABC's TV-movie of *Friendly Fire* (1979), and was disappointed when Carol Burnett snagged that role.

Although leery of the demands that a full-time acting career would bring, she continued to perform periodically during the next few years, making the expected guest appearance on *The Love Boat,* and playing an uncharacteristically coldhearted role as the headmistress of a posh boarding school in the TV-movie *Deadly Lessons* (1983). Then, unexpectedly, came the type of high-profile role she thought was behind her, when the producers of CBS' *Dallas* (1978–91) invited her to join the regular cast, replacing Barbara Bel Geddes as matriarch Miss Ellie.

After taking a meeting with the show's producers, Reed happily signed to make her *Dallas* debut in the fall of 1984. She loved the idea of playing a meaty role in a weekly series again, but without shouldering the responsibility for the entire production as she had done in *The Donna Reed Show*. If the show itself was a bit more risqué than what she had previously done on TV, the role of Ellie Barnes Ewing itself was dignified and distinctly non-villainous. It would also allow her to draw on her own Iowa roots in playing a woman bred in a rural environment.

Unfortunately, the role that Reed accepted so eagerly turned into the unhappiest episode of her entire career. Rather than trying to mimic her predecessor's performances, Reed wanted to interpret the character of Ellie as she saw her. However, she soon realized that the producers were fearful of alienating longtime viewers, and didn't much care for her innovative approach.

"She definitely brought a different take to the character," said series star Larry Hagman. "I first noticed it in her very first scene. She'd gotten off a plane and was running up the ramp toward Bobby and me. I

Donna Reed with Howard Keel in a 1984 publicity shot for CBS' *Dallas*. Reed's year playing Miss Ellie proved to be a miserable experience.

remember thinking running was something Mama would never do. By this time, viewers knew the character as well as we did, and as much as I adored Donna, she didn't have the strength or edge that Barbara had given Mama."[29]

As the 1984–85 season progressed, other actors' storylines grew while Reed was relegated to the background. In the spring of 1985, when Bel Geddes, after a year's rest, felt ready to return to work, Reed was abruptly fired.

Once again, the dispute with the *Dallas* company would show that Reed was made of sterner stuff than some of the women she played. Offered an "out" by Lorimar, the production company, she refused to go along with their fabrication that she had always intended to have a brief run on the show, and was happy to step aside once her predecessor was well. Instead, Reed bluntly told journalists she had been fired, and that she'd heard it from a reporter before the *Dallas* producers had had the courtesy to tell her. Angered, the actress asserted her contract had been violated, and promptly filed a lawsuit.

Ultimately, Lorimar would settle the lawsuit by agreeing to pay Reed her $17,250 per episode salary for the remainder of her three-year contract. While the payoff gave her some sense of a wrong righted, the *Dallas* debacle left her with a sour attitude toward Hollywood. As Hagman later admitted, the episode left Reed "with her trust in the business shattered, and rightfully so."[30] As the actress herself put it in a letter to a friend, "Just remember, nobody ever said show biz was easy, fair, fun, or filled with nice people. *Dallas* is the pits, obviously."[31]

By the time her lawsuit was settled, Reed's health was failing. In October 1985, entering Cedars-Sinai Medical Center in Los Angeles to be treated for ulcers, she was instead diagnosed with pancreatic cancer. Husband Grover Asmus was told that she had about six months to live, but that prognosis proved to be overly optimistic. With few treatment options available, doctors allowed her to go home at Christmastime, and Reed died on January 14, 1986, days short of her 65th birthday.

As it turned out, *Dallas* would be only a postscript to Reed's career. Her roles in classic MGM films of the 1940s, and *The Donna Reed Show*, would be her true legacy as a performer. In 1985, her series would be one of the baby boomer favorites chosen to launch Nickelodeon's "Nick at Nite" lineup, where it would play until 1994, giving a new generation a chance to discover Reed's work.

In the wake of Reed's death, several of her friends and colleagues formed The Donna Reed Foundation for the Performing Arts, based in her home state of Iowa. The organization works to assist Iowa students seeking a performing career, and presents a yearly festival commemorating Reed's work. Among those organizing the annual event was Reed's on-screen daughter Shelley Fabares, herself a highly successful television actress who said, "This comes from my absolute enduring love and admiration for Donna."[32] In 2004, the Donna Reed Heritage Museum, located in her hometown of Denison, Iowa, opened its doors to the public.

Given the nature of the role she played, Reed doesn't always get the credit she deserves as a pioneering sitcom star. Few other women have lasted for eight years on network television in a show that bears their name. Even fewer owned the production company that gave them that exposure.

According to Reed's co-star Fabares, "Donna gets lumped into a category she doesn't deserve—the perfect mom, a kind of plastic figure of that long-ago time. She was much, much more. She was a woman of enormous integrity, strength, will, humor, and a capacity to be curious."[33]

8

Ann Sothern

Private Secretary and
The Ann Sothern Show

FOLLOWING THE LEAD OF HER LONGTIME FRIEND and fellow B-movie actress Lucille Ball, Ann Sothern made the transition to television in 1953 with her popular sitcom *Private Secretary* (also known as *Susie*). Over the next decade, she would perform in more than 200 episodes of that show and its successor, *The Ann Sothern Show* (CBS, 1958–61). Playing a savvy, resourceful "career girl" onscreen must have come easily to the actress, whose off-screen accomplishments as a businesswoman were even more impressive.

Born January 22, 1909, as Harriette Lake, Sothern's parents were performers, her mother a singer and her father an actor, and were frequently on the road. Of her birthplace, Valley City, North Dakota, Sothern later said, "I've never seen the town. I was born there, then my mother and father moved on."[1] She grew up mostly in Minnesota, one of three daughters. Developing an interest in music early in life, Sothern learned to play the piano as well as composing her own tunes. She also cultivated a pleasant singing voice that would eventually help her gain a toehold in show business.

Sothern first came to Hollywood in the late 1920s, after a brief stint in college. Her newly divorced mother, who'd been hired as a vocal coach at Warner Brothers, tried to help Sothern get her entree into movies, but she was unable to progress much beyond uncredited bit parts. Retreating to the stage, she developed her craft further in musical theater. In the spring of 1931, Sothern (still as Harriette Lake) was featured in the Rodgers and Hart musical *America's Sweetheart*. The show was not a huge success, closing after only 135 performances, but after the summer hiatus she followed it up with another musical role in *Everybody's Welcome,* which ran until February 1932.

She returned to Hollywood in 1933, having achieved some renown for her abilities in musical theater. Offered the female lead in Columbia's musical comedy *Let's Fall in Love* (1935), Sothern's acting and singing impressed studio executives, and she was offered a contract. She had gone blonde for her first role at Columbia, and would retain that shade, along with the new stage name she had selected from a list offered by studio head Harry Cohn.

During those early years at Columbia, she met and befriended fellow starlet Lucille Ball, who became a lifelong friend. Both would be well-liked and employed steadily in the 1930s, but often found the roles they were given less than satisfying.

"We used to cry on each other's shoulder," Sothern said. "I said I got all the parts that Katy Hepburn didn't want and Lucille would say that she got all the ones *I* didn't want."[2] Also during this period, the actress renewed her acquaintance with bandleader Roger Pryor, whom she'd met a few years earlier, while on tour in Chicago. They were reunited when Pryor, now pursuing an acting career, was cast as Sothern's leading man in Columbia's *The Girl Friend* (1935). Their on-screen romance carried over to real life, and the couple was married on September 27, 1936. Unfortunately, the marriage would not be a success over the long haul, lasting only into the early 1940s.

Meanwhile, having slogged her way through numerous B movies, Sothern's better-than-average supporting role as a flighty stenographer in Tay Garnett's *Trade Winds* (1938) made an impression at MGM. The studio owned the rights to Wilson Collison's 1935 mystery novel "Dark Dame," which featured as contrast to the title character a brassy, cheerful showgirl, Maisie Ravier. The property had been purchased as a vehicle for Jean Harlow, but MGM put it on the shelf after that star's untimely death in 1937. Seeing Sothern's performance in *Trade Winds*, however, playing a similar character, studio executives signed her for *Maisie* (1939), opposite Robert Young. When that film cleaned up at the box office, MGM promptly launched a series, signing Sothern to crank out additional modestly budgeted Maisie films at the rate of two a year.

As film historian James Robert Parish noted, "All the *Maisie* films began with the established situation of luckless Maisie, a not so successful chorine, losing her job and being stranded, forced to fend for herself. Most of the entries gave saucy, scatterbrained Maisie the chance to sing a song, before coming into conflict and eventual harmony with the film's hero."[3]

The popularity of Maisie proved to be a double-edged sword for Sothern. While the B movies sold tickets on the strength of her name, and made her a valued commodity at MGM, she also worried that she was in danger of being pigeonholed. "So, me, I'm on this tightrope," she explained at the time. "Maisie is my pal and I love her but I don't want her to get her arms around my neck. When she falls off I don't want to fall off."[4]

In fact, she would spend most of the 1940s on the *Maisie* assembly line, rarely considered for any of the studio's more ambitious or challenging roles. Her starring role in the musical *Lady Be Good* (1941), opposite Robert Young, one that showcased her singing talent, was more of a plum than she usually rated, but MGM still liked her best as Maisie. Nor did she always benefit from the proper star buildup—in *Lady Be Good,* she's second-billed behind actress Eleanor Powell, though Sothern is clearly playing the lead character.

Ann Sothern as her popular movie character Maisie Ravier in *Swing Shift Maisie* (MGM, 1943), opposite leading man James Craig.

In 1945, she added to her workload a weekly *Maisie* radio comedy, initially heard Thursday nights as a summer replacement for Milton Berle's show. An early reviewer praised Sothern, noting that the "Metro star plays her role to the hilt, giving a performance that adds enjoyment to some fine writing."[5] The show quickly became popular enough to return as a regular attraction, and continued on CBS until 1947. It was revived in 1949 as a syndicated show, *The Adventures of Maisie*.

Because Sothern could get so far with material that was no better than average, she was somewhat taken for granted. Joseph Mankiewicz, who later directed Sothern in *A Letter to Three Wives*, said of her time at MGM, "Annie was a damned good Broadway musical comedy actress. She had the sexiest mouth any woman ever had. But, at Metro, poor Annie got stuck in the Sam Katz unit. She never got the big break Gene Kelly and others did, of being with the Arthur Freed steamroller of talent."[6]

On a personal level, however, Sothern's role as Maisie introduced her to her second husband. While shooting *Ringside Maisie* (1941), she met actor Robert Sterling, whom she married on May 23, 1943, not long after being granted her divorce from Roger Pryor. The second marriage did not prove an idyllic one either—Sothern and Sterling were separated for a time in the mid–1940s, and finally divorced in 1949. (Soon afterwards, he married Anne Jeffreys, with whom he would co-star in *Topper).* The union did, however, produce Sothern's only child, daughter Patricia, born on December 10, 1944.

She came to television in the early 1950s on the heels of a life-threatening health crisis that had sharply curtailed her career in recent years. A transfusion performed in an overseas hospital in 1949 infected the star with hepatitis, and she spent most of the next two years seriously ill. For a time, she was homebound, suffering from extreme sensitivity to light and sound. Unable to work on camera, she was mostly inactive professionally except for taping her role in the syndicated *Adventures of Maisie* radio series, recorded onsite at her home.

Ironically, just before her illness, she had played one of the best roles of her long film career, in Joseph L. Mankiewicz' *A Letter to Three Wives* (1949). The film, both a popular and critical success, gave Sothern a meaty role as successful radio scriptwriter Rita Phipps, whose marriage to schoolteacher George Phipps (Kirk Douglas) is threatened by his insecurity about her professional accomplishments. For Sothern, who'd toiled in B movies for most of her career, it was a plum role, but the unfortunate timing prevented it from reviving her film career.

Following her divorce from Robert Sterling, Sothern would never remarry. According to Kirk Douglas, he and his *Letter to Three Wives* co-star had a brief fling during shooting. "Ann Sothern played my wife," the married actor later said. "We rehearsed the relationship offstage."[7] She also enjoyed a few dates during this time with fellow film actor Ronald Reagan, not long before he married Nancy Davis, Sothern's co-star in *Shadow on the Wall* (MGM, 1950).

During her long recuperation from hepatitis, she became friendly with newcomer Richard Egan, twelve years her junior, and fan magazines reported that she declined a marriage proposal from the actor, who was a practicing Catholic. "Ann was not a Catholic. Even more serious, she was a divorcee. He couldn't marry her—not with the approval of the church. And could he marry without it?"[8] Ironically, Sothern herself would convert to Catholicism not long afterwards, and would practice that religion seriously for the rest of her life.

Once she had begun to put her illness behind her, Sothern resurfaced in the fall of 1951 with a starring role in the Broadway comedy "Faithfully Yours," opposite another soon-to-be TV stalwart, Robert Cummings (*Love That Bob*). Unfortunately, the show was not a hit, and closed after only 68 performances. By the time she did return to the silver screen, playing a critically praised supporting role in the *film noir* drama *The Blue Gardenia* (1953), she had already reached the conclusion that it was time to look into regular television work.

In the early 1950s, Sothern announced her availability in the new medium with guest appearances on shows like *Schlitz Playhouse of Stars* and *The Fred Waring Show.* Producers sent her scripts for prospective TV series, but the actress was choosy. When Jack Chertok offered her the lead role in *Private Secretary,* based on a concept by former MGM producer Ned Marin, Sothern decided that this was the right vehicle for her.

Although she would later try unsuccessfully to obtain the television rights to the Maisie character (which MGM would develop as a pilot for Janis Paige in 1960, but never sold as a series), Sothern's first series would present her as a new, if not radically different, character. A bit more educated and refined than the working-class Maisie, Susie MacNamara of *Private Secretary* was the invaluable assistant to New York talent agent Peter Sands (played by Don Porter). Her best friend and co-worker was switchboard operator Vi Praskins (Ann Tyrrell). Also seen occasionally were Susie's friendly rival Sylvia (Joan Banks) and Mr. Sands' scroungy competition, low-rent talent agent "Cagey" Calhoun (Jesse White, who alternated this recurring role with one as Danny Thomas' agent on *Make Room for Daddy*).

Not content to be hired merely as a performer, Sothern was active behind the scenes of *Private Secretary* as well, involving herself in casting, script editing, and other production chores. The savvy star had a sense of what would attract viewers, particularly women, and did her best to supply it. She did this not only by taking time with her appearance and costumes, giving them a look they might enjoy emulating, but also making sure that the show's basic setup was appealing as well.

"Women don't see competition in me," she said of her 1950s sitcom work, "they see a friend. I always make sure my scripts are written so the woman manages to tell off the big, hulking male at the finish. A happy female ending, you might say."[9]

In assembling *Private Secretary,* she was mindful of two goals that often conflicted—the need to create an attractive product, while simultaneously producing an attractive profit. "If you're trying to honestly do a show of quality, then you are constantly frustrated," she said. "In three days we have to shoot an entire 26-minute show. And we do it just like the movies, with close-ups, the whole works. But you know that isn't enough time. We start shooting promptly at 9 A.M., and never finish until 6. And still we don't have enough time. Some scenes that you see on the screen have never been rehearsed. I just read the script and they shoot it."[10]

In an era when the glass ceiling was firmly in place for women, Sothern played a clerical worker who routinely outshone her male supervisor. In the episode "What Every Secretary Knows" (11/11/56), Sands is eager to make inroads with opera impresario Bernard Hugo, whose upcoming Broadway production of "Samson and Delilah" is a golden opportunity for two of the agency's young clients. Offering to get him in the door by calling on her friendship with the producer's secretary, Susie is rebuffed by her boss, who deems the matter too important to be handled by the help.

Nor does he bide Susie's advice that he cultivate the producer's wife in order to achieve his goal: "You girls and your flighty romantic notion that behind every man is some noble, strong, long-suffering woman," he says high-handedly. "Fiddle faddle!"

Unperturbed, Susie makes friends with Mrs. Hugo, and devises an elaborate scheme to bring her boss and Mrs. Hugo together. Succeeding in getting them acquainted, she proceeds to arrange an impromptu audition where Mr. Hugo hears Sands' clients sing, and has a brainstorm—wouldn't they be perfect for his new show? Susie and Mrs. Hugo exchange winks, having made all the necessary arrangements while the supposedly powerful men remain oblivious of how skillfully they've been manipulated.

Like Eve Arden's *Our Miss Brooks,* the role of Susie (or Susan Camille MacNamara, as she was billed in the credits), made Sothern a favorite of women viewers, particularly those who were themselves employed in office jobs. Noted a fan magazine at the time, "Ann Sothern is perhaps the only secretary in the world who has three secretaries of her own to answer her sacks full of letters from stenos seeking her advice in love, marriage, how to handle the boss when he tells you his luckless yarns about how his wife doesn't understand him."[11]

In "How to Handle the Boss" (10/28/56), Susie's job is on the line after a practical-joking friend ghostwrites for her an unflattering newspaper article about her job, and Mr. Sands. Desperate to keep the insulting copy from seeing print, she calls upon her network of contacts—and smarts—to bail herself out. In an interesting plot twist for the 1950s, Susie ultimately succeeds in her goal by using a secret signal known only to secretaries (the SOS—"Save a Secretary"), but it is an important male executive, himself a former secretary, who sees it and comes to her aid.

Sothern herself, as if heeding the advice later given to aspiring career women as to how to avoid being pigeonholed into secretarial work, professed to be unable even to operate the typewriter that was seen so prominently in her show's closing credits. She enjoyed telling interviewers that her crew had removed most of the working parts from the typewriter on Susie's desk, so that Sothern could pretend to type during scenes without breaking the machine.

Unlike her friend Lucille Ball and other comediennes, Sothern did little physical comedy on her 1950s sitcoms. Her comedy was primarily verbal, her rich voice wrapping itself around a variety of sardonic and beguiling lines. Ball herself would later say, "The best comedian in this business, bar none, is Ann Sothern."[12]

Nor did her role as Susie really fall into the "dizzy dame" category. Though Susie occasionally gets into scrapes of her own making, as in "Dollars and Sense" (11/25/56), when her passion for new clothes has a devastating effect on her bank balance, she was more often the problem-solver. In "Crazy Mixed-Up Kid" (5/15/54), she not only tames a publicity-hungry young actor (Paul Picerni) whose stunts are hurting his professional reputation, but talks a reluctant investor into writing a $150,000 check to star him in a play. Boss Mr. Sands can do little but step aside, and watch her at work.

Sothern would have a slightly less intense workload than other sitcom stars of the period, producing only 26 segments of *Secretary* per season. For most of the year, her show alternated with *The Jack Benny*

Ann Sothern with actor Don Porter, her leading man in both *Private Secretary* and *The Ann Sothern Show.*

Show on CBS' Sunday night schedule. Still, after the relative ease of starring in a radio series, and given her health problems, she found TV work demanding. "I've been in show business for 20 years," she told *Time* magazine, "and this is the toughest thing I've ever done."[13]

Although Sothern, by then in her forties, was still highly attractive, her bout with hepatitis left her not only weakened but with residual side effects, among them a struggle with weight that would last the rest of her life. It's been reported elsewhere that the star, sensitive about her girth, would not allow her TV directors to shoot her below the waist. However, a viewing of *Private Secretary* episodes does not bear this out. Costume designer Elois Jenssen (also associated with *I Love Lucy*) did clothe the star mostly in black, and her flowing skirts seemed designed to avoid defining the specifics of her figure, but Sothern allowed herself to be seen full length at least now and then. In fact, the opening titles of her later *Ann Sothern Show*, set in a New York City hotel, show a full-length shot of her sweeping majestically through the revolving doors of the hotel entrance every week.

In 1955, *Private Secretary* became one of the first TV sitcoms to go into syndication even before its network run concluded. Television Programs of America, Inc. offered the first 52 episodes to local stations, re-titled *Susie* so as to avoid direct competition with the new episodes still airing in prime time. Though Sothern had been a well-known actress for almost twenty years, the TV show's ongoing popularity in reruns brought her a heightened level of audience recognition. While doing a nightclub appearance, she said, "a little girl walked out on the floor, threw her arms around me and said, 'I love you, Susie.' Nothing like that happened to me when I was in pictures as Maisie."[14]

Unfortunately for Sothern, the show's popularity didn't necessarily lead to critical acclaim, although its star would be repeatedly nominated for Best Actress Emmys. By 1957, when the show had been again overlooked for Emmy consideration, the actress was steamed. The Academy of Television Arts and Sciences' practice of sending a short "reminder list" of shows eligible for consideration, rather than a complete list, struck her as unfair, especially since the best series list was notably lacking *Private Secretary*.

"I'm on the warpath," she told reporters. "Out of the list of 20 series, my show has beaten more than half of them in the ratings. It's most unfair. Who is authorized to name those 20 shows on the list; who says it must be only those 20 shows. I think this could bear an investigation. My show has had a 39.8 rating this year, and isn't even on the list. They have no right to do this."[15] Other producers whose shows had been similarly snubbed, such as Alex Gottlieb of *The Gale Storm Show: Oh! Susanna*, echoed her complaints.

Although Sothern's show was still popular, it came to an abrupt end in 1957, when the star became embroiled in a legal battle with her producer. Chertok had sold *Private Secretary* in 1956 to TPA, the company that was successfully syndicating *Susie* reruns. TPA believed that it had bought not only the rights to the show, but also an option for Sothern to film new episodes. The actress, no less afraid to stand up to a man than her TV character, thought otherwise. She insisted that her contract be renegotiated before filming resumed, and said that she had not received her full payment for *Susie* reruns. Sothern professed to hold no grudge against producer Chertok, saying, "He's done a very creditable job. All he needs is a new accounting department."[16]

By the summer of 1957, when negotiations had completely broken down, Sothern began telling interviewers she might retire. "Five years of TV is a lot of hard work," she said. She claimed, probably as a negotiating ploy, to be making plans to leave the country—"I want to live in Europe for two years so my daughter Tish can go to school there. We'd live in Versailles."[17] Still, in the same interview, she admitted that she was at least contemplating the idea of a second TV series.

For a while, Chertok Television made noise about continuing *Private Secretary* with another star taking Sothern's place. June Allyson's name was bandied about as a possibility, as was Penny Singleton, star of the 1940s *Blondie* film series, but ultimately the impasse brought *Private Secretary* to an end in the spring of 1957.

Much as she sometimes professed to dislike Hollywood, and her workload, Sothern was soon busy with other projects. In 1958, she released an LP album, "Sothern Exposure: Ann Sothern Sings." The record consisted mostly of old standards like Irving Berlin's "Always." It was a return to old times for the actress, given her background in musical theater.

While the 104 episodes of Sothern's show continued to flourish in reruns, the star plotted a TV comeback. Her agent, William Morris, took the star to Desilu, where her first project was reprising Susie opposite Lucille Ball in the premiere of *The Ford Lucille Ball-Desi Arnaz Show*, "Lucy Takes a Cruise to Havana," which aired in November 1957. (The show, a flashback episode depicting how Lucy and Ricky first met, established Lucy Ricardo and Susie MacNamara as having been friends in New York in the 1940s). Meanwhile, the Desilu staff had begun to brainstorm a new vehicle for Sothern, which had the working title "Career Girl." Writers Bob Schiller and Bob Weiskopf, who had toiled on *I Love Lucy*, prepared the pilot script. The series would be a co-venture between Desilu and the star's Anso Productions, with Arnaz serving as executive producer.

Charged with replicating what had worked well in Sothern's previous series, without invoking legal complications as her lawsuit played out, the writers developed a format that would cast Sothern as Katy O'Connor, assistant manager of a hotel in New York City. In contrast to the setup of her previous series, here she would play not a support staff member but a supervisory role. The show's original concept called for her to be the capable second-in-command to a henpecked, meek manager, played by veteran character actor Ernest Truex. One of TV sitcom's most recognizable faces, character actress Reta Shaw, played his domineering wife, who not only ran roughshod over her husband, but looked askance at any pretty woman who appeared on the scene.

Initially, the only cast member familiar from *Private Secretary* was Ann Tyrrell, whose role as Katy's skittish secretary, roommate, and best friend Olive would be barely distinguishable from her characterization as Vi on *Secretary*. Other regulars that first year were a handsome French-born desk clerk (Jacques Scott), and a philosophical bellboy (Jack Mullaney). Before long, though, Tyrrell and Sothern would find themselves keeping company with some familiar faces.

Sothern admitted that her new venture didn't carry her too far into unfamiliar territory. "The character ... I played in *Private Secretary* on TV was only a more refined Maisie," she said. "And to push my luck, the character I'm playing now, Katy O'Connor ... is just a refinement of Susan."[18]

General Foods signed on to sponsor *The Ann Sothern Show*, using it mostly to promote its then-new Tang breakfast drink. Substantially increasing the show's chance for high ratings was CBS' agreement to slot it at 9:30 on Monday nights, following *The Danny Thomas Show*. It would take the place of Spring Byington's *December Bride*, shunted into a less desirable Thursday night slot that fall.

The Ann Sothern Show seemed to have it made. *Variety*'s reviewer called the show a "smart bet" to garner strong ratings, praising the opening installment as "a first night click."[19] Interviewed by *TV Guide* a few weeks into the new season, Sothern exuded enthusiasm about her new supporting cast. "They're dynamite performers, all of them," she said. "I hand-picked them myself. Ernest is delightful, the dames fall apart over Jacques. And as for that Mullaney kid—well, he's only terrific, that's all."[20]

More than a decade later, much would be made of how Mary Richards, the lead character of *The Mary Tyler Moore Show* (CBS, 1970–77), represented an early role model for working women. Without taking anything away from that notable show, though, we can look back further, and see that some of the elements thought to be groundbreaking in 1970 could be seen earlier in Sothern's TV work. As not only the star but the co-owner of her series, Sothern used her influence to place herself in a format that was progressive for its time.

In a first-season episode of *The Ann Sothern Show*, "Three Loves Has Katy" (1/19/59), a forthcoming college reunion causes Katy to muse, "Sometimes I wonder if I was right to choose a career instead of marriage." She tells friend Olive that she received eight marriage proposals in college—six of them from the same man. Of the three men she might have married, one was a star football player, another the student body president, but it's the third man, pre-med student Nathaniel Norcross, whom she particularly remembers. As Katy says to friend Olive:

KATY: Do you know that I was responsible for his going into medicine?
OLIVE: You were?
KATY: Mm-hm. He had to take a splinter out of me.
OLIVE: He did? Where?
KATY: *(giving her friend a sideways look)* In the infirmary, of course!

Left alone, Katy amuses herself with fantasies of what her life might have been had she married each of the three men, and become either the loving wife of a star athlete, a doctor's dedicated spouse, or the First Lady of the United States. The actual reunion, however, mostly fails to live up to her expectations. The football player is an immature boor whose wife has borne him five children, and says living with him is like having a sixth one. The politician is also married, but that doesn't stop him from putting the moves on Katy in his wife's absence.

As for Dr. Nat Norcross (John Beal), the attraction between him and Katy is still there, and at the reunion he proposes to her (for the seventh time). But Katy, who astutely sees that his first and foremost dedication is to his work, gently refuses him. Back home, when romantic Olive tries to console her about the fact that she didn't snag any of the three men, Katy sees it differently. She's content with her life, she tells her friend—"I have an exciting job, wonderful friends, complete independence." Not that she's opposed to the idea of getting married, she admits—but it's also OK if doesn't happen.

Unfortunately, the early predictions of success for *The Ann Sothern Show* were premature. Although the show was by no means a flop, by midseason it was evident that changes were needed. As Sothern had returned to network TV after a hiatus of only one year, playing a different character in a different setting, perhaps viewers in that more innocent age were confused. Perhaps her casting as an independent career woman was just a bit ahead of its time. But it became evident that some of the ways in which *The Ann Sothern Show* set itself apart from its predecessor were disappointing to the star's fans.

Near the end of the first season, a familiar face surfaced in the show's twenty-third episode, "Katy's Big Surprise" (3/9/59). Billed initially as a guest star, *Private Secretary*'s Don Porter played James Devery, who has just been named the new manager of the Bartley House. His arrival comes as a disappointment to Katy, who had envisioned herself stepping into that role.

Porter's appearance was part of a housecleaning that swept out much of the show's original cast. By the time *The Ann Sothern Show* returned for its second season that fall, most of the original players except Tyrrell had been dropped. Porter was on the regular payroll once again, given co-star billing after Sothern.

The star was frank about the reasons behind the cast changes, and Porter's return. "There isn't any mystery about why Don is back," she told *TV Guide*. "I wish I could show you the letters we got. 'Where is Mr. Sands?,' week after week. The simple psychological truth is, people don't want to see me dominating a man."[21]

Careful to emphasize that the decision to write out Truex's character was no reflection on the actor or his work, Sothern said that the show simply worked better with the byplay that Porter could provide. "[Viewers] want to see Don and me trying to outsmart each other. It's chemistry."[22]

Another familiar face on the show's second season opener was Lucille Ball, who guest starred as Lucy Ricardo in "The Lucy Story" (10/5/59). The episode's plot revolved around Lucy's visit to the hotel after an argument with workaholic Ricky, and her efforts to jump-start a romance between Katy and her boss. The script gave its leading ladies the chance to play out a cli-

Publicity photo for *The Ann Sothern Show*.

mactic scene in which both have been doped up with sleeping pills, which they carried off with style.

No fan of playing her comedy before a live audience, Sothern vetoed that and other of the usual Desilu production techniques in producing *The Ann Sothern Show*. In fact, for a time, the show's closing credits included an unusual disclaimer, "Audience Reaction Technically Produced." This may have been dictated by a nervous CBS in response to the late 1950s scandal surrounded rigged game shows, which for a time made network executives bend over backwards trying to avoid the implication that any aspect of its shows was phony, or simulated.

As she had done with *Private Secretary*, Sothern sought ways to make the show look good while not straining the budget. She took pride in innovations like the use of "flying" scenery (lightweight and portable) that could be moved quickly and inexpensively.

"I got talked into doing this series," she told *TV Guide*, "but as long as I was going to do it, I wanted to do it right. They call me the MGM girl over there. 'The things that girl *wants*!,' they say. But you have to do it. You have to do things yourself."[23]

Among the things that Sothern did herself was contribute the show's theme song, "Katy," which she composed with sister Bonnie Lake. She also joined her co-stars in appearing in weekly commercials for the sponsors' products, ending each week smiling into the camera and saying, "Well, good night, everybody. Stay happy!"

Busy with the series and other activities, Sothern was fond of professing that she would willingly give it all up for a more leisurely existence. "Frankly, I would much rather be married," she said, "and let someone else worry about making a living. I would love to be married to a diplomat, say, and give elegant dinners. I would like to live elegantly. Instead, I have to run five businesses."[24]

Aside from Anso Productions, those businesses included a music publishing firm and a cattle ranch. For a time, her Vincent Productions (named after her patron saint) also had two aspiring young performers under contract, whose careers Sothern guided. Another venture was a sewing shop in Sun Valley, Idaho, where she regularly vacationed. Struck by a sudden impulse to do some sewing during one trip, she was frustrated to find that there was nowhere nearby to purchase the supplies she needed. Soon, "Ann Sothern's Sewing Center" filled that gap.

Over the next two years, Sothern's second show would increasingly come to resemble her first one. Aside from Ann Tyrrell, Jesse White, who'd been featured as Cagey Calhoun on *Private Secretary*, was eventually written into the new show as well, playing the hotel's cigar stand operator, an inveterate conniver as White's previous character had been. As in the original series, there were hints of attraction between Sothern's character and her employer, though not much came of it. Instead, another running plot element during the 1960-61 season was Olive's romance and eventual marriage to dentist Delbert Gray, played by comic Louis Nye.

Toward the latter part of the show's run, Sothern also attempted to use her weekly vehicle as a springboard to launch new Anso Productions projects, often putting other funny women in the spotlight. Airing as the 2/23/61 episode of *The Ann Sothern Show*, "Always April" offered a lead role to fading film star Constance Bennett, cast as the mother of an aspiring actress. A few weeks later, "Pandora" (3/16/61), another lightly disguised series pilot, showcased actress-comedienne Pat Carroll, who played a gawky and self-conscious young woman hired as secretary to a matinee-idol movie star. She also gave her own daughter, Tisha, an aspiring actress, her television debut with a role in the episode "Loving Arms" (10/13/60).

Although the cast overhaul and story changes gave a boost to the show's ratings, *The Ann Sothern Show* would not enjoy quite as long a run as *Private Secretary* had. During the third season, a scheduling change placed Sothern's sitcom opposite one of TV's hottest shows at the time, ABC's gangster drama *The Untouchables* (1959–63). The competition sent Sothern's ratings plunging downward, and her series was unceremoniously cancelled in the spring of 1961 by CBS president James Aubrey. Left unresolved was the relationship between Sothern's character and "Mr. Devery," though he proposed to her in the final episode filmed.

Sothern walked away in a huff, telling reporters that the season had ended four episodes short by mutual agreement between her and the sponsor. *The Ann Sothern Show*, with almost 100 episodes in the hopper, joined *Private Secretary* in syndication, both shows raking in profits for savvy co-owner Sothern. By 1962, *Private Secretary* was reported to have grossed $4,000,000 over the course of its afterlife in syndication, a goodly portion of which Sothern collected.

At first, it looked as though the star's absence from series television might be brief. In the summer of 1962, *Variety* reported that Goodson-Todman, the production company better known for game shows like *To Tell the Truth* and *What's My Line?*, was pitching an Ann Sothern sitcom to NBC to be launched in the 1963-64 season. The projected show, which the trade paper said "casts the actress as a midwestern housewife,"[25] never materialized. Instead, the actress made plans for a Broadway comeback, but that too fell through.

On the heels of her TV series cancellation came a flurry of embarrassing and upsetting headlines for the star, when her mother sued her for support in 1961. Sothern defended herself to the press, explaining that she had withdrawn her support when her mother chose to live with other family members who the actress believed were usurping the money meant for her mother's care. The case was ultimately settled, but Sothern's mother died not long afterwards.

For a time in the early to mid–1960s, Sothern put television on the back burner while she pursued a career as a character actress. She spent time in New York City, studying acting under the highly regarded Stella Adler, then made a movie comeback in 1964. This time, though, she wasn't after the leading lady parts she'd done previously.

Putting on some of the weight she had fought while starring on TV, the star eschewed glamour for the creative challenge of playing a varied lot of character roles. In Gore Vidal's political drama *The Best Man* (1964), Sothern played Sue Ellen Gamadge, mover and shaker who is part of the team trying to elect Henry Fonda as president. Prone to spout advice about what "the women" do and don't like in their political candidates, Sothern's character is said by a former president to be a good choice to be the country's first female Chief Executive.

Nominated for a Golden Globe as Best Supporting Actress for that performance, Sothern appeared in a vastly different role a few months later, playing Sade, a cheap floozy, in Paramount's *Lady in a Cage*. Although this performance too was

Ann Sothern the character actress, menaced by Rafael Campos in *Lady in a Cage* (1964).

admired, 1964 audiences found the thriller, about a wealthy widow (Olivia de Havilland) terrorized by a home invasion, shockingly violent and intense, and Sothern believed that the controversy cost her recognition for her work.

Late that year, Sothern's longtime friend Lucille Ball approached her about appearing on *The Lucy Show*. Ill at ease without longtime second banana Vivian Vance, who was sitting out several episodes during the show's third season, Ball asked Sothern to join the show as a recurring guest star. With the help of writers like Leonard Gershe, who had contributed to Sothern's own shows in the 1950s, Sothern gave birth to the Countess Framboise, otherwise known as Lucy's old pal Rosie Hannigan, who had married very well, but was now a widow of straitened means.

Making her *Lucy Show* debut in "Lucy and the Countess" (2/1/65), Sothern appeared in three more episodes in quick succession, her chemistry with the star enlivening what was in danger of becoming a stale show. She would be seen intermittently on the show throughout 1965.

By that point in their careers, neither Ball nor Sothern was a shrinking violet, and there were occasional gossip column items reporting clashes of temper on the set. Though others were sometimes intimidated by Ball, Sothern knew her well, and held her own. "Despite what has been written," said Ball's longtime colleague Maury Thompson, "Lucille and Ann were very close friends, and on the set there was always girl talk between them. They could talk anyway [sic] they wanted to one another, and no one took offense."[26]

There was talk that she was offered the chance to become a series regular, when Vance quit the show altogether that spring, but Sothern was unwilling to accept the co-star billing that Ball had given Vance. Instead, with one foot already back in the sitcom world, Sothern took what seemed like a logical next step, unfortunately choosing a vehicle (pun intended) that would take her a long time to live down. In September 1965, NBC debuted *My Mother, the Car,* a fantasy sitcom about a suburban man (Jerry Van Dyke) who discovers that an antique car is the reincarnation of his late mother.

Producers wanted a name actress with a distinctive voice to read Mother's lines, and after giving thought to Eve Arden and film actress Jean Arthur, settled on Sothern. Initially, the new series seemed like an easy way to pick up a healthy paycheck— radio work for TV money, as she later put it. The gig didn't require her to doll up her appearance, worry about her weight, or shoulder any production responsibilities. All that was expected of her was to report to a sound studio every few weeks, where she could rattle off her dialogue for multiple episodes in one recording session and be home a few hours later. Still, there were signs that she missed being in the spotlight, and she told reporters that public demand might eventually see her role expanded to on-screen appearances, perhaps through flashback scenes.

In the meantime, she happily collected the paycheck, but the critical response to *My Mother the Car* was brutal, and the goofy show quickly became the laughingstock of the NBC prime time schedule, damaging the careers of everyone involved. At the end of the 1965-66 season, network programmers mercifully dropped the ax, though the show's notoriety would continue unchecked for years to come. It would be Sothern's last regular series role.

Perhaps that experience soured the star on sitcoms. A far more reasonable proposition soon came along, in the form of Sothern's friend and colleague Desi Arnaz, who offered her one of the lead roles in his projected sitcom *The Mothers-in-Law,* which he was developing for CBS. The series had been created by *Lucy* writers Bob Carroll, Jr. and Madelyn Davis with Sothern and Eve Arden in mind to play the co-leads, battling neighbors whose son and daughter had gotten married. Early on in the project, when it seemed that the stars lacked the right chemistry to play off each other effectively, Sothern withdrew, and the show ultimately premiered on NBC during the 1967-68 season, with Kaye Ballard opposite Arden.

In the mid- to late 1960s, Sothern largely occupied herself with theater engagements, starring in stock and dinner theater productions of crowd-pleasing shows like *Mame, Butterflies Are Free* (written by her former television colleague Leonard Gershe), and, on a more serious note, *The Glass Menagerie*. On television, she occasionally surfaced as a guest star in shows like *Family Affair* (CBS, 1965–71) and *Love, American Style* (ABC, 1969–74).

Unfortunately, Sothern's later years were often plagued with physical pain, much of it the aftermath of an injury she sustained in 1973, while starring in a dinner theater production in Florida. A piece of scenery crashed down on the actress during her opening night performance in the lightweight comedy *Everybody Loves Opal,* injuring her back. Sothern ultimately sued the theater owners, and collected a settlement, but her ability to walk was permanently impaired. She would use a cane for the remainder of her life.

More than most of her Golden Age peers from MGM, Sothern still found herself employable as a film actress in the 1970s. However, she did so, in part, by making herself available for roles that other leading ladies might have spurned. The low-budget thriller *The Killing Kind* (1973), released near the end of the "Scream Queen" cycle that had begun with Davis and Crawford's *What Ever Happened to Baby Jane?* (1962), cast Sothern as the blowsy, world-weary mother of a recently released convict (played by a young John Savage) who goes on a killing spree.

The Killing Kind's icky poster art, prominently featuring a limp rat being dangled by the tail, should have served notice to *Maisie* and *Susie* fans who might have ventured into the theater on the strength of Sothern's star billing. Those who forged ahead might have been a bit shell-shocked at the sight of their favorite leading lady being told by her onscreen son that she's "nothing but a fat old whore," or at Sothern playing the weirdly incestuous mom who cackles with delight when she snaps a candid photo of her adult son naked in the shower. Then there's the scene in which Sothern pays a $2 fee to drop off a trash can at the local dump—one that's stuffed with the corpse of future *Laverne & Shirley* star Cindy Williams. (Sothern grimaces expressively when, safely past the dump attendant, she notices that a limp arm is dangling from the bag).

If *The Killing Kind* was not Sothern's most dignified outing as an actress, it does have some moments of stylistic interest, thanks to director Curtis Harrington, and is something of a cult favorite today with horror buffs. Sothern herself, who'd long professed her fondness for character roles, was happy with the film itself, if not with its marketing. "It was a wonderful part," she said. "The film was distributed so badly that it never got the recognition it deserved."[27]

Nor did she denigrate *Crazy Mama* (1975), a cheap action film she made for veteran drive-in movie producer/director Roger Corman's company. Most appreciated today as an example of the early accomplishments of the young Jonathan Demme, *Mama* cast Sothern as the matriarch of a family that turns to crime during the Depression, opposite leading lady Cloris Leachman and ingénue Linda Purl. Sothern had lots of screen time, but little of interest to do. She made the film a year or so after her on-stage injury, and is conspicuously absent from most of the fast-paced action scenes. Later, as film offers lessened, she gradually moved into smaller roles, in forgettable productions like *The Little Dragons* (1980), and higher-budgeted stinkers like *The Manitou* (1978).

In 1987, after Sothern's shows had sat on the shelf for years, trade papers announced that the Nickelodeon cable network had acquired rerun rights to *Susie* and *The Ann Sothern Show*. The recently developed Nick at Nite service, which beamed classic sitcom reruns aimed at baby boomers on Nickelodeon's evening schedule, was an ideal outlet for rediscovering the actress' work. "(These) are the first series about working women," said network vice-president Linda Kahn in announcing the deal. "Mary Tyler Moore and all the others came later."[28] *Susie*, in particular, would continue to play for several years to come.

Also raising Sothern's profile that year was her best screen acting job in years, a co-starring role in the Bette Davis—Lillian Gish drama *The Whales of August,* which also featured Vincent Price. Director Lindsay Anderson, having seen Sothern play a featured role in the 1985 TV remake of *Letter to Three Wives*, offered her a role in his character drama about elderly sisters living together in Maine. She so charmed producer Mike Kaplan that he overcame some initial hesitation about her mobility, as she was still walking rather painfully with a cane. To Sothern, once she saw that the character's name, like that of her real-life daughter, was Tisha, it seemed that the role in *The Whales of August* was meant to be hers.

The Whales of August was something of an oddity in the youth-obsessed 1980s, with Sothern, by then in her late 70s, flanked by a cast almost entirely made up of her contemporaries (or those, like Gish, older than she). Playing a longtime friend and neighbor of sisters Sarah Webber (Gish) and Libby Strong (Davis), Sothern livens up the proceedings considerably with her candor and humor. (Upon arriving for a visit, and not seeing Libby, she asks, "Where's the old warhorse?")

Later, the three ladies enjoy a little gossip—"You will *never* guess who finally got a hearing aid!" Sothern exclaims, while Gish sighs over the unexpected death of a mutual friend, who died "so young"—though Davis points out the lady in question was over eighty. Although Sothern's screen time is limited, she gets the opportunity to create a full-fledged character, tearing up at one point over the suspension of her driver's license, summoning up an appreciative smile for the gentlemanly attentions of Price, and sprinkling her dialogue with a Maine "ayuh" now and then.

The movie set was not without tensions. Bette Davis played the cantankerous old lady even when the cameras weren't turning, endearing herself to few of her colleagues. Sothern, on the other hand, played poker with the film crew, did her work with a minimum of fuss, and walked away with an Oscar nomination for Best Supporting Actress (though she correctly predicted that she would not take home the award). Despite the critical acclaim, and warm reception from moviegoers and critics happy to see her showcased again, it was her last film role.

In 1999, on the eve of Sothern's 90th birthday, she was honored with a retrospective at the Museum of Modern Art, showcasing *A Letter to Three Wives* and ten more noteworthy selections from her more than 70 feature films. By that time, she had also been discovered by feminist scholars, who noted the intelligence and independence of the characters she played in the 1950s and earlier.

She spent her final years at home in her beloved Ketchum, Idaho, where she had lived full time since 1984, preferring to be away from the traffic, crime, and hubbub of Hollywood. The woman who had once owned five businesses was content to settle down in a rented house, saying, "I don't want to own anything anymore."[29] Aside from daughter Tisha, who is today a florist in nearby Hailey, Sothern had four cats to keep her company. Frustrated by the limitations of her body as she aged, she plowed ahead nonetheless. "I'm exactly like my grandmother," she told a reporter in 1987. "She lived to be 93. She never gave up. They pulled the sheet over her three times, and she pulled it down."[30]

Her prediction proved accurate. On March 15, 2001, Sothern died of heart failure at the age of 92. Despite her many successes, she was disappointed that she hadn't been allowed to accomplish more, saying, "I think Hollywood has been terrible to me. Hollywood doesn't respond to a strong woman, not at all. I was too independent. How dare a woman be competitive or produce her own shows?"[31]

♦ 9 ♦

Gale Storm

My Little Margie and *The Gale Storm Show: Oh! Susanna*

ALTHOUGH HER SHOWS SELDOM EARNED kudos from TV critics, and were conspicuously absent from the annual Emmy nominations, Gale Storm was a favorite of 1950s TV audiences, who consistently tuned in for the unpretentious fun they found on *My Little Margie* (CBS and NBC, 1952–55) and, later, *The Gale Storm Show: Oh! Susanna* (CBS and ABC, 1956–60). Not only did Storm's fans faithfully watch her sitcoms, they also bought her records, placing her on the *Billboard* charts as a pop singer, and later knew her as one of the first celebrities to talk unashamedly about her alcoholism and successful rehabilitation.

Before becoming a sitcom star in the early 1950s, Storm was a reliable B-movie player who enlivened a string of mostly low-budget genre films. Born on April 5, 1922, as Josephine Cottle, Storm grew up in rural Texas, her family often strapped for money. Nevertheless, the actress remembers her upbringing with fondness. "I'm sure life wasn't easy for Mother," she later wrote. "She was a seamstress and worked long hours, but she was serene and so were we. There just wasn't any pettiness in the Cottles."[1]

Looking back, she would comment, "You hear a lot about people 'going Hollywood.' That could only happen to those who've never had a secure childhood, a teenage where the values are sound. I was lucky. And all of you are lucky who live in a home where there's love and faith. Don't ever sell it short. It's something no money in the world can buy."[2]

Though enjoying chances to perform in school plays, Storm never entertained serious thoughts of a performing career. But in 1939, while still in high school, she gave in to the urging of two of her teachers, and entered a *Star Search*–type talent contest called "Gateway to Hollywood." This CBS radio show, produced as a tie-in with RKO Pictures, offered unknowns auditioned in regional competitions around the United States a shot at a movie contract.

The show's ultimate winners would be a young man and woman chosen to assume the pre-selected screen names Terry Belmont and Gale Storm. Finalists from around the country were sent to Hollywood, where each week three different pairs performed in brief playlets for CBS radio listeners. Against all odds, the teenager representing Texas emerged victorious. On December 31, 1939, she was presented with her RKO contract and membership in the Screen Actors' Guild, both bearing the stage name that seemed to have been invented by a weatherman, Gale Storm.

"At the time I was so impressed, I didn't even see the humor in the name," she later recalled. "It was so exciting and so thrilling. It's like a Cinderella story."[3] Adding to the fairy-tale quality was her real-life romance with "Terry Belmont"—her fellow "Gateway to Hollywood" winner, aspiring actor Lee Bonnell, whom she married on September 28, 1941.

Storm's tenure as an RKO contract player would be brief. She made her film debut in a minor role in *Tom Brown's School Days* (1940), and then advanced to playing the female lead in *One Crowded Night* the same year. While launching her acting career, she simultaneously worked to complete her senior year of high school in RKO's studio school.

Unfortunately for Storm, the fast track to stardom that the radio show seemed to promise didn't pan out. "I lasted a fast six months on the contract I won," she said, "and out I flew."[4] Having reaped the full benefit of the radio show publicity, the studio let Storm go, telling her that they did not see a substantial future for her in the industry. Bonnell, who'd fared no better, would soon leave the acting profession altogether. His wife, however, persisted.

While the "Gateway to Hollywood" proved no great boon at RKO, the tenacious young actress had gotten her foot in the door, and parlayed her skimpy resume into jobs at other studios. She would appear in three dozen films between 1940 and 1952, most of them low-budget genre films. Sure that a Texas-born girl could ride, studio executives assigned her to B Western films like Roy Rogers' *Red River Valley* (1941).

In 1942, she signed a contract at the Poverty Row studio Monogram, where she was cast in quickies like the East Side Kids comedy *Smart Alecks* (1942). In the early 1940s, moviegoers could see her multiple times per year in low-rent Monogram vehicles. Her comedy *Nearly Eighteen,* for example, issued on November 12, 1943, was followed seven days later by the release of a musical, *Campus Rhythm*. After that, eager fans had to bide their time until January, when *Where Are Your Children?*, a drama about juvenile delinquency, appeared.

Low-budget films had no time or patience for star temperament—Storm later recalled that the studio wouldn't even allow actors to watch dailies of the films being shot, for fear they'd demand retakes that definitely weren't in Monogram's minuscule budgets. (Only by pleading with producer Lindsley Parsons—"I just nagged at him, nicely, until I wore him down"[5]—was she allowed to view dailies, which she treated as a learning opportunity).

Her specialty was the "six-day wonder"—the B films cranked out in less than a week. The schedule was intense—she remembers that on one such film, they reached the end of the last day of shooting without having filmed the entire script. At Monogram, extra shooting days were out of the question, and so what had been completed was somehow edited into a releasable film, minus the missing footage.

Grateful for the career opportunities she'd been given, and held in higher regard at the low-rent studio than she might have been at a classier operation, Storm worked steadily and happily throughout the 1940s, earning a reputation as cheerful, cooperative, and extremely capable. Others might have been daunted by the workload, but Storm wasn't. "The hours weren't so bad," she says today. "I don't remember feeling overworked." Her ability to do creditable work on a tight shooting schedule would serve her in good stead as a sitcom star in the next decade.

Her own favorite vehicle of this period was the comic Western *The Dude Goes West* (1948), in which she co-starred with future *Green Acres* star Eddie Albert. She also had a fondness for the 1947 Christmas story *It Happened on 5th Avenue,* which enjoyed holiday reruns on TV for many years before *It's a Wonderful Life* became the perennial that it is today. More recently, she says that her horror melodrama, *Revenge of the Zombies* (1943), opposite John Carradine, has become a cult favorite for which she still receives frequent fan mail.

Glamorous Gale Storm attends a 1950s movie premiere with real-life husband Lee Bonnell.

While her career progressed at a steady if unspectacular pace, Storm also devoted herself to her family, which had grown with the birth of her first child, son Phillip, in the spring of 1942. Before the decade was out, she would add two more sons to her brood, interrupting her hectic moviemaking schedule only when sidelined by pregnancy and childbirth.

By the early 1950s, Storm's movie career was in a lull. Although she enjoyed working opposite future TV stars Eve Arden ("such a nice person to be with") and Donald O'Connor in *Curtain Call at Cactus Creek* (Universal, 1950), few noteworthy roles followed. By the spring of 1952, Storm was "at liberty," and, at the age of thirty, facing the possibility that her career had peaked.

Unbeknownst to her, producer Hal Roach, Jr. was then casting a sitcom to be called *My Little Margie,* centering on the relationship between an irrepressible young woman and her eligible bachelor father. The Roach Studios had earlier been home to the comic talents of Laurel and Hardy, and developed the *Our Gang* comedies, under the auspices of Hal Roach, Sr. His son wanted to establish the same type of leadership in TV comedy, and had begun to do so with *The Trouble with Father* (aka *The Stu Erwin Show),* which premiered as an ABC filmed series in the fall of 1950. The latest project, *Margie,* was being pitched to Philip Morris as a summer replacement for the sponsor's unexpectedly popular show *I Love Lucy,* which had just completed its first season.

Writer Frank Fox, who created the series' characters, was friendly with actress Marjorie Reynolds (later the TV wife of William Bendix on the 1953–58 NBC sitcom *The Life of Riley*), and Storm believes that he created "Margie" with her in mind. For reasons unknown, Reynolds wasn't cast in the role, however, and Roach was shopping for a star. Originally intended to be not much more than a place-holder, to keep the audience tuning in to CBS Monday nights at nine during *Lucy*'s summer hiatus, *Margie* needed not a temperamental, expensive star, but rather a recognizable face who could handle the show's comedy, and whose asking price was reasonable. Enter Gale Storm.

For the actress, by then a veteran of three dozen feature films, the offer to star in *My Little Margie* came out of the blue, and she wasn't certain why producer Roach had thought of her. He later told reporters he'd been aware of her work for some time. "I watched her for years," he explained, "and thought to myself that she had terrific possibilities that had never been exploited."[6]

Storm, shown a pilot script for the series, was hesitant, despite the fact that her movie career was going through a lull. She and her husband thought the script, which dealt with Margie's interference in her father's love life, "was pretty good, but we both thought the relationship between father and daughter seemed a little incestuous."[7] After a rewrite, she decided to take the plunge, signing on for an unimpressive $750 a week. Her co-star in the series would be Charles Farrell (1901–1990), a popular movie leading man of the late 1920s and early 1930s who'd done little or no acting in recent years.

My Little Margie cast its star as 21-year-old Margie Albright, who lived in New York City with her widowed father, an investment counselor. Not unlike Lucy Ricardo, Margie was an inveterate schemer, someone who constantly found herself mixed up in a mess (often of her own making), and could unfailingly develop a wild and impulsive plan to handle the situation. Her father Vern, whose function in the series was not terribly different from the husbands in *I Love Lucy* and *I Married Joan,* tried in vain to keep Margie under control, and her nose out of his business.

Storm had done comparatively little comedy in her days as a movie ingénue, and credits *Margie* director Hal Yates as a mentor. "I thought comedy was something you had a flair for, or you happened to have good timing," she says. "I had no idea that there were definite rules. It's a whole field of learning that Hal Yates knew. He was just a master at that." One of his key rules was that comedy required a brisk pace, and he kept his *Margie* actors hopping.

Storm did in fact have comedic gifts that the show spotlighted. She gave her TV character beauty, charm, and an uninhibited sense of fun. Like *I Married Joan,* which would make its bow a few months later, *My Little Margie* was nobody's idea of a highbrow show. Even *I Love Lucy* had more claim to substance and character development than Storm's and Davis' shows. The plots on *Margie* were pure fluff, a grab bag of mistaken identities, convenient coincidences, punches thrown, and setups for sight gags. Viewers lapped it up.

Critics, on the other hand, didn't cut the show much slack. After viewing the introductory episode, which aired on June 16, 1952, *Variety* predicted that *Lucy* fans would tune out, criticizing Storm's show for its "contrived situations and overly-coy dialog."[8] As the show continued to play out its thirteen-week summer run, however, ratings made it clear that viewers disagreed. The unambitious summer replacement sitcom was a bona fide hit. It was too late to find the show a spot on CBS' fall 1952 schedule, but it was clear that the audience wanted to see more.

When CBS was unable to find a vacant time slot for its unexpected hit, *Margie* resurfaced on NBC in October, in a 7:30 P.M. Saturday slot. By early 1953, CBS obliged Philip Morris with a spot for what was by then being acknowledged as "one of the prize situation comedy properties,"[9] having recently gone as high as #2 in the Nielsen ratings. In January, *Margie* jumped to a 10 P.M. Thursday berth.

The leapfrogging from network to network, and time slot to time slot, wasn't doing much to help the show maintain its following, and Philip Morris dropped its sponsorship at the end of the 1952-53 season. Some observers thought they'd seen the last of *My Little Margie*, but once again the little show that could would prove to be stronger than expected.

Scott Paper, which had been sponsoring a musical variety show on NBC, abruptly resurrected *Margie* in the fall of 1953. NBC placed Storm's show in a more favorable early evening time slot, as part of a Wednesday sitcom block that found it following the compatible *I Married Joan*. The combination gave fans of sitcoms—and funny ladies—a pleasant hour of undemanding fun that was very easy to take.

Aside from Storm and Farrell, the show drew on a larger-than-usual supporting cast, with five recurring characters aside from Margie and her father, not all of whom would be seen in any given episode. Vern's boss George Honeywell (played by Clarence Kolb) was a crotchety older man who, not unlike Larry Tate in the later *Bewitched* (ABC, 1964–72) left the show's leading man in weekly peril of losing his job. Elderly neighbor Mrs. Odetts (Gertrude W. Hoffman) was Margie's loyal sidekick, who, unlike *Lucy*'s Ethel Mertz, was always game for another crazy stunt and entered into them with relish.

Veteran African-American comic actor Willie Best played the apartment house's friendly elevator operator and general handyman, Charlie. It was a slightly more dignified role than some the talented actor had essayed in movies of the 1930s and 1940s, where he was cast as a succession of Stepin Fetchit-type porters and other characters generally addressed as "boy." With his character not seen in every episode, Best alternated this gig with a similar one on ABC's *The Stu Erwin Show* (1950–54), also filmed on the lot, and eventually with yet a third role on the syndicated adventure series *Waterfront*. Both Margie and her father had off-and-on love interests. Hers was genial, not especially bright Freddie Wilson (Don Hayden), whose inability to get and hold a steady job made him the object of Vern's scorn. Vern, meanwhile, kept company with attractive neighbor Roberta Townsend (Hillary Brooke), though he seemed in no hurry to make a commitment.

Most *Margie* episodes followed a fairly basic formula that found father and daughter scheming against one another, with the original scheme often received with a retaliatory counterattack. In "A Horse for Vern" (5/14/53), for example, Vern and Freddie conspire to put a damper on Margie's burgeoning relationship with a newspaper journalist, and her aspirations of becoming a cub reporter. When the men compromise Margie's credibility with her new beau by tricking her into reporting a wild horse loose in the apartment building, and then promptly hide the horse in question, Margie soon realizes she's been had.

Her own, even more elaborate scheme, enacted with the help of her reporter friend, soon has her father convinced that the disappearing horse incident has traumatized Margie, requiring the care of a psychiatrist. The phony psychiatrist recommends a remedy that first requires Vern to act out the presence of an invisible horse (to soothe his "disturbed" daughter), and then allow the real horse to sleep in their tenth-floor apartment, and join them for breakfast in the dining room. Naturally, boss Mr. Honeywell shows up with an important client, as he so often does, just in time to find Vern Albright pulling another crazy stunt, and, once again, barking, "Albright, you're fired!"

Unlike Lucy Ricardo, who tended to wind up with the short end of the stick by the end of most episodes, Margie Albright almost always emerged victorious from the weekly butting of heads with *her* male authority figure. When Vern, who does not want her to go on a trip, is unable to prevent her doing so, Honeywell suggests "one good swat with an old-fashioned razor strap" to bring her into line. Instead, they invent "Margie's Phantom Lover" (10/28/53), a secret admirer whose invitation to a rendezvous disrupts Margie's travel plans. Naturally, she soon grows wise to the gag, and leaves both her father and his boss with egg on their faces by episode's end. "I wonder if they'll ever learn not to try and trick Margie," she says with a satisfied grin.

If the show occasionally relied too heavily on far-out plots and wild coincidences, its saving grace was Storm, who played every scene with infectious enthusiasm. Another typically zany episode, "Corpus Delecti" (3/23/55), begins when Margie buys an old trunk at Charlie's church rummage sale. Margie finds a mysterious diary in the trunk, and thinks she's reading the written confessions of a murderer. Meanwhile, the writer of the diary, a novelist and screenwriter who coincidentally happens to be Vern's latest client, is desperate to retrieve it. Roping in Freddie, who's an aspiring detective, Margie tracks the author of the diary to a deserted movie studio. In the episode's fantastic final act, everyone winds up on a haunted house set, the kind that features spooky portraits with eyes cut out over the fireplace, and a hidden trap door in the floor. Once a gun or two has been drawn, and a vase crashed over Vern's head, each cast member in turn falls through the trap door into a giant net in the basement, and the episode is over.

Although the physical comedy Storm was given on *Margie* was a bit less restrained than what Lucille Ball or Joan Davis often tackled, nonetheless costumes, funny accents, and disguises were all in a day's work for the star, who in various episodes impersonates Vern's twelve-year-old daughter, an opera singer, a hillbilly, and a countess, among others. Still, starring in a raucous comedy had its risks. In October 1952, *Variety* reported that Storm "was kayoed when assistant director Nate Watt, indicating to audience of extras count of the ref during a wrestling match scene, accidentally brought his fist down on her, scoring a knockout."[10]

Storm doesn't remember that particular incident, but vividly recalls another one, in which the script called for her to struggle with a bad guy, trying to push a door closed in his face. A mistimed cue by the other actor resulted in his fist smashing into the actress' face. "He broke my nose," she says, remembering that she had to be rushed to the MGM studios for treatment, because the Roach facilities lacked an infirmary or medical personnel.

Even worse, though not for the star herself, was the accident that occurred during the filming of "Buried Treasure" (4/2/53). The script called for Margie to fall from a ceiling skylight while trying to throw a net over a couple of jewel thieves. Stunts of this type were accomplished with the use of a double, so Storm was able to go home while her stand-in took the fall. Thanks to faulty set construction, the stunt was more dangerous than it should have been, and Storm was horrified to learn the next day that her double had broken her back in the fall.

As Lucy Ricardo had her famous "spider" sound, Margie too had a way of expressing her dismay and frustration. When things were headed to hell in a hand basket for Margie, as they often were by the show's midway point, Storm would turn and look into the camera, making a gurgling, saliva-sloshing sound that became her trademark. "Wherever I would go, people would ask me to gurgle," she remembered. "It wasn't the classiest of sounds, but everyone loved it."[11]

If we credit *All in the Family* (CBS, 1971–79) as being a groundbreaking attempt to bring realism to the world of the TV sitcom, *My Little Margie* was surely the anti–*All in the Family,* the show that did its darndest to steer clear of same. Viewers never knew or cared whether Margie and her father were Democrats or Republicans, and if the characters had any opinions on the then-current Korean War, they kept them to themselves. *My Little Margie* was pure, unadulterated escapist entertainment.

It's the prototype of the show that scholars and media critics would later call upon to demonstrate what was wrong with television, and with the images of women on TV. Margie, as critics were quick to point out, was a young woman who didn't seem to have a job, or any serious career aspirations, and whose principal goal in life seemed to be to find a man. For those who wanted television comedy to be sophisticated, erudite, or reflective of the problems and concerns of contemporary life, criticizing the zany plots and innocent situations of *My Little Margie* was all too easy.

Did viewers tune in hoping to see stark reality? Not likely. Storm's show was never intended to be anything more than light entertainment, and at that it was quite successful. Though it's commonly said that the female sitcom characters of the 1950s were not overly imbued with brains, Margie is actually pretty clever, certainly more so than her father (who's somewhat reminiscent of *The Mary Tyler Moore Show*'s Ted Baxter in his handsome vacuousness). Her boyfriend Freddie was generally running neck-and-neck with Vern in the numbskull sweepstakes.

Nor can she be considered in any way downtrodden. Like other sitcom heroines of the era, Margie paid a minimal amount of lip service to the social codes of the day, such as the idea that she abides by her father's rules. Having done so, she then proceeds to do exactly as she pleases, her father helpless to prevent her. In "Margie and the Shah" (5/12/54), when Vern wants to keep his daughter from meeting a promising new client, it costs him a hefty bribe—"Just let me handle this business all by myself, and you get [a] new car, and a new wardrobe besides." Minutes later, she's been smuggled into the Shah's hotel suite in a laundry basket, dressed herself up as one of his harem of dancing girls, and is soon being offered a chance at becoming his sixty-sixth wife.

By the end of each episode, of course, everything came out all right. Each segment closed with a scene in which Margie and Vern's framed photo came to life, and the two stars exchanged a final bit of dialogue. Inevitably, after a few choice words from Storm, Farrell would say ruefully but lovingly, "That's my little Margie!" (Though, given Farrell's Boston-bred accent, the *r* was largely missing from "Margie").

Once it was clear that *My Little Margie* had caught on, even critics finally began to acknowledge that there might be *something* there—as when *Variety*, a year after publishing its initial pan, called the show "network quality programming ... [that has] proven its value as a property by the way it catapulted Gale Storm back into the public eye."[12] Another writer, Storm recalls, said of the show, "Nobody likes it but the people."

Unlike later sitcom stars who found the work confining, or disparaged their TV stardom, Storm was happy with *Margie*. "I loved the character, I loved my coworkers, I loved the show, I loved doing it," she later said. "I'd get tired, but I'd wake up every morning looking forward to the day's work."[13] Nor did she apologize for the show's focus on lightweight entertainment.

Much as she enjoyed the sitcom, Storm readily admits that the workload was demanding, much more so than her B movie work at Monogram in the 1940s. She and her colleagues shot two episodes of *My Little Margie* back-to-back each week, working every weekday and Saturdays. "You really had to love it to live through it," Storm says.

On the set from early morning until late in the day,

Gale Storm studying the script with *My Little Margie* co-star Charles Farrell (Vern).

she had little time even to learn lines. Falling into bed at night, "I'd put the script on my chest, and hope I got it by osmosis," she says with a laugh. Fortunately, she was able to remember the words with little rehearsal—"thank the Lord, that came easily to me." On the other hand, she remembers co-star Charlie Farrell struggling to get his lines down. "He would always have the pages from the next scene in his jacket pocket," she says, which allowed the actor some impromptu study anytime there was even a momentary break in the shooting schedule.

Unlike *I Love Lucy*, Storm's show was a "one-camera" sitcom, which was not played to a live audience. "We filmed *Margie* just as you film a motion picture," she explains. The method used was tiring for actors, as it required them to play scenes over and over, while different camera angles were captured. So that the film could be edited together seamlessly, it was important for Storm to repeat her actions each time exactly as she had before. Under those circumstances, the energy and spontaneity that she brings to her performances is even more impressive.

With her hectic workload, Storm says she never took the time to wonder whether she might have preferred doing a three-camera show in front of a studio audience. If anything, "I think it would have been a lot easier," she says today. She liked her co-stars—"everybody was very considerate, there was no jealousy"—but admits that the busy workday kept them from becoming close on a personal level.

My Little Margie show was so popular that, in a reverse of the usual circumstances of the early 1950s, the TV *Margie* spawned a radio offshoot. At first, when the possibility of a radio show was raised, she balked, protesting with good reason that there was no room left in her schedule. Hal Roach, Jr. grudgingly rearranged shooting of the TV episodes in order to accommodate the radio assignment.

Although some executives tried to maximize their profits by doing radio and TV versions using the same scripts, Storm and Farrell would instead star in original *Margie* segments for radio. Rather than using the TV supporting cast, however, radio's *Margie*, which would be broadcast live, featured seasoned talent from that medium, including Doris Singleton and Verna Felton of TV's *December Bride*. *Margie* also spawned a popular comic book series that would far outlast the show's original network run, surviving into the 1960s.

Some of Storm's contemporaries (like Lucille Ball and Joan Davis) were much more highly paid as sitcom stars than she was for *Margie*. She was amused when a fan magazine proclaimed her to be "the richest person in Hollywood." Still, she was earning what in most 1950s households would have been an astronomical salary, and was careful to see that her husband's pride wasn't threatened. "I learned very quickly to be really stupid about money," she says today. Though she was the primary breadwinner, husband Lee Bonnell gave her career guidance and emotional support, also handling her funds in addition to his work as an insurance agent.

Fortunately for Storm, she had never prized the financial rewards of movie or TV stardom over her personal life. "I wasn't working for the money," she explains. "I wasn't that aware of the money. I never had time to shop, anyway!"

Storm shot 126 episodes of the popular sitcom between 1952 and 1955. At the end of the show's third full season, Scott Paper executives pulled the plug on *Margie*, opting instead to sponsor a newer show called *Father Knows Best*, which would be moving to NBC after a season of so-so ratings on CBS.

My Little Margie's inventory immediately went on the auction block. A popular sitcom with a goodly bundle of episodes available was a hot property for the syndication market in 1955. *Margie* was ultimately sold to Official Films, which also acquired *The Stu Erwin Show* from Roach in the same deal. Storm's sitcom would quickly become one of the most frequently rerun shows of the decade, filling countless half hours on local stations across the country. When one of the first stations to air the show, the NBC affiliate in Philadelphia, drew the highest ratings of its entire daytime schedule with Monday-through-Friday *Margie* episodes, other stations were quick to follow suit. *Variety* reported that New York's WCBS paid $225,000 for the rights to five airings of the 126 *Margie* films, a hefty sum for the time but cheaper than the costs of producing local programming was by then.

In the wake of the show's cancellation, Storm launched an unexpected second career when she became a recording artist. She'd played her first professional singing gig a couple of years earlier, headlining a well-received musical act in Las Vegas. That led to bookings on TV variety shows. In the fall of 1955, shortly after *Margie* concluded its original run, Storm recorded her first song for Dot Records. Her cover of "I Hear You Knocking," released that October, would net the star a gold record. The songs she recorded were mostly chosen for her by her producer, Randy Wood. Although she doesn't have a favorite among them—"I don't believe in favorites," she says—she would place five more singles on the charts before winding down her brief recording career in 1957. Records like "Teen Age Prayer" and "Dark Moon" were promoted in the mid–1950s through her TV guest appearances with Milton Berle and Perry Como, among others.

Although she would soon curtail her career as a pop singer, largely because of husband Lee Bonnell's jealousy of the record producer with whom she worked, Storm was still popular with TV audiences. Busy with guest appearances and musical performances in 1956, she'd shied away from the possibility of a second TV series, leery of jumping back into the intense work schedule that a sitcom entailed.

Despite her hesitation, however, she couldn't resist an offer that came her way that spring, courtesy of former *Margie* colleague Lee Karson. His pitch consisted not of a sample script, or even a series outline. What he brought the star was a magazine ad.

"All he had was the back cover of a *Time* magazine with a beautiful luxury liner ad," Storm recalled. "It spoke of all the wonderful places and how your social director would see to it you had a grand time. A marvelous idea for a series because you could go anywhere."[14] If that wasn't temptation enough, Karson added that the series would naturally lend itself to sequences in which Storm could sing. She was sold, as was Hal Roach, Jr., who readily entered into a second major production with Storm.

Given Storm's track record, Nestlé quickly signed to sponsor the fledgling series, which would debut on CBS in the fall of 1956. Officially titled *The Gale Storm Show*, it would later be syndicated under its better-remembered subtitle, *Oh! Susanna*. Storm's character was named Susanna Pomeroy in order to justify the title. As it happened, Storm was pregnant when filming was set to begin, and would name her new daughter after her second TV character.

Also featured in *The Gale Storm Show* was the veteran movie comedienne ZaSu Pitts, who would play Susanna's best friend and "Ethel Mertz," Nugey, employed in the ship's beauty salon. For Pitts, working at the Roach Studio was like old home week. In the 1930s, she'd co-starred opposite Thelma Todd in a series of comedy shorts produced by Hal Roach, Sr. Pitts' expressive hands had long been her best-known feature, though she denied "fluttering" them, and said, "I never consciously plan to move them in any special way. They just go by themselves."[15]

Roy Roberts, in a characterization not unlike what he would later contribute to *The Lucy Show* (CBS, 1962–68) as stuffy bank president Mr. Cheever, played Susanna's boss, ship's captain Hurley. For the first three seasons, there was also a teddibly British steward, Cedric, played by Jimmy Fairfax, who was often a willing participant in Susanna's schemes.

A bit more settled than Margie Albright, Storm's new character was a fun-loving, impulsive, but basically responsible working woman who had a tendency to take a bit too much interest in the lives of her passengers. Late 1970s viewers who thought that ABC's *The Love Boat* (1977–86) was a fresh new concept might have been surprised to encounter *The Gale Storm Show*, which CBS would even air at the same night and time (Saturdays at 9 P.M.) that Aaron Spelling's show would later inhabit.

In an innovative format for the time, *The Gale Storm Show* would include a musical sequence in every third episode. Given that Susanna's job responsibilities entailed planning entertainment for the ship's passengers, as well as the star's singing ability, this was a logical feature that enhanced the show's appeal.

The show opened every week with the sound of a horn emitting from the ship's smokestack, followed by a view of Storm smiling through a porthole, then looking to the side, where ship's flags flapping in the breeze turned over to spell out the show's title. Seen later was a shot of each of Storm's co-stars in turn, spouting, "Oh, Susanna!," to which the star would cheerily reply, "Someone call me? I'll be with you in a moment!"

Storm had been somewhat underestimated since the days of *My Little Margie*, and in some ways for much of her career. Naysayers were surprised when *The Gale Storm Show* emerged as the actress' second hit series, drawing strong numbers despite considerable Saturday night competition from Lawrence Welk on ABC and Sid Caesar on NBC. Although not initially a Top Twenty show, *The Gale Storm Show: Oh, Susanna!* would attain that status during the 1957-58 season, when it landed in 16th place.

At a time when several big-name comedians were seeing their ratings drop, and when other sitcoms were falling by the wayside, *TV Guide* questioned why Storm's show was doing so well. Never one to take herself too seriously, the star provided a ready answer:

"The reason *Oh! Susanna* is so popular," she helpfully explained, "is because nobody watches it—so nobody complains. It's quite simple."[16] Pressed to expound on this theory, the actress admitted that her show's romantic and appealing setting might also be a factor in its popularity.

Thirty-five when the show began, Storm played a more adult character in her second series than she had in *My Little Margie*. Still, in the great tradition of sitcom characters everywhere, Susanna is, of course, a well-intended buttinsky who can't resist involving herself with the passengers. Her boss, Captain Huxley, tries in vain to squelch this impulse, as in the early episode "Passenger Incognito" (10/13/56):

HUXLEY: Now, for the millionth time, will you tell me what your job is?
SUSANNA (*holding up her hand as if taking an oath*): To entertain our passengers at all times.
HUXLEY: And *not* do what?
SUSANNA: And not to meddle in their private lives, nor try to solve their personal problems.
HUXLEY: I have never heard it said more insincerely!

Naturally, in the very next scene, she takes on the challenge of bringing a plain–Jane passenger (played by future *Beverly Hillbillies* "Jane" Nancy Kulp) out of her shell, taking her in for a makeover and spreading a rumor that she's really a countess traveling incognito.

Also a running theme in *The Gale Storm Show* was Susanna's own romantic life. A few weeks later, in "The Witch Doctor" (12/8/56), for example, Susanna takes an interest in a shy but handsome college professor who lacks the confidence to approach women. Taking him ashore when the ship docks, she persuades him to buy a love charm from a local witch doctor (in fact a relocated American, played by soon-to-be *Rifleman* Chuck Connors). Scornful of such superstitious nonsense, he begrudgingly agrees to wear the pendant. Trying to give him the extra bit of confidence he needs to make friends with some of the single women on board, Susanna flirts with him and boosts his confidence. Unfortunately for Susanna, whose boss has a tendency to show up just when she's making a little headway with the eligible bachelor, her would-be suitor warms up to a fellow passenger instead of her.

Publicity photo for *The Gale Storm Show: Oh! Susanna*.

The ambience of foreign travel that Storm's show attempted to convey was largely an illusion, as the series never left the soundstage. A set representing the *Ocean Queen*'s deck was perhaps the most frequently used, with Captain Huxley's office and the ship's dining room also seen regularly. Shore visits were largely depicted with the use of stock footage to set a scene, followed by a jump to an indoor set depicting a cafe or shop in the port city. Occasionally the studio's set designers would convert the soundstage into a facsimile of the Swiss Alps, or whatever other exotic setting was needed.

At lunchtime every day, she watched dailies of the previous day's work, as she had done since her employment at Monogram. "It's very easy when you're working so hard and so fast to fall into habits of overdoing—or underdoing," she explains. By doing her "homework" during her lunch hour, she felt more comfortable that she was keeping her characterization on track.

While Storm's recording career was still active, *The Gale Storm Show* also served as an effective promotional vehicle for her singles. The second-season opener, "Pat on the Back" (9/14/57), paired her with fellow Dot Records stalwart Pat Boone, whose *Pat Boone—Chevy Showroom* series premiered on ABC a couple of weeks later. The tuneful half hour featured the duo singing a duet of Boone's song "Would You Like to Take a Walk?" as well as individual solos for each, Storm's in a dream sequence in which Susanna fantasizes about a recording career. The main plot, which largely took a back seat to the music, concerned Susanna's attempts to spotlight Boone in a musical show on board, threatened by his confinement to sick bay with a diagnosis of measles. Susanna is, of course, not so easily dissuaded, and fills in for the downed singer herself, lip-syncing to his record album while she's silhouetted behind an opaque screen.

In 1959, *The Gale Storm Show* jumped to ABC, which would air a fourth season of the series, as well as retain the rerun rights to the show for two years, in a deal reported to be worth $2.5 million. The Roach Studios, in serious financial trouble, had sold the profitable show to Independent Television Corporation. Storm wasn't surprised when reports of Roach's problems surfaced. She'd seen him in the company of some "not very savory" associates, including one questionable character who visited the *Gale Storm Show* set and "was going to give me an emerald mine." (She's still waiting).

In hindsight, she says, "I think our show was paying for a lot of others." Warned that problems at the Roach studios were coming to a head, "we knew when they were going to lock the gates. We had to get all our sets off the lot and get them set up at Desilu," where the show's remaining episodes would be filmed.

ABC added Storm's still-popular sitcom to its Thursday night schedule, where sponsor Warner Lambert would use it to sell Listerine, and began "stripping" it in daytime reruns that would continue until 1961. That summer, awaiting the move to ABC, Storm sensed that her sitcom, despite its healthy ratings, had gotten off track. Wanting to pinpoint the problem, she asked cast and crew to take another look at the pilot episode that had originally sold the show to CBS three years earlier. "I knew we all needed a new grip on things," she said, "and boy, we got it."[17]

She sensed that the show's comedy and characterizations had grown too broad. "I remembered then the way I originally wanted Susanna to be. She was not a Margie. Susanna had to have intelligence and good taste or she couldn't hold down her job with an important steamship line."[18] Not exempting herself from criticism, Storm decided that her performances had grown too broad, and resolved to reel herself in. The show's producers also raised the budget allotted to scripts.

Despite the overhaul, during which supporting character Cedric fell by the wayside, critics were no more enchanted than they had ever been with the show, though its star sometimes received some grudging praise. Reviewing the fourth-season opener, *Variety* dismissed *Oh! Susanna* as "a haven for those who'd rather not look down the barrel of a rifle or maneuver their gray matter coping with pesky intellectual ideas. To 'escape,' viewers need only seek out Gale Storm."[19]

Ratings in the show's new berth on ABC were only so-so, despite being paired with the increasingly popular *Donna Reed Show,* and the show was canceled in the spring of 1960, after 126 episodes. Although the series vacated the prime time schedule that summer, viewers could still see Storm in reruns on ABC's afternoon schedule.

One of the biggest female sitcom stars of the 1950s, Storm would make a surprisingly quick exit from TV in the wake of her second sitcom's cancellation. In fact, she would be little seen on TV in the next decade, aside from frequent reruns of *My Little Margie* and *Oh! Susanna*. Although Storm herself preferred the latter show, it was the ubiquitous *Margie* for which she would always be best known. "I don't know why I'm not as well remembered for 'Susanna' as for 'Margie,'" she said years later, "but I'm not."[20]

She made two appearances on ABC's *Burke's Law* (1963–65), an early Aaron Spelling detective show that was among the first to introduce his guest-star policy that would later emerge on *The Love Boat* and *Fantasy Island*. In 1962, when Lucille Ball was having difficulty luring her sidekick Vivian Vance back to TV for *The Lucy Show,* Storm's name was said to be on the short list of candidates who could possibly take Vance's place, but nothing came of this. (Asked about this, she says she was never approached with an offer, though she has heard that such an idea was considered. "I don't know how I would have felt about it," she says about the prospect of playing such a role, though she knew Ball slightly, and liked her).

With few exceptions, Storm spent most of the 1960s and early 1970s pursuing her career onstage. Regional theater had become

Gale Storm dreaming up another fishy explanation for Captain Huxley (Roy Roberts) on *The Gale Storm Show: Oh! Susanna.*

extremely popular, and Storm welcomed the opportunity to share her gifts in productions of well-known shows like *The Unsinkable Molly Brown* and *Plaza Suite*. Having spent much of the 1950s playing to an audience composed of cameramen and other crew members, Storm enjoyed the live performances.

"It was hard work," she said of her theater days, "but there is a connection between a live actor and a live audience that is electric—more thrilling for the actor, I think, than any other kind of performance."[21]

By the 1970s, however, Storm's career, as well as her happy family life, was being threatened by her growing addiction to alcohol. Looking back, she would be unable to pinpoint exactly why she began to drink, as she was not unhappy with her life. But she had discovered, at midlife, after previously being a light drinker at best, that she liked the taste of vodka. Soon she was hooked.

Her initial efforts at treatment failed. "I went through three hospitals," she recalls. "They didn't know what to do with an alcoholic then." Detoxed while hospitalized, she found that the impact was short-lived. "I'd go home and I'd just make a beeline for the bottle." Nor was psychotherapy the answer.

She was ashamed of her inability to stop drinking. "At that time, alcoholism was really a stigma for women," she points out. Alcoholics were often regarded as being weak-willed, rather than sick.

In January 1979, Storm checked into Raleigh Hills Hospital in Oxnard, California.

Compounding her embarrassment over entering yet another treatment program was the celebrity factor, as she was readily recognized by other patients and hospital staff. "If I could have crawled under the rug, I would have," she says today of her initial visit to the facility. "I was just so humiliated."

Unbeknownst to Storm, however, the recovery program she was entering would be a turning point in her life. The program at Raleigh Hills Hospital used an intense form of aversion therapy that would permanently cure her taste for liquor. "After the fifth day, you felt like you could smell someone pouring a drink five miles away, and it's revolting!" she says. "I knew when I finished those treatments that it was done."

Just as important as the method of treatment was the outlook on alcoholism that she was given at Raleigh Hills. There she was told for the first time that alcoholism should be regarded as a disease, a belief not universally held in the 1970s. "That was like being given the greatest gift in the world," she says, emphasizing that for the first time she was able to begin letting go of her shame about her illness.

Storm says that, in the quarter-century since, she has never fallen off the wagon. "I never had 'white-knuckle' sobriety. I never ever needed it [liquor] or wanted it again." On the road to recovery in mid–1979, Storm made her most noteworthy public appearance in several years when she turned up as a guest star in an episode of *The Love Boat* aired in early November. It was a fitting tribute from a show that had often been compared to Storm's 1950s sitcom.

In early 1980 came the first of several TV commercials for the Raleigh Hills hospital chain that Storm would film. She was not asked by the hospital to do endorsements; "I begged to do those commercials." At a time when few celebrities talked openly about their addictions, Storm courageously "outed" herself in the hopes that others in her predicament would be encouraged to seek help. For those who remembered her fondly as girlish Margie Albright, it was a bit of a shock to see where life had taken Gale Storm. The publicity helped the hospital chain expand, reaching thousands of new patients, and Storm is proud of the times she was told that her candor led to someone seeking treatment. She later accepted a position as a consultant to the hospital chain, cutting ribbons at new facilities being opened, and regrets that management problems within the company, which she attributes to one highly placed executive, have since led to its demise.

Back in the spotlight, Storm not only made a second appearance on *The Love Boat*, but published her memoirs, *I Ain't Down Yet*, co-authored with Bill Libby, in 1981. She would continue to accept occasional TV acting jobs, such as a 1989 appearance on *Murder, She Wrote*, over the next several years.

In 1994, *Dark Moon: The Best of Gale Storm* made several of her key Dot recordings from the 1950s available on CD, including "Teen Age Prayer" and "I Hear You Knocking." More recently, she has recorded an inspirational CD called "Poems from the Heart," featuring selections from Rudyard Kipling and Emily Dickinson as well as excerpts from the Bible.

On a personal note, her longtime marriage to Lee Bonnell, who had a successful career in insurance after giving up acting, came to an end with his death from a heart attack in May 1986. Two years later, the widowed actress married for a second time, to former television executive Paul Masterson. Her second marriage was also a happy one—"I showed him the best eight years of his life," she says with a smile—though briefer, as she was again widowed in 1996.

Now in her eighties, the talented actress and singer remains active, appearing in recent years at numerous film festivals and nostalgic events. She is appreciative of the support and encouragement she has receive from fans of her television work, several of whom she says have become "just like my extended family." Her official fan club, the Gale Storm Appreciation Society, publishes a newsletter, *Gale Lore*, and recently hosted 50th anniversary commemorations of *My Little Margie* and *The Gale Storm Show: Oh! Susanna*. She has a website, *www.galestorm.tv*, and is flattered by the e-mails she regularly receives complimenting her work.

She also takes pride in the influence she has had on female sitcom stars of a later generation. Storm remembers meeting Cindy Williams of *Laverne & Shirley* (ABC, 1976–83) at a collectors' show, when the younger actress made a point of seeking her out. "She was so cute," Storm recalls of Williams. "She hugged me, she picked me up, and said, 'I want you to know that I learned everything I know from you and your show.'"

Modest about her professional accomplishments, and recognizing her good fortune in coming from a modest background to enjoy the career she did, Storm is hesitant to take personal credit. "Whatever I've done in my career, it's something that God gave me," she says today. "God gifted me—and I don't mean that I'm so gifted. God just plucked me up by the scruff of my neck and put me where I was supposed to be."

❖ 10 ❖

Betty White

Life with Elizabeth and
Date with the Angels

NINE OF THE TEN WOMEN PROFILED in this book came to television after first establishing themselves in film or radio (often both). And then there's Betty White, who entered the entertainment industry in television's infancy, and became its first home-grown female sitcom star. Although today's audiences know her best for her later roles as Sue Ann Nivens on *The Mary Tyler Moore Show* (CBS, 1970–77) and Rose Nylund on *The Golden Girls* (1985–92), White was also a pioneer in the early days of TV with her syndicated sitcom *Life with Elizabeth*, a show in which she not only starred, but also served as co-producer. Since then, she has gone on to have an amazing career in the medium that has now passed the fifty-year mark.

Of her early work with television, White has said, "When I started in television in 1949, television was ... just getting off the ground, and we had no idea that it would change the world as it has, and it really has. We just thought it was a wonderful new toy that everybody had...."[1]

Born January 17, 1922, in Oak Park, Illinois, Betty Marion White, an only child, relocated to Los Angeles with parents Horace and Tess when she was a toddler. From them she inherited what would become a life-long passion for animals. Despite the financial restrictions imposed by the Depression, the White family at one point gave food and shelter to more than two dozen dogs. She also credits "a mother and father with a great sense of humor"[2] for influencing her later career choices.

Instilled in the young White from the beginning was an enthusiasm for trying whatever life had to offer. "The one really dirty word in our house was 'bored,'" she later said. "If anyone ever said 'bored,' they would catch it, 'cause there were too many things that you'll never get time to do."[3] She would later bristle at the stereotypical assumptions made about those who were only children. "The idea that because a child grows up without sibling support and/or rivalry, he is inevitably doomed to be either a lonely little waif, a selfish spoiled brat, or both is absolutely specious."[4]

An aspiring performer from the time she starred in a grammar school play, White for a time thought that her singing talent would be her entree into the business. According to an article attributed to the star's mother, Tess White, in a mid–1950s fan magazine, that career path initially looked promising.

"Rather than go on to college when she finished high school," Mrs. White wrote, "she decided to continue her study of music, concentrating on her singing career. She had every reason to do so. She *did* have the raw material of a good voice; it was developing well; and she had the encouragement of her teacher, Felix Hughes, the brother of the writer, Rupert Hughes, and himself once a well-known opera singer. So, with all this behind her, Betty looked forward to a lifetime dream come true: a successful career on the opera stage."[5]

Unfortunately, a bout with strep throat left White bedridden for several weeks, and, according to her mother, took its toll on her voice. Mrs. White later credited this disappointment with helping to build her daughter's character, teaching her that most worthwhile things in life didn't come easily.

While still a teenager, White made her television debut, at a time when TV was still considered a pipe dream by many. In 1939, shortly after her high school graduation, she was asked to participate in an experimental television broadcast. Along with a classmate, she sang excerpts from the operetta *The Merry Widow*, performed in a makeshift studio on the top floor of a downtown office building. The experiment was successful, and a picture of sorts was in fact transmitted, though only to a lower floor in the same building. However, fascinated as White was by the experience, the real start of broadcast television was still several years away, as was White's professional debut in the medium.

During World War II, while volunteering with the American Women's Voluntary Services (AWVS), White met and married a pilot, but the union was a brief one, dissolved in 1945. At loose ends, she found her way to the little theater run by theatrical agents Lela Bliss and Harry Hayden (also the parents of *My Little Margie*'s Don Hayden). The training and exposure she received there led to her radio debut, saying exactly one word ("Parkay!") in an episode of *The Great Gildersleeve* that, thanks to a kindly producer, earned White her first union card. She was called back to play other small roles on *Gildersleeve*, giving her valuable professional experience though not a major breakthrough.

Had White been making the rounds a few years earlier, she probably would have tried to continue her radio career, or break into the movies. But in the late 1940s, the medium most accessible to inexperienced performers in Hollywood was television. Most established stars wouldn't go near it, and salaries were notoriously tiny. But for White, the brand-new KLAC-TV became her training ground—"my alma mater,"[6] as she later called it—with her first regular gig being a "phone girl" on a primitive viewer call-in game show called *Grab Your Phone*.

In 1949, White was offered a job as sidekick to radio disc jockey Al Jarvis, a fixture on KLAC's radio lineup who was launching the new TV station's first daytime show, to be called *Hollywood on Television*. Initially not much more than a televised version of Jarvis' radio show, the new venture would run for five hours daily, from 12:30 to

5:30 P.M., sometimes filling the time by allowing viewers to *watch* Jarvis and company play records, instead of just listening.

Within weeks, Jarvis, White, and their staff realized that TV was a vastly different medium from radio, and the show's format changed. On camera for hours on end every day, White's job was to play along with whatever conversational gambits Jarvis brought up, and to deliver a boatload of live commercials. She loved it. By the late 1940s, White was serious about her career, so much so that her second marriage, to agent Lane Allan, ended over her husband's discomfort with a working wife.

Starved for programming, KLAC tapped White for more work. Soon she and Jarvis also had a Saturday night live variety show on the station. The hour-long program consisted of an amateur contest spotlighting aspiring singers, and also featured musical numbers by White herself. That show would, unexpectedly, lead to *Life with Elizabeth*.

White and Jarvis began to perform brief comedy sketches tied to into her musical numbers, in which, as she explains, "the joke payoff was the title of the song." What began as casual, largely ad-libbed bits grew into something more, and one of them soon became a recurring skit—the adventures of a husband and wife named Alvin and Elizabeth. George Tibbles, originally her accompanist, showed a flair for the funny, and egged her on.

As her mother told it, "Betty started doing a little three-minute spot at night. It was Betty's brainchild, called 'Alvin and Elizabeth,' and it ... soon grew to five minutes—then more. There were no written sketches, just some things that Betty had dreamed up. She finally ran out of ideas and hired George Tibbles to write material for it—but, by then, it was a weekly one-hour show. It was later chopped down to a half-hour of just plain *Life with Elizabeth*."[7]

White's star was on the rise. When Al Jarvis departed KLAC, he was initially replaced as host of *Hollywood on Television* by movie and TV actor Eddie Albert (whose own sitcom, *Leave it to Larry*, ran only a few weeks on CBS in the fall of 1952). Then, when Albert accepted another job several months later, *Hollywood on Television* was turned over to White. "You've attracted a large following, and I think you're a good enough risk," said station manager Don Fedderson in awarding her the host's seat. "From now on, you get top billing."[8]

Not long afterwards, another opportunity was presented to White. Fedderson invited White to put together a half-hour comedy series, based on the husband-and-wife skits she and Jarvis had performed on their Saturday night program. Thus White's pioneering sitcom was born. The half-hour comedy, initially broadcast live on KLAC-TV Saturday nights at 8:30 P.M., cast White as Elizabeth, a slightly flaky young newlywed, with actor Del Moore replacing Jarvis as her befuddled husband Alvin. The new venture was a co-production of White, station manager Fedderson, and writer Tibbles, doing business as Bandy Productions (named after the star's pet dog, who would be seen on-camera occasionally).

Sitcoms were still in their formative years when White's show was assembled. Although *I Love Lucy* was taking the country by storm, and *The George Burns and Gracie Allen Show* was airing in biweekly, live broadcasts, there were few other models to draw upon when *Elizabeth* was being assembled. (Nor did White, still doing dozens of hours of live television on KLAC-TV each week, have much time to check out the competition). This left the actress and her producing partners free to experiment with format, not being bound by any particular expectations other than to make it funny.

Like *Burns and Allen*, *Life with Elizabeth* had an on-screen announcer, Jack Narz, who would introduce the show and provide some narrative continuity. Each 30-minute episode was divided into three brief sketches, running less than 10 minutes each.

As a reporter later put it, "They decided to stay away from the mean, the quarrelsome or the embittered husband and wife often depicted on TV and in the movies. There would be no ridiculing of either the wife or the husband in these skits. They would be neither stupid, nor idiotic geniuses. They'd simply be normal, wholesome, bright-eyed—and sometimes starry-eyed—persons. Normal Americans, with conventional dithers, getting into conventional messes and laughing their way out of them."9

According to White, each *Elizabeth* vignette was designed to have the feel of "a little anecdote that you would tell somebody," fleshed out and perhaps exaggerated slightly for the sake of humor. Since telling such a story in real life would take nowhere near 30 minutes, she and her production partners came up with the format of three brief sketches per episode. She and writer George Tibbles often car-pooled to work, and would trade ideas for skits as they rode. "On the drive home," she says, "we'd talk about what we could do next week."

A review of the live, local program's premiere, in May 1952, called it a "neat bundle of entertainment," but noted that some technical problems remained to be ironed out. "Production was on the loose side Saturday night," *Variety* reported, "with sound boom visible in a couple of shots, and dialogue by Miss White was cut off entirely by sound man, but show will undoubtedly acquire necessary polish since it has all the components and ingredients of a top package."10

Was that a mouse? Betty White clowns with *Life with Elizabeth* co-star Del Moore.

In the early 1950s, it was common practice for the TV networks to look to their local stations in markets such as Chicago and Los Angeles, which created and developed far more original programming than they do today, to generate shows that could graduate to the network schedule. *Elizabeth,* seen in one of the nation's biggest markets, was being noticed, even more so when White was given an Emmy Award as Best Female Personality in 1953.

While *Life with Elizabeth* didn't attract a network spot, White's live show did capture the attention of Guild Films president Reuben Kaufman, who was in the early stages of launching a business syndicating television shows. In an article written for *Variety,* Kaufman later explained that Guild had been set up initially solely for the purposes of distribution, but "reluctantly decided to produce our own shows"[11] when those already being done were either thought unsatisfactory, or could not be acquired on mutually acceptable financial terms.

Kaufman's most successful show was a musical program that introduced Liberace to audiences nationwide. With that show firmly established, he was on the lookout for new properties when he watched one of the local broadcasts of *Life with Elizabeth.* Calling for a meeting with White and her partners, Kaufman told the young actress, "You're wasting your talent on the California climate. You belong to the nation. I'll put you on film as I did Liberace."[12]

Kaufman was able to make a satisfactory deal with Bandy Productions to launch White's show nationwide. *Life with Elizabeth* would be produced as a filmed sitcom for first-run syndication, to be launched in the fall of 1953.

The filmed episodes would not be done for a live audience, but captured through the one-camera process used for shows like *My Little Margie.* White later confessed that she regretted the loss of audience reaction. "It was a little like doing comedy in a mortuary," she said, "and it threw our timing all off."[13] The finished episodes were shown to an audience, "so we would get their genuine laughs," but sometimes it was difficult to match the editing of the show to the unpredictable audience response.

Although network executives viewed syndicators as the enemy, and discouraged their affiliate stations from buying the shows, stations across the country were hungry for programming, and Guild Films had little trouble signing up *Elizabeth* in markets across the country. Within two weeks, the company had placed its new sitcom in 27 markets around the U.S. The flexibility of film allowed some stations the option of broadcasting each *Elizabeth* episode twice, filling two slots in their weekly programming schedules.

The first filmed episode of *Life with Elizabeth,* distributed nationwide in the fall of 1953, began with announcer Narz addressing the audience:

"Incident #1 in the life of Elizabeth occurred on one of her 'bad days,'" he says cheerfully. "Oh, yes, indeed, once in a while, she gets into a vile temper! But strangely enough, Alvin seems to understand. Let's go over to the house—maybe she's calmed down a little bit by now."

That introduction carries us into the first vignette, titled "Tree on the Freeway." It's a dialogue between White and her co-star about how she spotted a downed tree blocking the road, and her vain and frustrating attempts to report this safety hazard—to the police, the Department of Sanitation, and so on until she's spent most the money in her purse at a pay phone. Getting angrier (in a purely comedic way) as she relates the story, she's working up a head of steam that she defuses intermittently by smashing walnuts with a small mallet. The kicker? After spending all her money on phone calls, she doesn't have enough left to pay the attendant who filled her car with gas while she was using the phone, so he "kept the car for collateral," she explains tearfully. That's why she had to use her last nickel to take the bus home, where the last straw was—naturally—the bus crashing into the tree!

Following that first skit, which runs less than five minutes, announcer Narz leads us back in time to see Alvin and Elizabeth's first kiss, which takes place outside her parents' house at the conclusion of their seventh date. The third, and final skit, which runs the longest (almost ten minutes), concerns a dinner guest, Elizabeth's old flame, Jack (played by the ubiquitous comedic actor Hal March, whom White remembers today as keeping everyone laughing even when no cameras were rolling).

In what would what become another of the fledgling show's staples, the final skit concludes with the three actors all excitedly talking at once, until Narz' off-screen voice interrupts to say, "Hey! Say goodbye to the people!" White, Moore, and March look briefly into the camera, say "Goodbye, everybody!," and resume their argument.

It's clear watching early episodes of *Elizabeth* that the show was produced on a modest budget. Aside from its two stars, and announcer Narz, guest actors are few, rarely more than one per episode, and the sets are far from elaborate. There's little action, and anything that would have cost much to stage takes place off-camera, described rather than seen. "We had about a dollar and a quarter to do a show each week," White says today, claiming that the show's credits even gave billing to fictitious writers so as to make it look like a more fully staffed operation than it really was. The mom-and-pop operation, in fact, gave White a broadly-based education into the making of a TV sitcom.

Time has touched *Life with Elizabeth* more than some of the other shows commemorated in this book, and not all of its humor still works today. Still, the young (and then brunette) White has a charm and vitality that make it easy to understand why viewers took a shine to her, and if she hasn't yet fully hit the comedic peak that she would reach in the 1970s and 1980s, it's still interesting to watch her style develop. *Variety*, reviewing that first episode upon its debut on the DuMont station, WABD, in New York, mostly liked the show, saying it "shapes as an amusing, wacky series based on solid Americana situation material." As for its stars, the reviewer praised White and Moore as "highly attractive, and with good comedic sense and timing."[14]

By late 1953, *Life with Elizabeth* was being seen in dozens of markets nationwide, and White was rapidly becoming a known entity to TV audiences nationwide. NBC capitalized on her popularity by offering her a daily afternoon program to be called *The Betty White Show*, which premiered in February 1954. Her NBC show, originally a lunchtime half-hour, offered a pleasant mix of songs and conversation, part of the network's plan to fill the daytime schedule with a type of programming different from CBS' popular soap opera lineup.

Throughout the 1953-54 season, Guild Films reported sales of *Life with Elizabeth* to more and more markets. In early 1954, the company announced that production would begin shortly on a new batch of 34 episodes, with a larger budget allotted to each segment. Guild "has already allocated $1,093,000 for production of 74 half-hour telepix to be completed by April 20," *Variety* reported.[15]

The bigger budget would allow those later episodes to offer some slightly spiffier sets, and a few more actors other than the regulars. Otherwise, the show changed little. Because the vignettes were brief, the plots were simpler than in most sitcoms, usually just the playing out of a single basic idea. Often they seemed to spring from situations that had happened to the writers or performers in real life, such as a sketch about the complications that arise when Alvin's face has been immobilized by Novocain shots at the dentist, while Elizabeth's ears are plugged up from an airplane flight. Other vignettes revolved around the complications of operating an early home-movie projector, or the squabbling that a friendly game of Monopoly can produce.

By then, White had a firm grasp on her impish, practical-joking, but basically goodhearted character. Like other female sitcom characters, she was capable of being somewhat manipulative to get what she wanted, as in the segment "Driving Lessons."

Announcer Narz, in the show's opening minutes, interacts with White to set up the basic situation, her responses to his off-screen voice done purely through mime. As he explains, Elizabeth wants Alvin to buy a car, but he's resisting.

NARZ: Tell me something. Why won't Alvin buy a car?
WHITE: *(Looks annoyed, points to herself, mimes steering a car).*
NARZ: Oh, he thinks you'd always be borrowing it *(she nods and smiles).* You wouldn't do a thing like that, would you? *(She nods more emphatically).* How are you going to convince him that he needs a car, and you won't borrow it?
WHITE: *(Makes a 'moron' face, sticking out her tongue, while miming the steering wheel again).*
NARZ: Oh, you're going to try to make him think you're too *stupid* to learn to drive! *(She nods).* Pretty sneaky, Elizabeth!
WHITE: *(Taps her finger to her temple and nods—she's smart! Then, as she hears Alvin approaching, shushes the announcer).*

Throughout the series, the first vignette invariably closed with Narz' off-screen voice addressing the heroine chidingly with, "Elizabeth! Aren't you ashamed?" White's response, then and in every episode to follow, was to look directly into camera and shake her head fiercely *no*.

So believable as a young wife on TV, White herself remained single in the wake of her second divorce, leery of making another mistake. Fan magazine profiles at the time, playing up her clean-cut and somewhat innocent image, noted that she lived with her parents, and often implied that she had never been married. As to why she remained single, White told an interviewer in 1954, "I've seen so many career marriages go wrong and I know how hard it is for a woman like me to be fair to a husband and still keep a career.

"I try not to think just of my work but I guess I'm always carrying it around with me. But what else can I do? Working on my NBC shows and on *Life with Elizabeth*, I *have* to concentrate to do any kind of decent job. I can't just slide through it. And that reminds me—men concentrate a lot on their work so why should they expect a woman to be any less conscientious?"[16]

She went on to say that, should she marry again, it would probably be to a fellow performer, since he would be more likely to understand the ins and outs of maintaining a show business career. In fact, her prescription for personal happiness would ultimately be fulfilled just as she foresaw, though not until several years later.

Up to her ears in work in 1954, White was nonetheless disappointed when NBC cancelled her daytime *Betty White Show* in December. Though the show's initial ratings were promising, NBC programmers jerked *The Betty White Show* around the schedule three different times between July and September, the frequent changes in time slot losing its initial audience and resulting in the series' cancellation. *Life with Elizabeth*, however, would continue—for a time.

By 1955, with 65 episodes of *Elizabeth* on film, Guild ceased production of the show. The reason was apparently not lack of popularity, but rather, as a *Variety* article had put it, "How many first run personality telepix can producers make without reaching the point where reruns in secondary markets are being jeopardized?"[17] That article reported that popular syndicated shows like *Racket Squad* were being halted by their production companies while still in demand, so as to earn more profit from continuing to circulate the episodes already made. Guild would continue to syndicate *Elizabeth* reruns almost until the sprockets wore out on the films.

Now that station executives understood that film shows could be repeated multiple times while still drawing a respectable audience share, the *Elizabeth* films already in the can would continue to play multiple markets, second only to Liberace's first musical show as Guild Films' most successful offering. By 1956, trade ads boasted that Guild had "191 musicals, 143 mysteries, 208 comedies [and] dramas, and 370 cartoons" available for lease, as well as a package of children's shows and Western films. According to White, once the initial gloss wore off the oft-repeated *Elizabeth* films, the company tried a different approach, breaking apart the individual vignettes into 195 segments that, with commercials and credits added, could fill odd fifteen-minute slots on a station's schedule.

As for White herself, in the wake of *Elizabeth*'s demise, she and partner Don Fedderson pitched a new sitcom, this time for network airing. Wanting to make the show stand out from the many other sitcoms already on TV by the mid–1950s, they bought the rights to the Elmer Rice stage play, "Dream Girl," which had played to good reviews on Broadway in the mid–1940s as a vehicle for another Betty, film actress Betty Field. The basic concept, about a young woman who imagines her life as she wishes it were, was developed into a show White and her partner proposed to call *Date with the Angels*.

The new show again cast its star as a young housewife, this time named Vickie Angel (the pop single "I've Got a Date with an Angel," a hit for the Skinnay Ennis Orchestra in the late 1930s, would be used as the show's theme). Wanting to avoid too many similarities to the still widely-distributed *Life with Elizabeth*, White and her colleagues decided not to re-unite her with her former co-star Del Moore, and instead cast actor Bill Williams, previously the leading man of the syndicated Western series *The Adventures of Kit Carson*, as her husband Gus.

Date with the Angels would be launched under the sponsorship of Plymouth, whose executives were familiar with White's work on *Life with Elizabeth* and *The Betty White Show*. "They came to us as a sponsor, wanting to buy the whole show," she says. "They not only bought us, but they did a lot of promotion." With financial backing in place, a time slot for *Date with the Angels* was nailed down on ABC.

In an unusual scheduling pattern for the period, White's new show would make its debut in May, so as to help Plymouth get a jump on advertising its new year's models arriving in dealerships that summer. Originally slotted at 10 P.M. on Fridays, the show would air its first, abbreviated season of twelve episodes between May and early August, followed by a spate of reruns from late summer through Labor Day.

Producer Federson and his colleagues had high hopes for the show. White, he said, "is the most underrated comedienne in Hollywood. *Life with Elizabeth* never got the big network push it deserved, but this time she is getting the full treatment." Co-star Williams added, "Betty White should come out of this series as one of the biggest stars in the business."[18]

Having disliked the static feeling of filming *Life with Elizabeth* without a studio audience, White was pleased that her new show would be done three-camera style, with former *I Love Lucy* director James V. Kern overseeing the action. Unfortunately, despite the success of sitcoms like *Topper*, Plymouth disliked the fantasy element of the show, and she and Federson were unable to resist pressure to phase out what had promised to set the show apart from its competitors.

"Without our dream sequences," White said, "our show flattened out and became just one more run-of-the-mill domestic comedy, but without Del Moore's impeccable comedic timing."[19]

By the show's fifth aired episode, "Tree on the Parkway" (6/7/57), *Angels* was simply a sitcom about a young married couple. The plot of that episode (the name of which may have been an in-joke reference to *Life with Elizabeth*'s opener, "Tree on the Freeway") concerns Vickie's efforts to prevent a tree in her neighborhood from being cut down, which turns into a petition drive that spins so far out of control that she receives a personal visit from the mayor, imploring her to put it to a stop.

Increasingly the new show began to rely on supporting characters to provide the laughs. Although some strong character actors, like Richard Deacon (later Mel Cooley on *The Dick Van Dyke Show*) were there to lend White support, *Date with the Angels* was struggling. An early episode called "The Wheel," which introduced young actor Jimmy Boyd as Vickie's awkward, innocently troublemaking teenage nephew Wheeler, drew enough laughs that the actor would reprise the role intermittently throughout the show's run. Unfortunately, White's own character lacked some of the spirit and sense of mischief that Elizabeth had had, leaving her too often stuck with merely reacting to what was going on around her.

TV Guide's reviewer thought the show "harmless enough fun," but regretted that the lead characters did not themselves inspire much laughter. "One wishes Mr. Federson would bring his Angels down to earth and show us how funny they are with their halos down."[20]

Interviewed by *TV Guide* that summer, White was still guardedly optimistic. "We've already finished the first 13 films," she said. "Some of them are pretty funny. Others I'm not so sure about. But our big break, I think, is going to come in the fall when we move back to an earlier hour and follow *The Frank Sinatra Show*. If that doesn't help build our audience, nothing will."[21]

Angels returned to the ABC airwaves with new episodes in September 1957. A few weeks later, *The Frank Sinatra Show* premiered as White's Friday night lead-in. Despite its star power, that series was a surprising failure. When it crashed and burned,

Date with the Angels, despite only middleweight competition from *Schlitz Playhouse* on CBS and *The Thin Man* on NBC, was dead in the water.

In a drastic move, White and Fedderson pulled the plug on their show in January, with three months left to go on their contract with Plymouth and ABC. A schedule change that moved *Date with the Angels* to Wednesdays at 9:30 P.M. hadn't much helped the struggling show, and White believed that it had never really taken flight creatively. Relegating *Angels* to the dustbin after 33 episodes, ABC unveiled *The Betty White Show* (the third time around for this particular series title), in February 1958.

A half-hour skit comedy show, *The Betty White Show* allowed the star to play a wider variety of characters and scenes, with a plumped-up supporting cast that included Irene Ryan (later Granny of *The Beverly Hillbillies*), veteran character actress Reta Shaw, and her *Life with Elizabeth* co-star Del Moore.

Guests on her February 5 opener included movie actors Cornel Wilde and Charles Coburn. *Variety* commented that the new show, which was being broadcast live, "smacked of her long-ago show, *Life with Elizabeth*—a series of folksy skits. In those days, she restricted herself to husband-wife situations. The variation here was very slight—with one marital skit, a boarding house skit and the last, and perhaps the best, about temperamental actors." Despite the changes, the trade paper's reviewer found it "extremely difficult to see where the transition ... was going to hike her Nielsens significantly."[22]

Indeed, *The Betty White Show* didn't catch fire with Wednesday night viewers, and White's series came to a close upon the completion of her initial one-year contract with Plymouth that spring.

While White has never stopped performing on television since the early 1950s, she entered a relatively quiet period as an actress in the wake of *Date with the Angels'* failure. In the years following it, she became a favorite guest of *Tonight Show* host Jack Paar, logging more than 70 appearances during his tenure. She was also in demand for appearances on game shows like *To Tell the Truth* and *Password,* a painless paycheck for someone who had been an inveterate game-player from childhood. In addition, White was frequently tapped as commentator for events like the

Photograph sent to fans of *The Betty White Show.* Accompanying the original photo is a note dated April 11, 1958, thanking "Cynthia" for "your thoughtful response to our new show."

annual Rose Bowl Parade telecast. In 1962, she made a rare movie appearance, playing a supporting role as a senator in Otto Preminger's Washington drama *Advise and Consent* (Columbia, 1962). (Not until the late 1990s, when White was in her eighth decade, would she return to feature films).

Password proved to be far more than a career move for White. While guesting on the game show, she became friendly with host Allen Ludden, who had recently been widowed. Gun-shy after two marriages, White put him off when he proposed to her, but after a year of gentle pressure, she relented. They were married on June 14, 1963, and would remain a devoted couple until she was widowed in 1981.

When not appearing on TV, White kept busy with stage appearances. She relocated from the West Coast to Connecticut after marrying Ludden, since *Password* was then a New York–based broadcast. White also found work hosting a radio call-in show, *Ask Betty White*, in the early 1960s, replacing original star Betty Furness.

For most of the 1960s, her sitcom career was regrettably dormant. Not until after she and Ludden relocated to California in 1968, purchasing a home in Brentwood where she still lives today, did she stick a toe back into sitcom land. Already in her mid-forties, White had an ageless charm that kept her from being sidelined after the age of thirty-five, as so many of her fellow actresses would be.

Going into the 1970s, her most notable recent TV acting credit was a guest appearance as a librarian on the 2/1/69 episode of CBS' *Petticoat Junction*, "The Cannonball Bookmobile." (Meanwhile, her former producing partner Don Fedderson had enjoyed the most successful phase of his career in the 1960s, with *My Three Sons* and *Family Affair* becoming long-running favorites that made him a very wealthy man). In 1971, White briefly hosted a syndicated series, *The Pet Set*, drawing on her lifelong love of animals. Then, in 1973, a guest appearance on her friend Mary Tyler Moore's popular CBS sitcom unexpectedly kicked her sitcom career into high gear in middle age.

Cast as Sue Ann Nivens, WJM-TV's "Happy Homemaker" in the show's fourth-season opener, "The Lars Affair" (9/15/73), White played an outwardly sweet, pre–Martha Stewart "domestic goddess" who hosted a local TV show filled with cooking and housekeeping tips. Off-camera, she was a conniving, sharp-tongued home wrecker who was dallying with the unseen husband of series regular Phyllis (Cloris Leachman).

Latching onto the best role she'd had in years, White threw herself into the juicy character with a verve and skill that made Hollywood sit up and take notice. *The Mary Tyler Moore Show* quickly wrote in her one-shot character as a semi-regular, and she would continue to appear several times a year until it ended in 1977. Her peers awarded her two Best Supporting Actress Emmy Awards for her work on *Mary Tyler Moore*.

Her co-stars also admired her. Edward Asner, the often-irascible Lou Grant on-screen, noted White's moxie during the filming of "What Do You Want to Do When You Produce?" (12/20/75). In the show's hilarious climactic scene, Murray (Gavin MacLeod) plops Sue Ann down into a giant cake. Since there was only one cake, the gag had never been fully rehearsed before being done in front of the studio audience.

When the moment of truth arrived, White was set down with a force that caught her by surprise. Sinking through the layers of fluffy frosting, she came to rest with a jolt that unexpectedly injured her. Rather than ruining the take, which had the audience in hysterics, White rallied. "She went on with the show, and I knew she had to be hurting," Asner recalled. "And she had the wherewithal to reach behind her and take a finger and dip it into the icing coating her ass and taste it and say, 'It needs butter.' They kept the line."[23]

When *Mary* came to a close, its players, including White, were in demand for shows of their own. Twenty years after she had been tapped for her first network sitcom, *Date with the Angels,* White, at 55, was again offered her own show. MTM executives easily sold CBS on *The Betty White Show,* even though no one yet knew what its format would be.

"The first thing we considered, of course," said writer-producer Ed. Weinberger, "was to transfer Sue Ann, the Happy Homemaker, to some suitable environment and simply let her career continue along her woman-hating, man-hungry, acerbic course. But we had tried something like that with Cloris Leachman in *Phyllis* and it was becoming more and more apparent in the ratings that it hadn't been our most brilliant decision."[24] White, reckoning that a full thirty minutes of unrestrained Sue Ann each week would be too much of a good thing, concurred.

Instead, the MTM creative team devised a show-within-a-show format, casting White as actress Joyce Whitman, leading lady of a cheesy TV action drama, *Undercover Woman*. The obvious allusion to NBC's then-popular *Police Woman* (1974–78), starring Angie Dickinson, didn't escape that star's notice. *TV Guide* reported that Dickinson, after taking in a screening of the *Betty White Show* pilot that spring, told her friend White, "It's OK, darling. But if I notice your hair getting *one* whit blonder...."[25]

Co-starring John Hillerman (later of *Magnum, P.I.*) as White's acerbic ex-husband, and director, the series showed promise but wasn't given time to develop. Impatient with the initially sluggish ratings at a time when literate comedy was becoming an endangered species on TV, CBS rashly pulled the plug on *The Betty White Show* in early 1978, after only 13 weeks on the air.

Not long after, she suffered a personal crisis, when husband Allen Ludden, then hosting *Password Plus,* was diagnosed with cancer. Cutting back her work schedule, White spent time with him as they built their dream home in Carmel, realizing now that he might not live long enough to enjoy it. On June 9, 1981, White lost her husband of almost 18 years.

Focusing her energies on her work once again, White, newly acknowledged as one of TV's funniest actresses, would create an impressive gallery of unforgettable characters over the next decade. As a guest star on *The Carol Burnett Show* (CBS, 1967–78), she played Ellen Harper, snobbish and condescending sister to Burnett's pitiable Eunice in the popular "Family" skits. She continued the role when Vicki Lawrence later launched *Mama's Family,* which was only mildly successful in its 1983-84 run on NBC, but later enjoyed a long life as one of the highest-rated sitcoms produced originally for syndication.

While still working occasionally on the syndicated version of *Mama's Family,* she was sent a script for Susan Harris' new comedy *The Golden Girls,* about four older women happily sharing a home in Miami. Because of her association with lusty Sue

The Betty White Show, 1977 version: White playing an "Undercover Woman" with a beefy stunt double (Charles Cyphers).

Ann Nivens, White was originally considered for the role of sexy senior citizen Blanche Deveraux. Instead, after watching her and co-star Rue McClanahan in rehearsal, director Jay Sandrich suggested that the two actresses trade parts, and White became the endearingly loopy Rose Nylund. The result was stunning, a tribute to her versatility, and the show immediately became a critical and popular success.

The Golden Girls was a savvy combination of the classic and the contemporary—the best of both sitcom worlds. Franker than 1950s sitcoms, the show starred two veterans of Norman Lear's 1970s sitcom *Maude,* and occasionally had something potent to say about women's rights, or the health and welfare of senior citizens. Sassy Sophia (Estelle Getty), always ready to call 'em as she saw 'em—"You look like a prostitute!" she exclaims to McClanahan's Blanche in the pilot—tested the limits of mid–1980s TV censorship.

But the show also harkened back to the golden age of TV comedy, and to the rich tradition of funny leading ladies. White, bringing a lifetime of experience in television comedy to the table, likened the experience of co-starring with McClanahan, Getty, and Beatrice Arthur (Dorothy) to a tennis match. "When you threw out a line," she later said, "you had to brace yourself, because you knew it would be coming right back at you over the net and you'd better be ready."[26]

Perhaps the most difficult character to make credible, Rose was a lovable ding-dong who cheerfully told wildly improbable stories about the denizens of her hometown of Saint Olaf, Minnesota. Scarcely a trace of the calculating Sue Ann surfaced in Rose, a tribute to White's talents. The voters of the Academy of Television Arts and Sciences took notice, making her the first of the show's stars to collect a Best Actress Emmy.

The Golden Girls would keep White in the public eye until 1992, when it came to a close after a seven-year run. She and co-stars McClanahan and Estelle Getty continued their characters in a CBS spin-off called *The Golden Palace*, but that show lacked the magic of its predecessor, and ran for only one season.

Still very much active in her early eighties, White has been one of television's most valuable players for decades. Not all her series have been hits—some, like *Maybe This Time* (ABC, 1995-96), which teamed her with Marie Osmond, sank from view quickly. Still, even if a particular project doesn't work, she is widely acknowledged—and always in demand—for her versatility and ability to draw laughs.

Betty White (at far right) with her co-stars from NBC's hit sitcom *The Golden Girls* (left to right): Bea Arthur (Dorothy), Rue McClanahan (Blanche), and (seated) Estelle Getty (Sophia).

White has also been a favorite with Emmy voters, who have regularly taken notice of her work. Aside from her *Mary Tyler Moore* and *Golden Girls* wins, she took home a Daytime Emmy for her work as emcee of the short-lived game show *Just Men!* (NBC, 1983), a rare instance of a woman at the helm of a game show. She was named Outstanding Guest Actress in a Comedy Series for a 1996 appearance on *The John Larroquette Show* (NBC, 1993–96), only one of numerous nominations for TV guest appearances.

She is also the recipient of a Lifetime Achievement Award from the American Comedy Awards, and in 1995 was inducted into the Academy of Television Arts and Sciences' Television Hall of Fame. (Among the women previously inducted were Lucille Ball and Gracie Allen).

In 1998, White looked back to her television beginnings, participating in a 50th anniversary celebration for Los Angeles' former KLAC-TV, which had since become KCOP, the city's UPN affiliate. Resurrecting her 1950s TV character for a two-hour special aired in September 1998, White recreated one of her classic *Life with Elizabeth* skits for the historic broadcast. Original series announcer Jack Narz was on hand as well. Unfortunately, they could not be reunited with original co-star Del Moore (Alvin), who died in 1970.

In the late 1990s, after spending most of her career in television, White unexpectedly began racking up movie credits, playing featured roles in widely distributed features like *Hard Rain* (1998) and *Lake Placid* (1999). The latter role, which marked her first collaboration with writer-producer David E. Kelley (*The Practice)*, startled some longtime fans because it called for White to let loose with a few choice words she'd never uttered on television—to say nothing of the scene in which the longtime animal lover's character cheerfully fed a cow to a hungry crocodile. Since that particular scene was created through special effects, involving no real animals, and was so clearly unrealistic, she was able to find it funny.

On the other hand, when sought by friend and *MTM* colleague James L. Brooks for the role of Helen Hunt's mother in his acclaimed comedy-drama *As Good as It Gets* (1997), she politely declined. "I turned it down because of little Jill, the adorable little dog, being thrown down the garbage chute. Jim Brooks was kind enough to offer me the role, but I called him and told him that I just couldn't. He said, 'but the dog is fine. The dog is safe. The dog is the star of the movie.' I said, I know that, but there are a lot of kooks out there. They see that and say, oh, how convenient, there's a dog that barks down the hall that bothers me. I know what I'll do. And I said they don't all have happy endings like that. He understood."[27]

Attesting to the sincerity of White's love for animals, should anyone doubt it, is her 1950s sitcom colleague Gale Storm, who became friendly with White after they were teamed in the early 1990s for a Museum of Broadcasting retrospective of women's roles in television. Storm remembers walking down a Chicago sidewalk with White, who impulsively stopped a passerby holding a cat carrier. White insisted on meeting the stranger's cat, and soon had it out of the carrier, so that she could hold it and talk to it. White herself, Storm says, lives up to her image as friendly and approachable. "She's even better than that in person—naturally so funny, and such fun to be with."[28]

In the fall of 1999, she returned to weekly television as co-star of the CBS sitcom *Ladies' Man*, opposite Alfred Molina and Sharon Lawrence. At the age of 77, White was as enthusiastic about work as ever. "Don't let anybody doing a situation comedy say they work hard," she told a journalist. "We had to get up at the crack of 10 o'clock and the first three days, we go home early. Then on camera-blocking day, we're there till maybe 6 o'clock. It's just terrible.... It's stealing is what it is."[29] *Ladies' Man* struggled in the ratings, and after its first season was unceremoniously yanked from the CBS schedule. Revived briefly a year later, it was ultimately canceled in 2001, her last full-time sitcom venture to date.

In 2003, she was seen in a small role as a cranky, racist neighbor in the popular

Steve Martin–Queen Latifah comedy *Bringing Down the House*. She has also continued her association with writer-producer David E. Kelley *(The Practice, Ally McBeal)*, who cast her in a recurring role as suspected murderess Catherine Piper on *The Practice* (ABC, 1997–2004). After that show concluded its run, Kelley revived her character on its spin-off, *Boston Legal* (2004–), where she served as the outspoken administrative assistant of attorney Alan Shore (played by James Spader). During the 2005-06 season, Piper not only took up robbing convenience stores (armed with a rubber pistol), but also confessed to the murder of a client.

Away from work, White pursues her other lifetime passion throughout her ongoing involvement with the Los Angeles Zoo, the Morris Animal Foundation, and other organizations that promote animal welfare. She is also a published author, having penned *Betty White's Pet Love: How Pets Take Care of Us* (1983, co-authored with Thomas Watson), *Betty White in Person* (1987), *The Leading Lady: Dinah's Story* (1991, co-authored with Tom Sullivan), and *Here We Go Again: My Life in Television* (1995).

Not just a nostalgic figure, Betty White is still a busy working actress at a time when most people would be content to sit back and take life a bit more easily. And if the success and innovation of *Life with Elizabeth* is today less remembered than her classic roles as a character actress in the oft-repeated *Mary Tyler Moore Show* and *The Golden Girls*, her early work has still earned her a place in television history as one of the first—and now, as one of the most enduring, of TV's funny ladies.

Interviewed a few weeks past her 84th birthday, White exuded enthusiasm for her current TV project—"I'm having a *wonderful* time on *Boston Legal*," she says. Modest about her professional successes, she tends to attribute them to others. She's quick to praise "the kind of writers that I've been blessed with," citing Kelley as well as the talents behind *The Mary Tyler Moore Show* and *The Golden Girls*. "Believe me, so much of it is on that page," she says. As a performer, "you can screw up a good show, but you can't save a bad one."

What comes across clearly in all of White's performances, from *Life with Elizabeth* to her current endeavors, is her love for what she does. While she admits that she still suffers from stage fright—"you can't help it, it goes with the territory"—she clearly isn't ready to retire, and rest on her laurels. Nor is it an accident that, despite her occasional forays into movies and stage work, she has remained primarily a television fixture since 1949.

"I just love the fact that you only play to two or three people at most," she says of what she readily acknowledges is her favorite medium. "It's a very personal medium, and a very personal audience."

Of her fifty-plus years of employment on television, awards too numerous to count, and the demand that still exists for her services today, she says simply, "I'm the luckiest old broad on two feet."

Appendix I: Casts and Credits

The Ann Sothern Show
(October 6, 1958–September 25, 1961)

Ann Sothern (Katy O'Connor), Don Porter (James Devery), Ann Tyrrell (Olive Smith), Jack Mullaney (Johnny Wallace), Ernest Truex (Jason Macauley), Reta Shaw (Flora Macauley), Louis Nye (Dr. Delbert Gray), Jacques Scott (Paul Martine), Jesse White (Oscar Pudney), Ken Berry (Woody Hamilton)

Produced by Devery Freeman, Arthur Hoffe; directed by James V. Kern, Sidney Miller, Oscar Rudolph, Richard Whorf, others; associate producer, William Andrew; written by Ray Allen, Art Baer, Dick Chevillat, Richard Deroy, Fred S. Fox, Ben Joelson, Bob Ross, Danny Simon, others. Anso Productions, in association with Desilu Productions.

Aired Mondays at 9:30 P.M. on CBS-TV *(seasons 1 and 2)*; Thursdays at 7:30 P.M. on CBS-TV *(season 3)*; Mondays at 9:30 P.M. on CBS-TV *(summer 1961)*. 93 episodes.

Date with the Angels
(May 10, 1957–January 29, 1958)

Betty White (Vickie Angel), Bill Williams (Gus Angel), Richard Deacon (Roger Finley), Maudie Prickett (Cassie Murphy), Jimmy Boyd (Wheeler)

Executive producer Don Fedderson; produced by Fred Henry; directed by James V. Kern; written by George Tibbles, Fran Van Hartesveldt, Bill Kelsay. Don Fedderson Productions.

Aired Fridays at 10 P.M. on ABC-TV *(May–June 1957)*; Fridays at 9:30 P.M. on ABC-TV *(July–December 1957)*; Wednesdays at 9:30 P.M. on ABC-TV *(January 1958)*. 33 episodes.

December Bride
(October 4, 1954–September 24, 1959)

Spring Byington (Lily Ruskin), Dean Miller (Matt Henshaw), Frances Rafferty (Ruth Henshaw), Harry Morgan (Pete Porter), Verna Felton (Hilda Crocker)
Created and produced by Parke Levy; produced by Samuel Marx; directed by Jerry Thorpe; written by Parke Levy, Bill Davenport, Lou Derman, Ben Gershman, Arthur Julian, others. Desilu Productions.
Aired Mondays at 9:30 P.M. on CBS-TV *(seasons 1–4)*; Thursdays at 8 P.M. on CBS-TV *(season 5)*. 157 episodes.

The Donna Reed Show
(September 24, 1958–September 3, 1966)

Donna Reed (Donna Stone), Carl Betz (Dr. Alex Stone), Shelley Fabares (Mary Stone), Paul Petersen (Jeff Stone), Patty Petersen (Trisha Stone), Bob Crane (Dr. Dave Kelsey), Ann McCrea (Midge Kelsey)
Produced by Tony Owen; directed by Lawrence Dobkin, Jeffrey Hayden, Andrew McCullough, E.W. Swackhamer, others; associate producers Phil Sharp, Paul West; written by Tom and Helen August, Barbara Avedon, Sam Locke, Sumner Long, Nate Monaster, Joel Rapp, Henry Sharp, Paul West, John Whedon, others; based on characters created by William Roberts. Screen Gems; Todon Productions.
Aired Wednesdays at 9 P.M. on ABC-TV *(season 1)*; Thursdays at 8 P.M. on ABC-TV *(fall 1959–Jan. 1966)*; Saturdays at 8 P.M. on ABC-TV *(Jan.–Sep. 1966)*. 274 episodes.

The Eve Arden Show
(September 17, 1957–March 25, 1958)

Eve Arden (Liza Hammond), Allyn Joslyn (George Howell), Frances Bavier (Nora), Gail Stone (Jenny Hammond), Karen Greene (Mary Hammond)
Produced by Al Lewis; directed by John Rich, William D. Russell; associate producer, Brooks West; based on Emily Kimbrough's novel *It Gives Me Great Pleasure*; written by William Cowley, Peggy Chantler. Westhaven Productions, in association with the CBS Television Network; filmed by Desilu.
Aired Tuesdays at 8:30 P.M. on CBS-TV. 26 episodes.

The Gale Storm Show: Oh! Susanna
(September 29, 1956–March 24, 1960)

Gale Storm (Susanna Pomeroy), ZaSu Pitts (Esmerelda "Nugey" Nugent), Roy Roberts (Captain Huxley), Jimmy Fairfax (Cedric)
Executive producer, Hal Roach, Jr.; produced by Alex Gottlieb *(seasons 1–3)*, Lou Derman *(season 4)*; directed by William A. Seiter, Richard Kinon, James V. Kern; based on characters created by Lee Karson; written by Alex Gottlieb, others. Hal Roach Studios.
Aired Saturdays at 9 P.M. on CBS-TV *(first three seasons)*; Thursdays at 7:30 P.M. on ABC-TV *(fourth season)*. 126 episodes.

The George Burns and Gracie Allen Show
(October 12, 1950–September 22, 1958)

George Burns (Himself), Gracie Allen (Herself), Bea Benaderet (Blanche Morton), John Brown, Hal March, Larry Keating (Harry Morton), Bill Goodwin (Himself), Harry Von Zell (Himself), Ronnie Burns (Himself)

Produced and directed by Ralph Levy *(seasons 1–3)*, Frederick de Cordova *(seasons 4–6)*, Rod Amateau *(seasons 6–8)*; written by Paul Henning, William Burns, Sid Dorfman, Keith Fowler, Jesse Goldstein, Harvey Helm, Nate Monaster, Norman Paul. McCadden Productions.

Aired Thursdays at 8 P.M. on CBS-TV *(seasons 1–3)*; Mondays at 8 P.M. on CBS-TV *(seasons 4–8)*. Episodes: 52 live broadcasts; 239 on film.

I Love Lucy
(October 15, 1951–June 24, 1957)

Lucille Ball (Lucy Ricardo), Desi Arnaz (Ricky Ricardo), Vivian Vance (Ethel Mertz), William Frawley (Fred Mertz), Richard Keith *a.k.a.* Keith Thibodeaux (Little Ricky), Jerry Hausner (Jerry), Elizabeth Patterson (Mathilda Trumbull)

Executive producer, Desi Arnaz; produced by Jess Oppenheimer *(seasons 1–5)*, Desi Arnaz *(season 6)*; written by Jess Oppenheimer, Bob Carroll, Jr., Madelyn Pugh, Bob Schiller, Bob Weiskopf. Desilu Productions.

Aired Mondays at 9 P.M. on CBS-TV. 179 episodes.

I Married Joan
(October 13, 1952–April 6, 1955)

Joan Davis (Joan Stevens), Jim Backus (Brad Stevens), Beverly Wills (Beverly), Hope Emerson (Minerva Parker), Elvia Allman (Vera), Sheila Bromley (Janet Tobin), Dan Tobin (Kerwin Tobin), Adele Jergens (Helen Cavanaugh)

Produced by P.J. Wolfson; directed by Marc Daniels, John Rich, Ezra Stone, others; written by Jesse Goldstein, Sherwood Schwartz, Phil Sharp, Arthur Stander, Hugh Wedlock, others. Volcano Productions; Joan Davis Enterprises.

Aired Wednesdays at 8 P.M. on NBC-TV. 98 episodes.

Life with Elizabeth
(produced 1952–1955)

Betty White (Elizabeth), Del Moore (Alvin), Ray Erlenborn (Mr. Fuddy), Loie Bridge (Mrs. Skinridge)

Produced by George Tibbles; directed by Duke Goldstone, Betty Turbiville; written by George Tibbles, Milt Kahn; a Guild Films production in association with Don Fedderson; Bandy Productions.

Aired Saturdays at 8:30 P.M. on KLAC-TV, Los Angeles *(May 1952–1953)*. Various times in first-run syndication *(fall 1953–spring 1955)*. Episodes: 65 filmed, plus live broadcasts.

Love That Jill
(January 20–April 28, 1958)

Anne Jeffreys (Jill Johnson), Robert Sterling (Jack Gibson), James Lydon (Richard), Betty Lynn (Pearl)
Executive producer, Hal Roach, Jr.; written and produced by Alex Gottlieb. Hal Roach Studios.
Aired Mondays at 8 P.M. on ABC-TV. 13 episodes.

My Little Margie
(June 16, 1952–August 24, 1955)

Gale Storm (Margie Albright), Charles Farrell (Vern Albright), Willie Best (Charlie), Hillary Brooke (Roberta Townsend), Don Hayden (Freddie Wilson), Gertrude W. Hoffman (Mrs. Odetts), Clarence Kolb (George Honeywell)
Produced by Hal Roach, Jr.; directed by Hal Yates; associate producer, Guy V. Thayer, Jr.; characters created by Frank Fox; written by G. Carleton Brown, Nathaniel Curtis, Frank Fox, Frank Gill, Jr., John Kohn, Audrey Lives, Alan Woods, others. Roland Reed TV Productions.
Aired Mondays at 9 P.M. on CBS-TV *(summer 1952)*; Saturdays at 7:30 P.M. on NBC-TV *(fall 1952)*; Thursdays at 10 P.M. on CBS-TV *(January–June 1953)*; Wednesdays at 8:30 P.M. on NBC-TV *(fall 1953–summer 1955)*. 126 episodes.

Our Miss Brooks
(October 3, 1952–September 21, 1956)

Eve Arden (Connie Brooks), Gale Gordon (Osgood Conklin), Robert Rockwell (Philip Boynton), Dick [Richard] Crenna (Walter Denton), Jane Morgan (Mrs. Davis), Gloria McMillan (Harriet Conklin), Nana Bryant (Angela Nestor), Bob Sweeney (Oliver Munsey), Gene Barry (Gene Talbot)
Directed by Al Lewis; production executive, Larry Berns; written by Al Lewis, Joe Quillan, others. Desilu Productions.
Aired Fridays at 9:30 P.M. on CBS-TV *(first three seasons)*; Fridays at 8:30 P.M. on CBS-TV *(fourth season)*. 127 episodes.

Private Secretary (aka *Susie*)
(February 1, 1953–September 10, 1957)

Ann Sothern (Susie MacNamara), Don Porter (Peter Sands), Ann Tyrrell (Vi Praskins), Jesse White ("Cagey" Calhoun), Joan Banks (Sylvia)
Produced by Jack Chertok; directed by Oscar Rudolph, others. Written by Leonard Gershe, Tom Seller, others. Jack Chertok TV Productions.
Aired Sundays at 7:30 P.M. on CBS-TV *(in-season, Feb. 1953–March 1957)*; Saturdays at 10:30 P.M. on NBC-TV *(summer 1953 and summer 1954)*; Tuesdays at 8:30 P.M. on CBS-TV *(April–September 1957)*. 104 episodes.

Topper
(October 9, 1953–October 14, 1956)

Anne Jeffreys (Marion Kerby), Robert Sterling (George Kerby), Leo G. Carroll (Cosmo Topper), Lee Patrick (Henrietta Topper), Thurston Hall (Mr. Schuyler), Kathleen Freeman (Katie), Edna Skinner (Maggie)

Produced by John W. Loveton; directed by Paul Landres, Lew Landers; written by Robert Riley Crutcher, Stanley Davis, George Oppenheimer, Elon Packard, Philip Rapp, Stephen Sondheim, others; based on the characters originally created by Thorne Smith. John W. Loveton—Bernard L. Schubert Productions.

Aired Fridays at 8:30 P.M. on CBS-TV *(seasons 1–2)*. Mondays at 7:30 P.M. on ABC-TV *(season 3; reruns of CBS episodes)*. Sundays at 7 P.M. on NBC-TV *(Jun.–Oct. 1956; reruns)*. 78 episodes.

Appendix II: Chronology

1950

October 12 — *The George Burns and Gracie Allen Show* premieres on CBS' Thursday night schedule, as a live, biweekly broadcast.

1951

October 15 — *I Love Lucy*, starring Lucille Ball, premieres on CBS' Monday night schedule. It is TV's first sitcom filmed before a live audience, and will soon become the first show of any kind to be watched by 10 million viewers.

1952

May — Betty White's *Life with Elizabeth* premieres as a local show on Los Angeles' KLAC-TV.

June 16 — *My Little Margie*, starring Gale Storm, premieres on CBS' Monday night schedule, as a summer replacement for *I Love Lucy*. It returns for a second season on NBC in October, then moves to CBS in early 1953.

October 3 — *Our Miss Brooks*, starring Eve Arden, premieres on CBS' Friday night schedule.

October 9 — *The George Burns and Gracie Allen Show* begins its run as a weekly, filmed show, after two years of biweekly live broadcasts.

October 15 — *I Married Joan*, starring Joan Davis, premieres on NBC's Wednesday night schedule.

1953

February 1 — *Private Secretary*, starring Ann Sothern, premieres on CBS' Sunday night schedule.

February 5	Lucille Ball wins an Emmy as Best Comedienne of 1952. *I Love Lucy* is named Best Situation Comedy.
October	*Life with Elizabeth* makes its debut in first-run syndication, on film, after a successful run on local TV in Los Angeles. It is soon seen on more than 70 stations around the U.S.
October	NBC pairs *I Married Joan* and *My Little Margie* on its Wednesday night lineup.
October 9	*Topper*, starring Anne Jeffreys, premieres on CBS' Friday night schedule.

1954

February 11	Eve Arden wins an Emmy as Best Female Star of Regular Series in 1953. *I Love Lucy* is again named Best Situation Comedy.
October 4	*December Bride* premieres on CBS' Monday night schedule, following *I Love Lucy*.

1955

April 6	*I Married Joan* has its final prime time broadcast on NBC.
Spring	Guild Films ceases production of new *Life with Elizabeth* episodes.
August 24	*My Little Margie* has its final prime time broadcast on NBC.
Fall	Reruns from *Private Secretary*'s first three seasons are sold in syndication, under the title *Susie*, while new episodes continue to air Sunday nights on CBS.
September	*Topper* has its final prime time broadcast on CBS, but returns with prime time reruns on ABC's Monday night schedule in October.

1956

March 17	Lucille Ball receives an Emmy as Best Actress of 1955 (Continuing Performance).
September 21	*Our Miss Brooks* has its final prime time broadcast, but will continue in CBS daytime reruns until 1957.
September 29	*The Gale Storm Show: Oh! Susanna* premieres on CBS' Saturday night schedule.

1957

May 10	*Date with the Angels*, Betty White's first network sitcom, premieres on ABC's Friday night lineup.
June 24	*I Love Lucy* concludes its sixth and final season. Lucille Ball will return to prime time in September with an occasional series of hour-long Lucy specials. CBS will show prime time reruns of the original series until 1961, and daytime reruns until 1967.
September 10	*Private Secretary* has its final prime time telecast. Ann Sothern is embroiled in a lawsuit with the production company over the terms of her contract.

September 17	*The Eve Arden Show* premieres on CBS' Tuesday night schedule.
November 6	*The Ford Lucille Ball-Desi Arnaz Show* premieres on CBS, with Ann Sothern guest starring as her *Private Secretary* character.

1958

January 20	*Love That Jill,* starring Anne Jeffreys, premieres on ABC's Monday night schedule. Low ratings will kill the show by April, after only 13 broadcasts.
February 5	Disappointed with the ratings of *Date with the Angels,* ABC and the sponsor agree to convert it into *The Betty White Show,* a live sketch comedy program. The new series is not a success, and comes to an end in April.
March 25	*The Eve Arden Show* has its final prime time telecast.
September	*The George Burns and Gracie Allen Show* has its final prime time telecast on CBS. *The George Burns Show,* without Gracie Allen, premieres on NBC in October, but will be canceled in 1959.
September 24	*The Donna Reed Show* premieres on ABC's Wednesday night schedule. The show will continue in prime time until 1966, and in ABC daytime reruns until 1968.
October 6	*The Ann Sothern Show,* a Desilu product, premieres on CBS' Monday night schedule, in the time slot previously allotted to *December Bride.* It will survive in prime time until 1961.
October 13	*Westinghouse Desilu Playhouse,* which includes occasional hour-long *Lucy* episodes, premieres on CBS' Monday night schedule, following *The Ann Sothern Show.*

1959

September	*December Bride* concludes its fifth and final season. CBS will revive the show for prime-time reruns in 1960 and 1961, and will air its spin-off *Pete and Gladys* from 1960 to 1962.
October	*The Gale Storm Show: Oh! Susanna* moves to ABC after a three-year run on CBS. The show will continue in prime time until 1960.

Appendix III: Ten More Leading Ladies

Aside from the actresses spotlighted in this book, there were others integral to the history of television comedy in the 1950s. The TV success of Gracie Allen, Eve Arden, Lucille Ball, and others inevitably led to imitation, particularly at CBS, the reigning home of the sitcom. CBS would, in fact, introduce at least one new female-centered sitcom every year until 1958. While not all their shows enjoyed success, here are ten more women who made 1950s sitcom history headlining their own half-hour comedy shows:

Lynn Bari (1913–1989) was one of the first film actresses to tackle a TV sitcom. A former contract player at 20th Century Fox, where she was typecast in other-woman roles, Bari starred in a live sitcom, *Detective's Wife,* aired Fridays at 8:30 P.M. on CBS during the summer of 1950. She played Connie Conway, wife of a private investigator, who usually got involved in his cases. That show was short-lived, as was her second effort, *Boss Lady* (NBC, July–September 1952), another summer replacement series that cast her as the CEO of a construction company. Lee Patrick (later Henrietta on *Topper*) played Bari's secretary on the latter show.

Joan Caulfield (1922–1991) seemed poised for sitcom stardom in the 1950s, but neither of her two starring roles caught fire with the public. Gifted at musical comedy, she was a Paramount contract player in the 1940s, appearing in movies like *Blue Skies* (1946) before plunging into TV. Her first thankless assignment was to replace Lucille Ball as Liz Cooper in CBS' TV adaptation of *My Favorite Husband*. She played that role from 1953 to 1955, when she was replaced by Vanessa Brown. Two years later, Caulfield made a sitcom comeback as the star of *Sally* (NBC, 1957-58), playing a former salesgirl hired as traveling companion to rich, eccentric Myrtle Banford (Marion Lorne, later *Bewitched*'s Aunt Clara). Stuck in a rough Sunday evening time slot, opposite *The Jack Benny Show* on CBS and *Maverick* on ABC, *Sally* expired after one season. Caulfield spent much of her later career onstage, making only sporadic television appearances.

Celeste Holm (1919–), winner of a Best Supporting Actress Oscar for *Gentleman's Agreement* (Fox, 1947) and famous for her Broadway role as Ado Annie in *Oklahoma!*, was considered quite a catch when CBS signed her for *Honestly, Celeste!*, a sitcom that premiered in the fall of 1954. Holm played a former journalism professor who went to work on a New York newspaper. The highly publicized filmed show was a complete bust, and was canceled in December 1954, after only eight telecasts. Her more recent video ventures have included supporting roles in the sitcom *Nancy* (NBC, 1970-71), and the drama *Promised Land* (CBS, 1996–99).

Betty Hutton (1921–) was, like Holm, widely touted as a catch when CBS signed her for *The Betty Hutton Show* in 1959. A gifted musical comedy performer, she'd been a Paramount star in the 1940s, notably in Preston Sturges' classic *The Miracle of Morgan's Creek*, and later played Annie Oakley in MGM's film version of *Annie Get Your Gun* (1950). Her sitcom concerned manicurist Goldie Appleby, forced to mingle with the rich folks when longtime customer Mr. Strickland died and left her a fortune, also naming her guardian of his children. Competition from ABC's *The Donna Reed Show* translated into low ratings for Hutton, whose show was canceled in 1960 after one season. For Hutton, who'd had an unhappy experience starring in a highly promoted but ill-fated musical special, *Satins and Spurs*, on NBC in 1954, television was generally a disappointment.

Ida Lupino (1918–1995) was a highly regarded movie actress (and pioneering female director) who co-starred with then-husband Howard Duff in the CBS sitcom *Mr. Adams and Eve* (1957-58). Like Lucille Ball, Lupino took the series largely for the opportunity to team up with her husband. She played Eve Drake, half of a husband-and-wife team of movie stars, in a show purportedly based on some of her and Duff's real-life experiences. The series was only a moderate success, and Lupino would later lose her enthusiasm for acting, preferring to spend most of her time in the 1960s directing. As a director, she worked on shows ranging from *Bewitched* (ABC, 1964–72) and the horror anthology *Thriller* (1960–62) to, most incongruously, *Gilligan's Island* (CBS, 1964–67).

Peg Lynch (1916–) created and starred in *Ethel and Albert,* a husband-and-wife comedy that enjoyed only moderate success on TV, though highly popular as a radio attraction in the 1940s. The low-key suburban adventures of Mr. and Mrs. Arbuckle first came to TV as a segment of NBC's popular daytime show, *The Kate Smith Hour*. Spun off into a half-hour prime time sitcom in 1953, the show aired on NBC through late 1954, then resurfaced as a summer replacement

In the shadow of Lucy: Joan Caulfield, with on-screen husband Barry Nelson, in CBS' *My Favorite Husband.*

for *December Bride* on CBS in 1955. That fall, it moved to ABC's Friday night schedule, but was dropped in the summer of 1956.

Janis Paige (1922–) was CBS' 1955 candidate for sitcom stardom. A Warner Brothers' contract player in the 1940s, she later made a splash on Broadway as the star of *The Pajama Game*, but lost the lead in the movie to Doris Day. *It's Always Jan* (1955-56) cast her as Janis Stewart, nightclub singer and single mom to daughter Josie (Jeri Lou James), mixing music into the standard sitcom format. The show's time slot, Saturdays at 9:30 P.M., had proved a tough row to hoe for *My Favorite Husband,* and would be no luckier for *Hey, Jeannie!,* starring Jeannie Carson, a year later. *Jan* was canceled after one season. Paige continued to be a busy stage and TV actress for the next several decades, seen in regular roles during the 1980s and 1990s on the soap operas *Santa Barbara* and *General Hospital.*

Elena Verdugo (1926–) starred in CBS' live sitcom *Meet Millie* from 1952 to 1956. The former Universal contract player, who'd toiled in films like *House of Frankenstein* (1944) and Abbott and Costello's *Little Giant* (1946), replaced Audrey Totter, who'd launched *Millie* as a radio show in 1951. Verdugo played a New York–based secretary whose interfering mother (Florence Halop) worked overtime trying to fix her up with eligible men. *Meet Millie* featured two faces familiar to viewers of later sitcoms—Halop played matron Florence on *Night Court* (NBC, 1984–92), while Marvin Kaplan, *Millie*'s aspiring poet Alfred Prinzmetal, resurfaced as nerdy diner regular Henry on CBS' *Alice* (1976–85). As for Verdugo, she later co-starred in another CBS sitcom, *Many Happy Returns* (1964-65), but is better remembered by TV viewers for her long run as Nurse Consuelo Lopez on *Marcus Welby, M.D.* (ABC, 1969–76).

Ethel Waters (1896–1977) was the first African-American actress to play the lead in a TV sitcom. She was the first star of ABC's *Beulah* (1950–53), adapted from a long-popular radio series about a sassy maid in a white household. Waters, critically praised for her role in the stage and film versions of *The Member of the Wedding,* and Oscar-nominated for *Pinky* (Fox, 1949), didn't much care for the stereotypical TV role, and left *Beulah* after two years. Oscar winner Hattie McDaniel (who had played the character on radio) signed to replace her, but soon fell ill, leaving Louise Beavers to step in. Although less criticized than *The Amos 'n' Andy Show* (CBS, 1951–53), *Beulah* too was controversial in a time when African-American viewers were beginning to demand more respectful representation on TV. Waters was later seen on many religious TV broadcasts, and penned two memoirs, *His Eye Is on the Sparrow* and *To Me It's Wonderful.*

Marie Wilson (1916–1972) practically patented the role of the dumb blonde, most notably as the star of *My Friend Irma*. Irma, scatterbrained secretary to a crabby lawyer, was a ubiquitous character in the early 1950s. Heard on a CBS radio series that had begun in 1947, Wilson also starred in movies like *My Friend Irma Goes West* (Paramount, 1950), which gave Jerry Lewis and Dean Martin some of their first national exposure. *My Friend Irma*, the TV sitcom, aired live from 1952 to 1954, going through several cast changes in search of the perfect formula. Wilson had the biggest success of her career playing dumb blondes, but sometimes regretted that the public's ready acceptance of this persona stood in the way of her being offered other roles.

Chapter Notes

Introduction

1. Rick Mitz, *The Great TV Sitcom Book* (New York: Perigee Books, 1988), p. 311.

1. Gracie Allen

1. George Burns, *Gracie: A Love Story* (New York: Putnam's, 1988), p. 175.
2. *Ibid*, p. 164.
3. *Ibid*, p. 241.
4. "Burns & Allen To Join TV Parade," *Variety*, August 23, 1950, p. 31.
5. "B&A's 18G Weekly As Carnation Buys CBS Video Series," *Variety*, September 6, 1950, p. 29.
6. *Variety*, October 18, 1950.
7. Burns, *Gracie*, p. 245.
8. Cynthia Clements and Sandra Weber, *George Burns and Gracie Allen: A Bio-Bibliography* (Westport, CT: Greenwood Press, 1996), p. 31.
9. Fred De Cordova, *Johnny Came Lately: An Autobiography* (New York: Simon and Schuster, 1988), p. 109.
10. Burns, *Gracie*, p. 157.
11. Max Wilk, *The Golden Age of Television: Notes from the Survivors* (New York: Delacorte Press, 1976), p. 177.
12. Martin Gottfried, *George Burns and the Hundred-Year Dash* (New York: Simon and Schuster, 1996), p. 166.
13. Burns, *Gracie*, p. 274.
14. Yvonne Lime Fedderson, letter to the author, December 2, 2005.
15. "Burns Without Allen." *Time*, March 3, 1958, p. 46.
16. Cheryl Blythe and Susan Sackett, *Say Good Night, Gracie!: The Story of Burns & Allen* (New York: Dutton, 1986), p. 187.
17. *Variety*, September 2, 1964.
18. Maria Efantis Brennan, telephone interview with the author, December 12, 2005 (all subsequent quotes from Brennan are from this interview).

2. Eve Arden

1. James Gregory, *The Lucille Ball Story* (New York: New American Library, 1974), p. 45.
2. Alvin Krebs, "Eve Arden, Actress, Is Dead at 83," *New York Times*, November 13, 1990, p. 26.
3. *Current Biography* (1953), p. 32.
4. "Eve Arden: One-Man Woman," *TV Guide*, April 2, 1954, pp. 6–7.
5. "No Competition," *Time*, October 13, 1952, p. 88.
6. Jack Gould, "TV's Top Comediennes," *New York Times Magazine*, December 27, 1953, p. 17.
7. Hyman Goldberg, "'Our Miss Brooks' America's Favorite Schoolmarm," *Cosmopolitan*, June 1953, p. 71.
8. "No Competition," p. 91.
9. Gerald Nachman, *Raised on Radio: In Quest of the Lone Ranger ... And Other Lost Heroes from Radio's Heyday* (New York: Pantheon Books, 1998), p. 219.
10. Douglas Brooks West, telephone interview with the author, January 10, 2006 (all subsequent quotations from West are from this interview).
11. "Goodbye, Miss Brooks?" *TV Guide*, April 28, 1956, p. 14.
12. *TV Guide*, March 3, 1956, p. 18.
13. "Goodbye," p. 14.
14. *Variety*, September 25, 1957.

15. *TV Guide*, December 28, 1957.
16. Eve Arden, *Three Phases of Eve: An Autobiography* (New York: St. Martin's Press, 1985), p. 268.
17. *New York Times*, February 23, 1983.
18. *New York Post*, February 23, 1983.
19. Bert A. Folkart, "Eve Arden, 82; Portrayed TV's Beloved 'Our Miss Brooks,'" *Los Angeles Times*, November 13, 1990, p. 24.
20. Arden, *Three Phases of Eve*, p. 70.
21. *Ibid*, p. 121.

3. Lucille Ball

1. Hector Arce, *Groucho* (Putnam, 1979), p. 261.
2. Warren G. Harris, *Lucy & Desi: The Legendary Love Story of Television's Most Famous Couple* (New York: Simon & Schuster, 1991), pp. 120–121.
3. Bob Johnson, "What Is Lucy Really Like?" *TV Star Parade*, April 1965, p. 72.
4. *Variety*, September 20, 1950.
5. Eleanor Harris, *The Real Story of Lucille Ball* (New York: Farrar, Straus & Young, 1954), p. 56.
6. Jess Oppenheimer, *Laughs, Luck, and Lucy: How I Came to Create the Most Popular Sitcom of All Time* (New York: Syracuse University Press, 1999), p. 139.
7. Diane Haithman, "The Industry's Debt to Lucy," *Los Angeles Times*, April 30, 1989, p. 3.
8. Oppenheimer, *Laughs, Luck, and Lucy*, p. 170.
9. Steven Bender, *Greasers & Gringos: Latinos, Law, and the American Imagination* (New York: New York University Press, 2003), p. 17.
10. Lucille Ball, *Love, Lucy* (New York: Putnam, 1996), p. 217.
11. Jim Brochu, *Lucy in the Afternoon: An Intimate Memoir of Lucille Ball* (New York: Morrow, 1990), p. 152.
12. Johnson, "What Is Lucy," p. 72.

4. Spring Byington

1. Brandon Tartikoff and Charles Leerhsen, *The Last Great Ride* (New York: Turtle Bay Books, 1992), p. 150.
2. Jordan R. Young, *The Laugh Crafters: Comedy Writing in Radio and TV's Golden Age* (Beverly Hills, CA: Past Times Publishing Co., 1999), p. 19.
3. Warren G. Harris, *Lucy & Desi: The Legendary Love Story of Television's Most Famous Couple* (New York: Simon & Schuster, 1991), p. 209.
4. Boze Hadleigh, *Hollywood Lesbians* (New York: Barricade Books, 1994), p. 26.
5. Desi Arnaz, *A Book* (New York: Morrow, 1976), p. 277.
6. Elsa Molina, "Happiness Knows No Season," *TV Radio Mirror*, November 1955, p. 94.
7. *Current Biography* (1956), p. 94.
8. Molina, "Happiness," p. 94.
9. *New York Times*, October 25, 1950, p. 45.
10. Charles Stumpf, "Spring Byington: Eternal Spring!" *Classic Images*, June 2000, <www.classicimages.com/2000/june00/byington.shtml>
11. Pressbook, *According to Mrs. Hoyle*, Monogram Pictures, 1951.
12. *Daily Variety*, May 31, 1951.
13. "The Female of the Species," *TV Guide*, September 21, 1957.
14. Jeff Kisseloff, *The Box: An Oral History of Television, 1920–1961* (New York: Viking, 1995), p. 543.
15. "Spring Byington: Flying Grandmother," *TV Guide*, March 10, 1956, p. 15.
16. Hadleigh, *Hollywood Lesbians*, p. 27.
17. Axel Madsen, *The Sewing Circle: Hollywood's Greatest Secret: Female Stars Who Loved Other Women* (New York: Birch Lane Press, 1995), p. 144.
18. Hadleigh, *Hollywood Lesbians*, p. 27.
19. Molina, "Happiness," p. 93.
20. Spring Byington, "What Should I Do?" *Photoplay*, October 1956, pp. 8–16.
21. *Variety*, October 8, 1958.
22. Robert Fuller, telephone interview with the author, December 7, 2005 (all subsequent quotations from Robert Fuller are from this interview).
23. Molina, "Happiness," p. 94.

5. Joan Davis

1. "Joan Davis: Crazy Mixed-Up Kid?" *TV Guide*, July 2, 1954, p. 16.
2. "Sneak-In Success," *Time*, September 10, 1945, p. 57.
3. Jack Gaver and Dave Stanley, *There's Laughter in the Air!: Radio's Top Comedians and Their Best Shows* (New York: Greenberg, 1945), p. 269.
4. Jordan R. Young, *The Laugh Crafters: Comedy Writing in Radio and TV's Golden Age* (Beverly Hills, CA: Past Times Publishing, 1999), p. 151.
5. Gregory Koseluk, *Eddie Cantor: A Life in Show Business* (Jefferson, NC: McFarland, 1995) p. 315.
6. Goldman, *Banjo Eyes: Eddie Cantor and the Birth of Modern Stardom* (New York: Oxford University Press, 1997), p. 238.
7. "Campbell, United Drug in Bid for Davis-Haley Package; Upped to 25G," *Variety*, January 17, 1945, p. 27.
8. "Joan Davis Drops Off Sealtest For United in Fall," *Variety*, January 31, 1945, p. 19.

9. "Joan Davis' No. 3 Spot Cues Trade O.O. at Web Maneuvers on Drug Deal," *Variety*, March 7, 1945, p. 30.
10. "Sealtest's 'You Can't Say Goodby' Irks Joan Davis," *Variety*, July 4, 1945, p. 27.
11. "Agency, Sponsor, RKO in Joan Davis Promotion Parlay for CBS Teeoff," *Variety*, August 29, 1945, p. 24.
12. "Sneak-In Success," p. 57.
13. Fredda Dudley, "Leave it to Joan," *Radio & Television Mirror*, November 1949, p. 54.
14. Gaver and Stanley, *There's Laughter in the Air!*, p. 267.
15. "Joan Davis TV Show Prepped as CBS Kine," *Variety*, January 24, 1951, p. 25.
16. "CBS Preps Situation TV Comedies As Answer to NBC's Star Lineup," *Variety*, February 7, 1951, p. 27.
17. "Heavy Switch to Film; 46 Shows Now Set for Lensing This Fall," *Variety*, September 17, 1952, p. 33.
18. Jim Backus and Henny Backus, *Forgive Us Our Digressions: An Autobiography* (New York: St. Martin's Press, 1988), p. 154.
19. *Variety*, October 22, 1952.
20. Backus, *Forgive Us Our Digressions*, p. 157.
21. "Joan Davis: Crazy Mixed-Up Kid?" pp. 15–17.
22. "I Married Joan," *Radio-TV Mirror*, October 1953, p. 73.
23. Sherwood Schwartz, telephone interview with the author, May 23, 2006 (all subsequent quotes from Schwartz are from this interview).
24. Jack O'Brian, "TV Off-Guard in New York," *TV Star Parade*, May 1955, p. 82.
25. Jim Backus, "Jim Backus Takes A Long, Humorous Look at TV Ratings," *TV Guide*, July 27, 1957, p. 9.
26. James Robert Parish, *The Slapstick Queens* (New York: Castle Books, 1973), p. 166.
27. *Ibid.*

6. Anne Jeffreys

1. *Variety*, June 13, 1945, p. 34.
2. "Anne Jeffreys: TV's Loveliest Ghost," *TV Guide*, June 4, 1954, p. 12.
3. Michael Mallory, "Ghosts with the Most! Anne Jeffreys and Robert Sterling." *Scarlet Street*, no. 38, 2000, p. 45.
4. Atkinson, Brooks, "New York to Music," *New York Times*, January 19, 1947, section II, p. 1.
5. Steffen Silvis, "First Rose," *Willamette Week*, March 23, 2005, <www.wweek.com/story/php?story=6134>
6. Douglas Hunt, "Anne Jeffreys: 'Sickly Child' Overcomes Tragedy to Become Hollywood Star," *Journal of Longevity*, vol. 8, no. 9 (2002), p. 11.
7. Mallory, "Ghosts with the Most!" p. 48.
8. Meryle Secrest, *Stephen Sondheim: A Life* (New York: Knopf, 1988), p. 97.
9. *Variety*, October 14, 1953.
10. Jack Holland, "Thank You, Darling," *TV Star Parade*, May 1955, p. 57.
11. Chris Pustorino, "Fly on the Wall: Kathleen Freeman," *Scarlet Street*, no. 37, 2000, p. 51.
12. "Anne Jeffreys: TV's Loveliest Ghost," p. 11.
13. Steven Lance, *Written Out of Television: The Encyclopedia of Cast Changes and Character Replacements, 1945–1994* (Lanham, MD: Scarecrow Press, 1996), p. 407.
14. *Variety*, November 30, 1955.
15. *Variety*, January 22, 1958.
16. Mallory, "Ghosts with the Most!" p. 51.
17. Mark Teschner, telephone interview with the author, March 30, 2006 (all subsequent quotations from Teschner are from this interview).
18. Harry Haun, "Playbill on Opening Night: *Match*'s Frank Langella Chex It Out," *Playbill*, April 9, 2004, <www.playbill.com/features/article/85471.html>
19. Kulzer, Dina-Marie, *Television Series Regulars of the Fifties and Sixties in Interview* (Jefferson, NC: McFarland, 1992), p. 73.

7. Donna Reed

1. Freeman, Donald. "Donna Reed: Fire and Ice," *Saturday Evening Post*, March 28, 1964, p. 22.
2. "Donna Reed, Farmer's Daughter," *TV Guide*, May 6, 1961, p. 14.
3. *Ibid*, p. 12.
4. Jay Fultz, *In Search of Donna Reed* (Iowa City: University of Iowa Press, 1998), p. 75.
5. James Jones, *From Here to Eternity* (New York: Delta, 1998), p. 847.
6. Fred Zinnemann, *A Life in the Movies: An Autobiography* (New York: Scribner's, 1992), p. 124.
7. "Just What the Doctor Ordered," *TV Guide*, December 13, 1958, p. 10.
8. Fultz, *In Search*, p. 119.
9. Roseanne Arnold, *My Lives* (New York: Ballantine Books, 1994), p. 5.
10. Fultz, *In Search*, p. 118.
11. "Donna Reed, Farmer's Daughter," p. 13.
12. *Variety*, October 1, 1958.
13. "Just What the Doctor Ordered," p. 9.
14. *Variety*, October 7, 1959.
15. "Just What the Doctor Ordered," p. 11.
16. "No Prima Donna," *TV Guide*, March 26, 1960, p. 26.
17. Richard F. Shepard, "Star on a Campaign: Busy Exploitation Schedule Devised for Donna Reed of A.B.C.-TV," *New York Times*, November 1, 1959, p. X-13.

18. Marian Dern, "'Sweet, Sincere, and Solvent,'" *TV Guide,* June 20, 1964, p. 11.
19. Jay S. Harris, ed., *TV Guide: The First 25 Years* (New York: Simon & Schuster, 1978), p. 96.
20. Freeman, "Donna Reed: Fire and Ice," p. 22.
21. Dern, "Sweet, Sincere," p. 12.
22. *Ibid.*
23. "Legends of the Games: Paul Petersen of *Dream Girl of '67*," <www.tvgameshows.net/paulpetersen3.htm>
24. Brenda Scott Royce, *Hogan's Heroes: A Comprehensive Reference to the 1965–1971 Television Comedy Series, with Cast Biographies and an Episode Guide* (Jefferson, N.C.: McFarland, 1993), p. 34.
25. Fultz, *In Search,* p. 156.
26. "Donna Reed, 64, Dies of Cancer at Her Home," *Los Angeles Times,* January 14, 1986, p. 1.
27. "Legends of the Games," <www.tvgameshows.net/paulpetersen3.htm>.
28. Michael Seiler, "Donna Reed, Oscar Winner and TV Star, Dies at 64," *Los Angeles Times,* January 15, 1986, p. 3.
29. Larry Hagman with Todd Gold, *Hello Darlin': Tall (and Absolutely True) Tales About My Life* (New York: Simon and Schuster, 2001), p. 212.
30. *Ibid.*
31. Fultz, *In Search,* p. 191.
32. Patricia Brennan, "Waiting for Word on *Coach*: Another Chapter in Her 43-Year Success Story," *Washington Post,* April 29, 1990, p. Y-7.
33. Don Freeman, "Outtakes: Simply Fab," *Emmy,* January/February 1995, p. 72.

8. Ann Sothern

1. Richard G. Hubler, "A Belle Named Sothern," *Coronet,* June 1959, p. 93.
2. Hubler, "Belle," p. 92.
3. James Robert Parish, ed., *The Great Movie Series* (South Brunswick, N.J.: Barnes, 1971), p. 241.
4. Kyle Crichton, "Amazing Maisie," *Collier's,* July 12, 1941.
5. *Variety,* July 18, 1945.
6. Aljean Harmetz, "Ann Sothern Dauntless," *New York Times,* October 11, 1987, p. A-1.
7. Kirk Douglas, *The Ragman's Son: An Autobiography* (New York: Simon & Schuster, 1988), p. 145.
8. Wender, Susan, "I Can Never Marry You (Richard Egan-Ann Sothern)," *Modern Screen,* June 1956, p. 93.
9. Hubler, "A Belle Named Sothern," p. 92.
10. "Sympathetic Susie," *Time,* April 20, 1953, p. 64.
11. "Those Beverly Hills Beauties," *Complete TV,* August 1957, p. 19.
12. Elaine Woo, "Ann Sothern; Gave Strong Women a Voice in Film and TV," *Los Angeles Times,* March 17, 2001, p. B-6.
13. "Sympathetic Susie," p. 62.
14. "Singing Secretary," *TV Guide,* September 18, 1954, p. 21.
15. "Ann Sothern in Tirade at Emmy; Demands a Probe," *Variety,* February 6, 1957, p. 25.
16. "Ann Sothern to Scrap 'Secretary' Unless TPA Works Out a New Deal," *Variety,* February 27, 1957, p. 31.
17. "A Belle Named Sothern," p. 93.
18. "Everything Is In Limbo," *TV Guide,* July 20, 1957, p. 21.
19. *Variety,* October 8, 1958.
20. "Ann Sothern Is Playing That Blonde Again," *TV Guide,* October 18, 1958, p. 18.
21. "Don Porter's Back, and Ann Sothern's Got Him," *TV Guide,* April 16, 1960, p. 14.
22. *Ibid.*
23. "Ann Sothern, Businesswoman," *TV Guide,* March 21, 1959, p. 14.
24. *Ibid.*
25. "Goodson-Todman Pitch New Ann Sothern Show," *Variety,* July 18, 1962, p. 22.
26. Geoffrey Mark Fidelman, *The Lucy Book: A Complete Guide to Her Five Decades on Television* (Los Angeles: Renaissance Books, 1999), p. 200.
27. Michael Buckley, "Ann Sothern," *Films in Review,* March 1988, p. 138.
28. "Nick to Dust off Two Sothern Skeins," *Variety,* January 28, 1987, p. 54.
29. Buckley, "Ann Sothern," p. 140.
30. Harmetz, "Ann Sothern Dauntless," p. A-1.
31. Aljean Harmetz, "Ann Sothern Is Dead at 92; Savvy Star of B-Films and TV," *New York Times,* March 17, 2001, p. C-17.

9. Gale Storm

1. Gale Storm, as told to Jane Morris, "You Can't Buy Happiness," *TV Star Parade,* December 1954, p. 33.
2. Storm, "You Can't Buy Happiness," p. 58.
3. McLellan, Dennis, "A Star with a Place in the Sun: Gale Storm Is Looking Ahead to a Marriage and New Film Roles," *Los Angeles Times,* April 14, 1988, p. 3.
4. Jean Lewis, "Dreams Do Come True," *TV Picture Life,* April 1957, p. 52.
5. Gale Storm, telephone interview with the author, January 19, 2006. All subsequent quotations from Gale Storm, where not otherwise noted, are from interviews on January 19 and 24, 2006.
6. Lewis, "Dreams Do Come True," p. 52.
7. Gale Storm. *I Ain't Down Yet: The Autobi-*

ography of My Little Margie (Indianapolis: Bobbs-Merrill, 1981), p. 64.
   8. *Variety,* June 18, 1952.
   9. "'Margie' Coming Home to Roost on CBS-TV Sked," *Variety,* October 22, 1952, p. 23.
   10. "Storm Battered," *Variety,* October 15, 1952, p. 20.
   11. Storm, *I Ain't Down Yet,* p. 68.
   12. *Variety,* September 9, 1953.
   13. Storm, *I Ain't Down Yet,* p. 75.
   14. Boyd Magers and Michael G. Fitzgerald, *Westerns Women* (Jefferson, NC: McFarland, 1999), p. 231.
   15. "The Hands Have It," *TV Guide,* April 6, 1957, p. 14.
   16. "Gale Storm Tells Why She Has Lasted," *TV Guide,* June 29, 1957, p. 18.
   17. "Gale Storm Changes Her Course," *TV Guide,* June 6, 1959, p. 26.
   18. *Ibid.*
   19. *Variety,* October 7, 1959.
   20. Storm, *I Ain't Down Yet,* p. 89.
   21. *Ibid,* p. 94.

10. Betty White

   1. "Betty White: My First 46 Years in Television." Lecture recorded at the Smithsonian Institution, September 7, 1995, <http://smithsonianassociates.org/programs/white/white.asp>
   2. Betty White, telephone interview with the author, February 27, 2006. All subsequent quotations from Betty White, except where otherwise noted, are from this interview.
   3. "Biography: Betty White." New York: A & E Home Video, 2003.
   4. Betty White, *Betty White: In Person* (New York: Doubleday, 1987), p. 111.
   5. Tess White, "My Daughter, Betty White," *TV Radio Mirror,* February 1955, p. 30.
   6. Betty White, *Here We Go Again: My Life in Television* (New York: Scribner's, 1995), p. 34.
   7. White, "My Daughter," p. 78.
   8. Brent Mark, "The Girl Who Reversed the Trend ... in Necklines," *TV and Movie Starland,* May 1954, p. 61.
   9. *Ibid.*
   10. *Daily Variety,* May 19, 1952.
   11. *Variety,* January 6, 1954, p. 104.
   12. Mark, "Girl Who," p. 61.
   13. White, *Here We Go Again,* p. 88.
   14. *Variety,* October 21, 1953.
   15. "Guild Films Set $2,200,000 Budget for '54 Product," *Variety,* January 27, 1954, p. 27.
   16. Jack Holland, "Can I Ever Be a Wife?" *TV Star Parade,* December 1954, p. 38.
   17. "Vidpix Producers Face a Dilemma," *Variety,* December 9, 1953, p. 29.
   18. "The Angels Rush In." *TV Guide,* July 27, 1957, p. 19.
   19. White, *Here We Go Again,* p. 110.
   20. *TV Guide,* July 9, 1957.
   21. "The Angels Rush In," p. 20.
   22. *Variety,* February 12, 1958, p. 34.
   23. Valerie J. Nelson, "Naughty Lady of Shady Lane," *Los Angeles Times,* July 13, 1999, p. 1.
   24. Bill Davidson, "Kidding the Network for Fun and Profit," *TV Guide,* September 24, 1977, p. 22.
   25 *Ibid,* p. 21.
   26. White, *Here We Go Again,* p. 249.
   27. Lori Golden, "Betty White: A Golden Girl to All Animals," *The Pet Press,* January 2001, <www.-thepetpress-la.com/articles/bettywhite.htm>
   28. Gale Storm, telephone interview with the author, January 24, 2006.
   29. Nelson, "Naughty Lady," p. 1.

Selected Bibliography

Arden, Eve. *Three Phases of Eve: An Autobiography*. New York: St. Martin's, 1985.

Arnaz, Desi. *A Book*. New York: Morrow, 1976.

Backus, Jim, and Henny Backus. *Forgive Us Our Digressions: An Autobiography*. New York: St. Martin's, 1988.

Bartelt, Chuck, and Barbara Bergeron, eds. *Variety Obituaries*. New York: Garland, 1988.

Blythe, Cheryl, and Susan Sackett. *Say Good Night, Gracie!: The Story of Burns & Allen*. New York: Dutton, 1986.

Brooks, Tim, and Earle Marsh. *The Complete Directory to Prime Time Network and Cable TV Shows, 1946–Present*. 8th ed. New York: Ballantine, 2003.

Burns, George. *Gracie: A Love Story*. New York: Putnam, 1988.

Clements, Cynthia, and Sandra Weber. *George Burns and Gracie Allen: A Bio-Bibliography*. Westport, CT: Greenwood, 1996.

De Cordova, Fred. *Johnny Came Lately: An Autobiography*. New York: Simon and Schuster, 1988.

DeLong, Thomas A. *Radio Stars: An Illustrated Biographical Dictionary of 953 Performers, 1920 Through 1960*. Jefferson, NC: McFarland, 1996.

Dunning, John. *Tune in Yesterday: The Ultimate Encyclopedia of Old-Time Radio, 1925–1976*. Englewood Cliffs, NJ: Prentice Hall, 1976.

Fidelman, Geoffrey Mark. *The Lucy Book: A Complete Guide to Her Five Decades on Television*. Los Angeles: Renaissance, 1999.

Fultz, Jay. *In Search of Donna Reed*. Iowa City: University of Iowa Press, 1998.

Gaver, Jack, and Dave Stanley. *There's Laughter in the Air! Radio's Top Comedians and Their Best Shows*. New York: Greenberg, 1945.

Goldberg, Lee. *Unsold TV Pilots: 1955 Through 1988*. Jefferson, NC: McFarland, 1990.

Gottfried, Martin. *George Burns and the Hundred-Year Dash*. New York: Simon and Schuster, 1996.

Hyatt, Wesley. *Short-Lived Television Series, 1948–1978: Thirty Years of More Than 1,000 Flops*. Jefferson, NC: McFarland, 2003.

Kulzer, Dina-Marie. *Television Series Regulars of the Fifties and Sixties in Interview*. Jefferson, NC: McFarland, 1992.

Lance, Steven. *Written Out of Television: The Encyclopedia of Cast Changes and Character Replacements, 1945–1994*. Lanham, MD: Scarecrow, 1996.

Martin, Linda, and Kerry Segrave. *Women in Comedy*. Secaucus, NJ: Citadel, 1986.

Mitz, Rick. *The Great TV Sitcom Book*. New York: Perigee, 1988.

Nachman, Gerald. *Raised on Radio*. New York: Pantheon, 1998.

O'Neil, Thomas. *The Emmys: The Ultimate, Unofficial Guide to the Battle of TV's Best Shows and Greatest Stars*. 3rd ed. New York: Perigee, 2000.

Parish, James Robert. *The Great Movie Series*. South Brunswick, NJ: Barnes, 1971.

_____. *The Slapstick Queens*. New York: Castle, 1973.

Royce, Brenda Scott. *Donna Reed: A Bio-Bibliography*. New York: Greenwood, 1990.

_____. *Hogan's Heroes: A Comprehensive Reference to the 1965–1971 Television Comedy Series, with Cast Biographies and an Episode Guide*. Jefferson, NC: McFarland, 1993.

Sanders, Coyne Steven, and Tom Gilbert. *Desilu: The Story of Lucille Ball and Desi Arnaz*. New York: Morrow, 1993.

Schultz, Margie. *Ann Sothern: A Bio-Bibliography*. New York: Greenwood, 1990.

Shapiro, Mitchell E. *Television Network Daytime and Late-Night Programming, 1959–1989*. Jefferson, NC: McFarland, 1990.

Silverman, Stephen M. *Funny Ladies: The Women Who Make Us Laugh*. New York: Abrams, 1999.

Smith, Sally Bedell. *In All His Glory: The Life of William S. Paley, The Legendary Tycoon and His Brilliant Circle*. New York: Simon and Schuster, 1990.

Smith, Thorne. *Topper: A Ribald Adventure*. Thorndike, ME: Thorndike, 1985.

Storm, Gale, with Bill Libby. *I Ain't Down Yet: The Autobiography of My Little Margie*. Indianapolis: Bobbs-Merrill, 1981.

Terrace, Vincent. *Radio Program Openings and Closings, 1931–1972*. Jefferson, NC: McFarland, 2003.

Variety Television Reviews. New York: Garland, 1989–1991.

White, Betty. *Here We Go Again: My Life in Television*. New York: Scribner, 1995.

Wilk, Max. *The Golden Age of Television: Notes from the Survivors*. New York: Delacorte, 1976.

Young, Jordan R. *The Laugh Crafters: Comedy Writing in Radio and TV's Golden Age*. Beverly Hills, CA: Past Times, 1999.

Index

Page numbers in *bold italics* indicate photographs.

Abbott, Bud 185
ABC Afternoon Playbreak 35
Academy Awards 22, 61, 112, 140
Academy of Television Arts and Sciences 131, 170–171
According to Mrs. Hoyle 63
Ackerman, Harry 8, 34, 81
Adams, Donna *see* Reed, Donna
Adler, Stella 136
The Adventures of Kit Carson 164
The Adventures of Maisie 127, 128
The Adventures of Ozzie and Harriet 17, 88, 113, 115, 119, 120
The Adventures of Topper 94
Advise and Consent 167
Ah, Wilderness! 61
Albert, Eddie *41*, 143, 159
Albertson, Mabel 64
Albright, Margie (*My Little Margie* character) 48, 68, 144, 145–146, 147–148, 151, 156, 176
The Aldrich Family 9
Alfred Hitchcock Presents 72
Alice 36, 185
All in the Family 2, 3, 56, 147
Allan, Lane 159
Allen, Bessie 6
Allen, Fred 11
Allen, Gracie 1, 2, 3, 5–20, 42, 53, 67, 78, 82, 85, 91, 171, 175, 181, 183
Allen, Hazel 6
Allen, Pearl 6
Allen, Ray 173
Allen, Woody 36
"Allen Sisters" Quartet 6
Allison, Fran 10
Allman, Elvia 87, 175

Ally McBeal 172
Allyson, June 110, 132
Amateau, Rod 19, 175
American Comedy Awards 170
American Movie Classics 107
American Women in Radio and TV 20
American Women's Voluntary Services (AWVS) 158
America's Sweetheart 125
The Amos 'n' Andy Show 8, 23, 46, 185
Anatomy of a Murder 33
Anderson, Lindsay 140
Anderson, Margaret (*Father Knows Best* character) 49
Anderson, Scott M. 108
Andrew, William 173
Andrews, Dana 106
The Andy Griffith Show 32, 105
Angel 55
Angel, Vickie (*Date with the Angels* character) 164, 165, 173
The Ann Sothern Show 1, 3, 53, 70–71, 125, 131, 132–136, 139, 173, 181
Annie Get Your Gun 184
Another Mother for Peace 121–122
Anso Productions 4, 132, 135, 173
Appleby, Goldie (*The Betty Hutton Show* character) 184
Arden, Eve 1, 2, 3, 21–38, 47, 52, 82, 85, 86, 129, 138, 143, 174, 176, 179, 183
Arnaz, Desi 23, 24, 27, 31, 34–35, 39, 40, 42, 43, 44, 46, 47–48, *49*, 50–51, 52, 53, 54, 55, 60, 65, 66, 67, 82, 96, 132, 138, 175
Arnaz, Desi, Jr. 50, 86
Arnaz, Lucie 11
Arthur, Beatrice 2, 35, 36, 57, 169

195

Arthur, Jean 138
Arthur Godfrey and His Friends 86
As Good as It Gets 171
Asher, William 24, 34
Ask Betty White 167
Asmus, Grover 122, 124
Asner, Edward 167–168
At the Circus 22
Atkinson, Brooks 95
Aubrey, James 136
August, Helen 174
August, Tom 174
Auntie Mame 33
Avedon, Barbara 121, 174
Ayres, Lew 110

B.F.'s Daughter 62
B.J. and the Bear 36
Backus, Henny 86
Backus, Jim 83, 85–86, 89, 91, 175
Baer, Art 173
Ball, Lucille 1, 10, 19, 22, 23, 26–27, 31, 34, 39–57, 60, 67, 71, 75, 76, 82, 85, 86, 96, 116, 125, 126, 130, 132, 137, 138, 146, 149, 154, 175, 179, 180, 183, 184
Ballard, Kaye 34, *35*, 65, 138
Bandy Productions 159, 161, 175
Bankhead, Tallulah 53
Banks, Joan 129, 176
Bari, Lynn 183
Barnes, Clive 37
Barr, Roseanne 1, 113
Barry, Gene 29, 176
Bat Masterson 29
Batman 73
Bavier, Frances 32, 174
Baywatch 107
"Be Careful—It's My Art" 34
Beal, John 133
Beavers, Louise 185
Beggar on Horseback 61
Bel Geddes, Barbara 122, 123
Belmont, Terry 142; *see also* Bonnell, Lee
Benaderet, Bea *10*–11, 13, 16, 44, 175
Bender, Steven 49
Bendix, William 99, 144
Bennett, Constance 93, 97, 135
Bennett, Joan 61, 106
Benny, Jack 7, 15, 19, 55, 66
Berg, Gertrude 10
Bergen, Edgar 70
Bergen, Edward 25
Berle, Milton 7, 39, 46, 53, 115, 127, 150
Berlin, Irving 132
Bernds, Edward 82
Berns, Larry 176
Berry, Ken 173
Best, Willie 145, 176
The Best Man 136
The Best Place to Be 122
The Betty Hutton Show 115, 184

Betty White in Person 172
The Betty White Show 162, 164, *166*, 168, *169*, 181
Betty White's Pet Love: How Pets Take Care of Us 172
Betz, Carl 113, *114*, 116, 121, 122, 174
Beulah 9, 185
The Beverly Hillbillies 31, 152, 166
Bewitched 32, 34, 64–65, 87, 100, 105, 145, 183, 184
Beyond Mombasa 12
The Bickersons 102
Bicknell, Arthur 36–37
The Big Street 40
Bigelow Theatre 63
Billboard 141
Billingsley, Barbara 118
Biography 20
Blake, Arthur *83*
Bledel, Alexis 118–119
Bliss, Lela 158
Blondie 132
The Blue Gardenia 128
Blue Skies 183
Bonanza 72
Bonnell, Lee 142, *143*, 144, 149, 150, 156
Bonnell, Philip 143
Bonnell, Susanna 150
Boone, Pat 153
Booth, Shirley 23
Boss Lady 99, 183
Boston Legal 172
Boyd, Jimmy 165, 173
Boys' Night Out 106
Bradbury, Ray 69
The Brady Bunch 88
Brennan, Maria Efantis 20
Brennan, Walter 113
The Brian Keith Show 121
Brice, Fanny 90
Bridge, Loie 175
Bright Promise 106, 107
Bringing Down the House 172
Broadway 20, 22, 36–37, 53–54, 61, 93, 94, 95, 96, 128, 136, 164, 184, 185
Brocco, Peter 17
Brochu, Jim 52
Bromley, Sheila 89, 175
Brooke, Hillary 145, 176
Brooks, Connie (*Our Miss Brooks* character) 3, 11, 21, 23, 24–25, 26, 28–29, 30–31, 37–38, 85, 176
Brooks, James L. 171
Brown, G. Carleton 176
Brown, John 175
Brown, Vanessa 45, 183
Bryant, Nana 29, 176
Buck Rogers in the 25th Century 106
Bunker Bean 76
Burke, Billie 97
Burke's Law 29, 154

INDEX

Burnett, Carol 122
Burns, George 5–20, 78, 175, 176
Burns, Ronnie *15*, 16–17, *18*, 175
Burns, Sandra *15*
Burns, William 175
Burns and Allen see *The George Burns and Gracie Allen Show*
Butterflies Are Free 33, 138
Byington, Spring 1, 3, 59–74, 133, 174

Caesar, Sid 46, 151
Cagney & Lacey 121
Calhoun, Rory 70
Camelot 106
Campbell's Soup 78, 113, 115
Campos, Rafael *137*
Campus Rhythm 142
Canova, Judy 94
Cantor, Eddie 6, 77–78
Capra, Frank 60, 61, 110
Carlson, June 61
Carmichael, Anne Jeffreys see Jeffreys, Anne
Carmichael, Kate 94
Carmichael, Lucy (*The Lucy Show* character) 28
Carnation 8, 9, 11, 14
The Carol Burnett Show 168
Carr, Allan 36
Carr, Geraldine 87
Carradine, John 143
Carroll, Bob, Jr. 34, 35, 41, 43, 54, 55, 138, 175
Carroll, Leo G. 93, 98, *102*, 105, 177
Carroll, Nancy *97*
Carroll, Pat 136
Carson, Jeannie 185
Carson, Johnny 31
Castle, Peggie *83*
Caulfield, Joan 45, 183, 184
Champion, John 72
Chandler, Jeff 24
Chandler, Roy Carey 60–61
Chaney, Frances 94
Channing, Carol 19
Chantler, Peggy 174
Chaplin, Charlie 76
Charlie's Angels 105
Chase, Chevy 36
Cheers 66
Chertok, Jack 128, 131–132, 176
Chertok Television see Jack Chertok Television Productions
Chevillat, Dick 173
cigarette advertising on television 103
Cleaver, June (*Leave It to Beaver* character) 49, 113, 118
Clift, Montgomery 112
Climax 14
Coach 121
Coburn, Charles 61, 63, *64*, 166
Coca, Imogene 10

Cohn, Harry 111, 126
The Colgate Comedy Hour 46
Collison, Wilson 126
"The Colonel's Lady" 34
Communist Party 50
Como, Perry 150
Conn, Didi 20
Connelly, Marc 61
Connors, Chuck 152
Conried, Hans 65
Conway, Connie (*Detective's Wife* character) 183
Cooper, Daisy (*Laramie* character) 72–73
Cooper, Liz (*My Favorite Husband* character) 183
Corman, Roger 139
Costello, Lou 76, 185
Cottle, Josephine see Storm, Gale
Couric, Katie 20
The Courtship of Andy Hardy 110
Cowley, William 174
Craig, James *127*
Crane, Bob 119–120, 174
Crawford, Joan 22, 62, 99, 139
Crazy Mama 139
Crenna, Richard (Dick) 21, 24, 27, 29, 176
Croft, Mary Jane 28
Crothers, Rachel 61
Crowther, Bosley 63
Crutcher, Robert Riley 177
Cukor, George 69
Cummings, Bob 128
Curtain Call at Cactus Creek 143
Curtis, Nathaniel 176
Cyphers, Charles *169*

Dailey, Dan 110, *111*
Dallas 122–124
Daniels, Marc 44, 45, 82, 175
Dann, Mike 46, 67
The Danny Kaye Show 22
The Danny Thomas Show 32, 70, 133; see also *Make Room for Daddy*
Darin, Bobby 34
The Dark at the Top of the Stairs 33
Dark Dame 126
Dark Moon: The Best of Gale Storm 156
Dark Shadows 106
Date with the Angels 53, 157, 159, 164–166, 173, 180, 181
Davenport, Bill 174
Davis, Bette 139, 140
Davis, Joan 1, 2, 3, 16, 22, 47, 53, 75–91, 175, 179
Davis, Madelyn Pugh see Pugh, Madelyn
Davis, Madonna Josephine see Davis, Joan
Davis, Nancy 128
Davis, Stanley 177
Day, Dennis 66, 77
Day, Doris 72, 118, 185
Deacon, Richard 165, 173
Deadly Lessons 122

Dean, James 87, 89
Deane, Shirley 61
December Bride 1, 2, 3, 63–71, 74, 133, 174, 180, 181, 185
December Bride (radio) 59–60, 65
de Cordova, Frederick 15, 175
de Havilland, Olivia 137
Dell Comics 31
The Delphi Bureau 106
Demme, Jonathan 139
Denning, Richard 39, 43
Dennis the Menace 72, 81
Derman, Lou 174
Deroy, Richard 173
Desilu Playhouse see *Westinghouse Desilu Playhouse*
Desilu Productions 1, 14, 23, 24, 25–26, 27, 32, 34, 50, 52, 54, 55, 60, 63, 65, 66, 67, 70—71, 82, 83, 85, 132, 135, 153, 173, 174, 175, 176, 181
The Detectives Starring Robert Taylor 72
Detective's Wife 183
Dick Tracy 94
Dick Tracy vs. Cueball 94
The Dick Van Dyke Show 25, 48 165
Dickinson, Angie 168
Dillinger 94, 95
Ding Dong Williams 95
Disney, Walt 118
Disneyland 89
Dobkin, Lawrence 174
Dr. Kildare 73
Don Fedderson Productions 173
Donna Reed Foundation for the Performing Arts 124
Donna Reed Heritage Museum 124
The Donna Reed Show 1, 53, 87, 109, 112, 113–121, 122, 123, 154, 174, 181, 184
Dorfman, Sid 175
Dot Records 150, 153, 156
Douglas, Kirk 128
Dozier, William 117
Dragnet 65
Dragonwyck 62, 65
Drake, Alfred 106
Drake, Eve (*Mr. Adams and Eve* character) 184
Dream Girl 164
DuBarry Was a Lady 40
The Dude Goes West 143
Duff, Howard 32, 106, 184
"Dumb Dora" 5

The Ed Sullivan Show 34
Eden, Barbara 105
Egan, Richard 128
Elitch Gardens Summer Stock Company 60
Elizabeth (*Life with Elizabeth* character) 159, 160, 161–162, 163, 175
Emerson, Faye 10
Emerson, Hope 81, 87, 175
Emery, John 90

Emmy Awards 16, 26, 33, 35, 51, 56, 67, 86, 116, 131, 141, 161, 167, 170, 180
Erlenborn, Ray 175
Ernest, George 61, *62*
Ethel and Albert 184
The Eve Arden Show 21, 31–33, 34, 53, 174, 181
Every Saturday Night 61–62
Everybody Loves Opal 138
Everybody's Welcome 125
Eyes in the Night 112
"The Eyes of Texas" 36

Fabares, Shelley 113, *114*, 119, 121, 124, 174
The Facts of Life 53
Fairfax, Jimmy 151, 174
Faithfully Yours 128
Falcon Crest 37, 106
A Family Affair (film) 61
Family Affair (TV) 138, 167
Fantasy Island 106, 107, 154
Fargé, Annie *54*
Farrell, Charles 144, 145, *148*, 149, 176
Father Knows Best 49, 67, 122, 149
The FBI 34
Fedderson, Don 159, 164, 165, 166, 167, 173, 175
Fedderson, Yvonne Lime 18
Felton, Verna 66, 67, 71, 72, 149, 174
The Feminine Mystique 117–118
Field, Betty 164
Field, Mary 99
Finder of Lost Loves 107
Fisher, Carrie 36
The Flying Nun 73
Ford, John 110
The Ford Lucille Ball–Desi Arnaz Show 53, 132, 181
Ford Television Theatre 112
Forever, Darling 31, 51
Fowler, Keith 175
Fox, Frank 144, 176
Fox, Fred S. 173
Franciosa, Tony 107
The Frank Sinatra Show 165
Franklin, Bonnie 2
Frawley, William 44, 51, 55, 87, 175
The Fred Waring Show 128
Freed, Arthur 127
Freeman, Devery 173
Freeman, Kathleen 99, 100, 101, 177
Friedan, Betty 117–118
Friendly Fire 122
From Here to Eternity 111–112
Fuller, Robert 72, 73
The Fuller Brush Girl *41*–42, 46
Fultz, Jay 110
Furness, Betty 167

Gale Storm Appreciation Society 156
The Gale Storm Show: Oh! Susanna 1, 53, 105, 131, 141, 150–154, 156, 174, 180, 181
Garland, Judy 62

Garnett, Tay 126
"Gateway to Hollywood" 141–142
General Electric Theater 112
General Hospital 93, 107, 185
General Service Studios 86
Gentleman's Agreement 184
The George Burns and Gracie Allen Show 1, 2, 3, 5–20, 39, 44, 46, 68, 82, 87, 91, 105, 159, 160, 175, 179, 181
The George Burns Show 19, 181
George White's Scandals 79
Gershe, Leonard 137, 138, 176
Gershman, Ben 174
The Get-Away 110, *111*
Getty, Estelle 169, *170*
The Ghost and Mrs. Muir 105
Gill, Frank, Jr. 176
Gilligan's Island 86, 88, 120, 121, 184
Gilmore Girls 118–119
The Girl Friend 126
Gish, Lillian 139
The Glass Menagerie 138
Gobel, George 89
Godfrey, Arthur 89
Goldberg, Hyman 26
The Goldbergs 9, 10, 39
The Golden Girls 3, 20, 35, 36, 59, 67, 74, 157, 168–170, 172
Golden Globe Awards 106, 136
The Golden Palace 170
Goldstein, Jesse 175
Goldstone, Duke 175
Good Times 2
Goodwin, Bill 9, 10, 175
Goodyear Playhouse 72
Gordon, Gale 21, 24, 28, 44, 176
Gorshin, Frank 20
Gottfried, Martin 15
Gottlieb, Alex 105, 131, 174, 176
Gould, Jack 26
Gould, Sandra 86–87
Grab Your Phone 158
Gracie: A Love Story 15
Gracie Allen Awards 20
"Gracie Allen: The Better Half" 20
The Gracie Allen Murder Case (book) 6
The Gracie Allen Murder Case (film) 15
Grady, Billy 110
Graham, Lauren 118–119
The Gramercy Ghost 96
Grant, Cary 93, 97
Grayson, Kathryn 96
Grease 20, 28, 36
The Great Gildersleeve 158
Green Acres 13, 143
Greene, Karen 32, 174
Gwenn, Edmund 63, *64*

Hagman, Larry 123–124
Hal Roach Studios 105, 144, 147, 150, 151, 153, 174, 176

Haley, Jack 77, 78
Hall, Thurston 99, 177
Halop, Florence 185
Hammond, Liza (*The Eve Arden Show* character) 31–32, 174
Happy Days 50
Hard Rain 171
Hardy, Oliver 144
Harem Girl 82, *83*
Harlow, Jean 126
Harrigan and Son 54
Harrington, Curtis 139
Harris, Susan 168
"Harry and Maggie" 36
Hart, Lorenz 125
Hart, Moss 61
Hasselhoff, David 107
Hausner, Jerry 87, 175
Having Wonderful Time 22
Hawkins, Jimmy 117
Hayden, Don 145, 158, 176
Hayden, Harry 158
Hayden, Jeffrey 174
Heaven Can Wait 69
Heflin, Van 110
Hello, Dolly! 33
Helm, Harvey 175
Henie, Sonja 76
Henning, Paul 175
Henry, Fred 173
Hepburn, Katharine 22, 41, 61, 126
Here Comes Cookie 6
"Here Comes Melinda" 72
Here We Go Again: My Life in Television 172
Here's Lucy 28, 50, 56
Hey, Jeannie! 185
Hickman, Darryl 54
Hillerman, John 168
His Eye Is on the Sparrow 185
Hoffe, Arthur 173
Hoffman, Gertrude W. 67, 145, 176
Hogan's Heroes 119, 120
Hold That Ghost 76–77
Holden, William 27, 52, 70
Holliday, Judy 27
Hollywood on Television 158–159
Hollywood Walk of Fame 73
Holm, Celeste 184
Holmes, Dennis 72
Holmes, Rupert 20
Honestly, Celeste! 184
Hope, Bob 7, 53, 78, 88, 89
Hot Off the Wire: The Jim Backus Show 91
Hotel 106
House of Frankenstein 185
House Un-American Activities Committee 50
How to Become President 6
Howell, Kenneth 61, *62*
Hubbard, Eve (*The Mothers-in-Law* character) 34
Hughes, Felix 158

Hughes, Langston 95
Hughes, Rupert 158
Hunt, Helen 171
Hunter, Ross 122
Hunter, Tab 69
Hurwitz, Alvin 87
Hussey, Ruth 63
Hutton, Betty 184

I Ain't Down Yet 156
I Dream of Jeannie 73, 98, 100, 105
"I Love Her Anyway" 19
I Love Her, That's Why! 12
I Love Lucy 1, 2, 3, 7, 11, 12, 13—14, 23, 24, 27, 28, 34, 39, 40, 41, 42–53, 55, 56, 70, 75, 77, 80, 82, 83, 85, 86, 103, 132, 144, 145, 149, 159, 175, 179, 180
I Married Joan 1, 2, 11, 12, 47, 75, 79, 82–89, 90, 91, 144, 145, 175, 179, 180
Ichabod and Me 106
If You Knew Susie 77
Imitation of Life 122
In the Good Old Summertime 60
Independent Television Corporation 153
Inge, William 33
interracial marriage, *I Love Lucy* and 49–50
It Gives Me Great Pleasure 32, 174
It Happened on 5th Avenue 143
It's a Wonderful Life 110, 117, 143
It's Always Jan 185
It's Garry Shandling's Show 13

The Jack Benny Show (radio) 66
The Jack Benny Show (TV) 7–8, 14, 19, 130–131, 183
Jack Chertok Television Productions 132, 176
Jackson, Kate 105
James, Jeri Lou 185
Jarvis, Al 158–159
The Jeffersons 49, 51
Jeffreys, Anne 1, 2, 3, 93–108, 128, 176, 177, 180, 181
Jenssen, Elois 131
Jergens, Adele 88, 175
Joan Davis Enterprises 75, 79, 82, 90, 175
The Joan Davis Show 78–80, 89, 90
Joan Davis Time 80
"Joan of Arkansas" 90–91
Joan of Ozark 95
Joanie's Tea Room see *The Joan Davis Show*
Joelson, Ben 173
The John Larroquette Show 170
John Robert Powers Agency 94
John W. Loveton-Bernard L. Schubert Productions 177
Johnson, Jill (*Love That Jill* character) 176
Jones, Henry 9
Jones, James 111
Josefsberg, Milt 55
Joslyn, Allyn 31–32, 33, 174
Judd, for the Defense 121

Julian, Arthur 174
Junior Miss 79
Just Men! 170

Kahn, Linda 139
Kahn, Milt 175
Kampen, Irene 55
Kaplan, Marvin 185
Kaplan, Mike 140
Karson, Lee 150, 174
The Kate Smith Hour 184
Katz, Sam 127
Kaufman, George S. 61
Kaufman, Reuben 161
Kaye, Danny 102
Kearns, Joseph 81
Keating, Larry *10*, 175
Keaton, Buster 40, 117
Keel, Howard 96, 123
Keith, Richard 175
Kelley, David E. 171, 172
Kelly, Gene 127
Kelsay, Bill 173
Kerby, Marion (*Topper* character) 3, 93, 101, 102–103, 105, 177
Kern, James V. 165, 173, 174
The Killing Kind 139
Kimbrough, Emily 32, 174
The King and I 106
Kinon, Richard 174
Kipling, Rudyard 156
Kismet 106
Kiss Me, Kate (film) 96
Kiss Me, Kate (play) 93, 96
KLAC-TV 158–159, 171
Knotts, Don 36
Kohn, John 176
Kolb, Clarence 145, 176
The Kraft Music Hall 115
Kulp, Nancy 152

Ladies' Man 171
Lady Be Good 126
Lady in a Cage 136–*137*
Lake, Bonnie 135
Lake, Harriette see Sothern, Ann
Lake Placid 171
Lambchops 6
Landers, Lew 177
Landres, Paul 177
Lansbury, Angela 67
Laramie 72–73
Latifah, Queen 172
Laurel and Hardy 144
Laverne & Shirley 139, 156
Lawrence, Sharon 171
Lawrence, Vicki 168
Leachman, Cloris 139, 167, 168
The Leading Lady: Dinah's Story 172
Lear, Norman 2, 3, 36, 49, 169
Leave It to Beaver 49, 118, 121

INDEX

Leave It to Joan 80
Leave It to Larry 159
Leonard, Sheldon 11, 32, 33
Let's Face It 22
Let's Fall in Love 126
"Let's Join Joanie" 80–82, 87
A Letter to Three Wives 127, 128, 140
Levy, Parke 59, 60, 65, 71, 174
Levy, Ralph 16, 175
Lewis, Al 23, 25, 174, 176
Lewis, Jerry 185
Libby, Bill 156
Liberace 31, 161, 164
The Life and Loves of Joan Davis 77
Life Begins in College 76
The Life of Riley 99–100, 103, 113, 144
Life with Elizabeth 1, 104, 157, 159–164, 165, 171, 172, 175, 179, 180
Life with Lucy 56, 57
Life Without George 55
Lights Out 46
Lime, Yvonne *see* Fedderson, Yvonne Lime
Little, Rich 36
The Little Dragons 139
Little Giant 185
Little Me 33
The Little People 121
Little Women 61, 69
Lives, Audrey 176
Livingstone, Mary 15
Locke, Sam 174
Long, Sumner 174
The Long, Long Trailer 51, 86
Lorne, Marion 183
Louisa (film) 63, *64*, 65
Louisa (radio) 63
Love, American Style 138
The Love Boat 36, 122, 151, 154, 155, 156
Love of Life 113
Love That Bob 14, 128
Love That Jill 93, 105–106, 176, 181
Loveton, John W. 94, 177
Lucille Ball Productions 56
The Lucille Ball Show see I Love Lucy
Luckinbill, Laurence 106
Lucy-Desi Comedy Hour 53
The Lucy Show 19, 28, 50, 55, 56, 137, 138, 151, 154
Ludden, Allen 167, 168
Lupino, Ida 32, 184
Lydon, James (Jimmy) 105, 176
Lynch, Peg 184–185
Lynn, Betty 105, 176

Mack, Dick 82
MacLeod, Gavin 167
MacMurray, Fred 53, 70
MacNamara, Susie (*Private Secretary* character) 129, 130, 132, 133, 176, 181
Madsen, Axel 69
The Magic Carpet 45

"The Magnificent Morgans" 41
The Magnificent Seven 114
Magnum, P.I. 168
Mahan, Billy 61
Main, Marjorie 60, 69, 70
Maisie (film) 126, 139
Maisie (radio) 127
Make Room for Daddy 63, 70, 113, 129; *see also The Danny Thomas Show*
The Maltese Falcon 99
Mama 9, 10, 100
Mama's Family 168
Mame (film) 57
Mame (play) 138
The Manitou 139
Mankiewicz, Joseph 127, 128
Many Happy Returns 185
March, Hal 10, 65, 152, 175
Marcus Welby, M.D. 185
Marin, Ned 128
Martin, Dean 185
Martin, Madelyn Pugh *see* Pugh, Madelyn
Martin, Steve 172
Martin, Tony 115
Marx, Groucho 9, 40, 44
Marx Brothers 22, 40
Mary Kay and Johnny 9
The Mary Tyler Moore Show 2, 20, 25, 28, 133, 147, 157, 167–168, 170, 172
*M*A*S*H* 65
Mason, James 68
Masterson, Paul 156
Maude 2, 35–36, 56, 57, 169
Maverick 183
"Max Liebman Presents" 105
Maybe This Time 170
Mayor of the Town 101
McCadden Productions 14, 19, 175
McCarthy, Eugene 122
McClanahan, Rue 169, *170*
McCrea, Ann 119–120, 174
McCullough, Andrew 174
McDaniel, Hattie 185
McDowall, Roddy 105
McMillan, Gloria 21, 176
Meet Millie 185
The Member of the Wedding 185
The Men 106
The Merry Widow 158
Mertz, Ethel (*I Love Lucy* character) 10–11, 27, 43, 44, 45, 46, 47, 64, 145, 175
Mertz, Fred (*I Love Lucy* character) 27, 28, 43, 44, 45, 47, 175
The Mickey Mouse Club 113
Mildred Pierce 22, 99
Miller, Ann 22
Miller, Dean 64, 65, 174
Miller, Sidney 173
The Millionaire 115
A Minor Consideration 121
The Miracle of Morgan's Creek 184

Miss Grant Takes Richmond 40
Mr. Adams and Eve 32, 184
Mr. and Mrs. North 14, 94
Mister Ed 73, 99, 101
Mitchell, Thomas 101
Molina, Alfred 171
Monaster, Nate 174, 175
Montgomery, Elizabeth 105
Monty, Gloria 107
Moore, Candy 120
Moore, Constance 78
Moore, Del 159, *160*, 162, 164, 166, 171, 175
Moore, Mary Tyler 1, 4, 48, 139, 167
Moorehead, Agnes 34, 64–65
Moose Murders 36–37
Morgan, Harry 64, 65–66, 67, 71, 174
Morgan, Jane 21, 176
Morison, Patricia 96
Morton, Gary 54, 57
The Mothers-in-Law 34, *35*, 36, 65, 138
Mullaney, Jack 132, 133, 173
Mullenger, Donnabelle *see* Reed, Donna
The Munsters 120
Murder, She Wrote 67, 74, 156
Museum of Broadcasting 171
Museum of Modern Art 140
Music Theater of Lincoln Center 106
Mutiny on the Bounty 61
My Favorite Husband (radio) 10, 39, 41, 42, 45
My Favorite Husband (TV) 45, 183, *184*, 185
My Favorite Martian 99, 100, 120
My Friend Irma 26, 59, 85
My Friend Irma Goes West 85
My Little Margie (comic book) 149
My Little Margie (radio) 149
My Little Margie (TV) 1, 2, 11, 48, 67, 82, 85, 141, 143–150, 151, 154, 156, 176, 179, 180
My Mother, the Car 138
My Three Sons 55, 120, 167

Nancy 184
Narz, Jack 160, 161, 162, 171
Nearly Eighteen 42
Nelson, Barry *184*
Nelson, Craig T. 121
Nelson, Harriet 113, 114
Nelson, Ozzie 113
Nelson, Ricky 17
Nelson, Tony 73
Nicoletti, Louis A. 46
Night Court 185
Nivens, Sue Ann (*The Mary Tyler Moore Show* character) 157, 167, 168–169, 170
"Nuts and Bolts" 36
Nye, Louis 135, 173
Nylund, Rose (*The Golden Girls* character) 20, 157, 169

Oakie, Jack 80
O'Connor, Donald 143

O'Connor, Katy (*The Ann Sothern Show* character) 3, 132, 133–134, 173
Oh Doctor! 22
Oh God! 19
Oh! Susanna see *The Gale Storm Show: Oh! Susanna*
Oklahoma! 184
Oliver, Edna May 35
On Their Own 61–*62*
One Crowded Night 142
One Day at a Time 2
Oppenheimer, George 94, 101, 177
Oppenheimer, Jess 41, 42, 43, 44, 45, 46, 47, 51, 52, *54*–*55*, 175
Osmond, Marie 170
Our Gang 144
Our Hearts Were Young and Gay 32
Our Miss Brooks (comic book) 31
Our Miss Brooks (film) 30–*31*
Our Miss Brooks (radio) 23, 34, 44
Our Miss Brooks (TV) 1, 3, 11, 21–31, 34, 37, 47, 60, 66, 82, 86, 100, 129, 176, 179, 180
Owen, Mary Anne 116
Owen, Timothy 111
Owen, Tony 80, 110, 111, 112, 115, 116, 118, 119, 120, 122, 174
Owen, Tony, Jr. 110
Ozzie and Harriet see *The Adventures of Ozzie and Harriet*

Paar, Jack 166
Packard, Elon 177
Paige, Janis 128, 185
The Pajama Game 185
Paley, William S. 7, 23, 66
Palmer, Stuart 35
Papa's Slay Ride 61
Parish, James Robert 126
Parsons, Lindsley 142
Password 167
Password Plus 168
Pat Boone—Chevy Showroom 153
Patrick, Lee 90, 98–99, *102*, 177
Patterson, Elizabeth 67, 175
The Patty Duke Show 120
Paul, Norman 175
Pepe 118
Pepper, Barbara 46
The Pet Set 167
Pete and Gladys 66, 71, 181
Petersen, Patty 119, 174
Petersen, Paul 113, *114*, 119, 120, 121, 174
Petticoat Junction 167
The Phil Silvers Show 32, 104
Philip Morris 43, 44, 103, 144, 145
Photoplay 69–70
Phyllis 168
Picerni, Paul 130
The Picture of Dorian Gray 110
Pinky 185
Pitts, ZaSu 150–151, 174

Plaza Suite 155
Please Don't Eat the Daisies 72
Plymouth 164–165, 166
Police Woman 168
Pomeroy, Susanna (*The Gale Storm: Oh! Susanna* character) 150, 151–152, 153, 174
Port Charles 93, *107*–108
Porter, Cole 22, 96
Porter, Don 30, 129, *130*, 134, 173, 176
Powell, Eleanor 126
Powers, Stefanie 105
The Practice 121, 171, 172
Preminger, Otto 33, 167
Presenting Lily Mars 62
Price, Vincent 140
Prickett, Maudie 173
Private Secretary 1, 125, 128–132, 134, 135, 136, 176, 179–180
Promised Land 184
Prouty, Jed 61–62
Pryor, Roger 126, 127
Pugh, Madelyn 34, 35, 41, 42, 43, 47, 54, 55, 138, 175
Pulitzer Prize Playhouse 63
Purl, Linda 139

Quedens, Eunice *see* Arden, Eve
Quillan, Joe 23, 176

R.J. Reynolds Tobacco Company (Camel cigarettes) 97, 99, 103–104
Racket Squad 164
Radio Hall of Fame 37
Rafferty, Frances 64, 65, 71, 174
Raleigh Hills Hospital 155
Rapp, Joel 174
Rapp, Philip 90, 101–102, 177
Ravier, Maisie (film series character) 126, *127*, 129
The RCA Victor Show Starring Dennis Day 66
Reagan, Ronald 11, 63, 128
The Real McCoys 113
Reed, Donna 1, 3, 87, 109–124, 174
The Restless Gun 105
Return of the Bad Men 96
Revenge of the Zombies 143
Reynolds, Marjorie 144
Rebel Without a Cause 89
The Red Buttons Show 66–67
Red River Valley 142
Rhoda 3, 31
Ricardo, Lucy (*I Love Lucy* character) 1, 11, 24, 27, 39, 43, 45, 46, 47–49 51, 52, 55, 56, 65, 68, 83, 84, 88, 132, 134, 144, 146, 147, 175
Ricardo, Ricky (*I Love Lucy* character) 12, 42, 43, 45, 47–49, 50, 51, 52, 56, 132, 134, 175
Rice, Elmer 164
Rich, Frank 37
Rich, John 174, 175
Richard III 108

The Rifleman 152
Ringside Maisie 127
Ritz Brothers 76
Rivers, Joan 77
Roach, Hal, Jr. 106, 143, 144, 149, 150, 174, 176
Roach, Hal, Sr. 144, 151
Roach Studios *see* Hal Roach Studios
Roberts, Roy 151, *154*, 174
Roberts, William 114, 174
Rockwell, Robert 21, 24, 28, 29, *30*, 176
Rodgers, Richard 125
Roger Wagner Chorale 83
Rogers, Ginger 22
Rogers, Roy 142
Roland Reed TV Productions 176
Roman Scandals 40
Room Service 40, 94; see also *Step Lively*
Rooney, Mickey 70
Rose, Glenn 37
Roseanne 25, 113, 116
Roseanne *see* Barr, Roseanne
Ross, Bob 173
Rudley, Herbert 34
Rudolph, Oscar 173, 176
Ruggles, Charles 72
Run for Your Life 34
Ruskin, Lily (*December Bride* character) 3, 62, 64, 65, 67–69, 70, 73, 174
Russell, Kurt 36
Russell, William D. 174
Ryan, Irene 166

Sadie McKee 98
Saks, Sol 32, 33
Sally 183
Sandrich, Jay 169
Santa Barbara 185
Satins and Spurs 184
Savage, John 139
Say Goodnight, Gracie 20
Schiller, Bob 55, 132, 175
Schlitz Playhouse of Stars 128, 166
Schubert, Bernard L. 94
Schwartz, Sherwood 87, 88, 175
Scott, Jacques 132, 133, 173
Scott, Lizabeth 69
Scott, Randolph 96
Screen Actors Guild 142
Screen Writers Guild 42
The Sealtest Village Store 22, 23, 77, 78
Sedgwick, Eddie 40
Seinfeld 11
Seiter, William A. 174
Seller, Tom 176
Sennett, Mack 76
Serena, Joseph 96
Shadow of the Thin Man 110
Shadow on the Wall 128
Sharp, Henry 174
Sharp, Phil 174, 175
Shaw, Reta 132, 166, 173

She Wrote the Book 79, *81*
Shore, Dinah 16, 89
Show Business 77–78
Simon, Al 14, 82
Simon, Danny 173
Sinatra, Frank 94
Sincerely Yours 31
Singleton, Doris 65, 88, 149
Singleton, Penny 132
The $64,000 Question 50
Skinnay Ennis Orchestra 164
Skinner, Edna 100, 177
Skylarks 9
Sleeping Beauty 72
Smart Alecks 142
Smith, Cecil 57
Smith, Cleo 41, 57
Smith, John 72, 73
Smith, Thorne 93, 97, 177
Sondheim, Stephen 101, 177
Sothern, Ann 1, 3, 21, 30, 34, 52, 96, 125–140, 173, 176, 179, 180, 181
Sothern Exposure: Ann Sothern Sings 132
Spader, James 172
Spelling, Aaron 57, 106, 107, 151, 154
Stage Door 22
Stander, Arthur 175
Stanwyck, Barbara 22, 62, 115
Step by Step 95
Step Lively 94, 95
Sterling, Anne Jeffreys *see* Jeffreys, Anne
Sterling, Dana 106
Sterling, Jeffreys 101, 106
Sterling, Patricia Ann *see* Sterling, Tisha
Sterling, Robert 93, 96–106, 110, 127–128, 176, 177
Sterling, Tisha (Patricia Ann) 128, 132, 136, 140
Stevens, Andrew 105
Stevens, Connie 19
Stevens, Joan (*I Married Joan* character) 83, 86, 88, 90, 175
Stewart, Janis (*It's Always Jan* character) 185
Stewart, Jimmy 110
Stone, Donna (*The Donna Reed Show* character) 109, 113, 115–116, 118, 119, 174
Stone, Ezra 82, 175
Stone, Gail 32, 174
Storm, Gale 1, 4, 53, 82, 85, 141–156, 171, 174, 176, 179
The Story of Alexander Graham Bell 61
Stoska, Polyna 95
The Stratton Story 110
Streep, Meryl 20
Street Scene 95–96
The Strongest Man in the World 36
The Stu Erwin Show 144, 145, 150
Stuhlmueller, Dean *see* Miller, Dean
Sturges, Preston 184
Sullivan, Tom 172
The Sunshine Boys 19
Susie see *Private Secretary*

Swackhamer, E.W. 174
Swan Soap 78, 79, 80
Sweeney, Bob 29, 176
Swing Shift Maisie 127

"Take Him—He's Yours" 34
Talbot, Lyle 68
Taming of the Shrew 96
Tartikoff, Brandon 59
Tarzan's New York Adventure 94
Tashlin, Frank 41
Television Programs of America, Inc. 131
Teschner, Mark 108
Texaco Star Theatre 46
The Texan 70
Thayer, Guy V., Jr. 176
They Were Expendable 110
Thibodeaux, Keith 175
Thin Ice 76
The Thin Man 166
Thomas, Danny 63, 113, 129
Thomas, Marlo 1
Thompson, Marshall 54
Thompson, Maury 137
Thorpe, Jerry 66
Three Phases of Eve: An Autobiography 37
Three Stooges 40
Three Wishes for Jamie 96
Three's Company 20
Thriller 184
Tibbles, George 159, 160, 173, 175
Tierney, Lawrence *95*
To Me, It's Wonderful 185
To Tell the Truth 32, 136, 166
Toast of the Town 14
Tobin, Dan 89, 175
Todd, Thelma 151
Todon of California, Inc. 112, 174
Tom Brown's School Days 142
The Tom Ewell Show 54
The Tonight Show 166
Too Many Girls 40
Topper (book) 93, 97
Topper (film) 93, 97
Topper (TV) 1, 2, 3, 93, 96–105, 108, 128, 165, 177, 180, 183
Topper Returns (film) 93
"Topper Returns" (TV pilot) 105
Topper Takes a Trip 93
Totter, Audrey 185
Tracy, Spencer 41
Trade Winds 126
The Traveling Saleswoman 80, 88
The Trouble with Father see *The Stu Erwin Show*
Truex, Ernest 132, 133, 134, 173
Truth or Consequences 44
Turbiville, Betty 175
Turner, Lana 122
Turner, Ted 121
Tuttle, William 110
Tyrrell, Ann 129, 132, 134, 135, 173, 176

Ullman, Tracey 20
Under the Rainbow 36
The Unsinkable Molly Brown 155
The Untouchables 54, 136

Vallee, Rudy 71, 76, 77
Vance, Vivian 11, 44, 51, 55, 87, 137, 138, 154, 175
Van Dine, S.S. 6
Van Dyke, Dick 48
Van Dyke, Jerry 138
Van Hartesveldt, Fran 173
Van Slyke, Helen 122
vaudeville 3, 5, 6, 17, 43, 75, 76
Vega$ 106
Verdugo, Elena 185
"A Very Missing Person" 35
Vidal, Gore 136
Vincent Productions 135
Volcano Productions 175
Von Zell, Harry 9, 12, 18, 175

Wagon Train 106
Walley, Deborah 34
Waterfront 145
Waterman, Ruth 23
Waters, Ethel 9, 185
Watson, Thomas 172
Watt, Nate 146–147
Way Up Thar 76
Wedlock, Hugh 175
Weill, Kurt 95
Weinberger, Ed 168
Weiskopf, Bob 55, 77, 132, 175
Welk, Lawrence 151
Welles, Orson 70
Wendy and Me 19
WereWolf of London 60
West, Brooks 25–26, 27–28, 32, 33–34, 37, 174
West, Douglas Brooks 26, 27–28, 33, 36–37
West, Duncan 26
West, Paul 174
Westhaven Productions 32, 174
Westinghouse Desilu Playhouse 53, 181
The Whales of August 139–140
What Ever Happened to Baby Jane? 139
What's My Line? 14, 136
Whedon, John 174
When Ladies Meet 61, 62
Where Are Your Children? 142
White, Betty 1, 3, 53, 104, 157–172, 173, 175, 179, 180
White, Horace 157
White, Jesse 129, 135, 173, 176
White, Tess 157, 158, 159
Whorf, Richard 173
Wildcat 53–54
Wilde, Cornel 166
William Morris Agency 78
Williams, Bill 164, 165, 173
Williams, Cara 71
Williams, Cindy 139, 156
Williams, Esther 117
Wills, Beverly 76, 79, 87, 89, 91, 175
Wills, Serenius (Si) 76, 78
"Wills and Davis" 76
Wilson, Marie 185
Winters, Shelley 27
Without Love 41
Wolfson, P.J. 175
Wood, Peggy 10
Wood, Randy 150
Woods, Alan 176
Wyatt, Jane 67, 113, 114
Wyler, William 60
Wyman, Jane 22, 37, 106
Wynn, Keenan 41

Yates, Hal 144, 176
You Bet Your Life 9, 44
You Can't Take It with You 61, 62
You'll Never Get Rich see *The Phil Silvers Show*
Young, Robert 126
Young, Roland 93, 97, 98
Young and Rubicam 79
Your Show of Shows 10, 46

Zahn, Paula 20
Ziegfeld Follies 22
Zinnemann, Fred 112

www.ingramcontent.com/pod-product-compliance
Ingram Content Group UK Ltd.
Pitfield, Milton Keynes, MK11 3LW, UK
UKHW050527150426
5217IPUK00026B/1829